"Angela Adams brings us a candid and informative look at PowerSellers. In The eBay Success Chronicles, she provides a look at some of the best in our field. This book explains what it takes to become – and to remain – a PowerSeller. The 70 PowerSellers interviewed in The eBay Success Chronicles reveal their insights and techniques for staying on top. I especially enjoyed each seller's 'Final Piece of Advice.' It reminded me of the magic of eBay: each seller is unique and that's what makes eBay such a success."

— Cindy Shebley
Author of *Easy Auction Photography*
eBay Certified Business Consultant
and Education Specialist

"An important part of success on eBay is learning to cross market merchandise between stores and auctions and to find a niche and brand your name. This assures return customers which is what every business thrives on. Angela's book is a serious lesson on how to do both. From cover to cover it teaches you success on eBay from those who are successful. Highly recommended for anyone who hopes to have a business on eBay—part-time or full-time."

— Joyce Banbury, eBay Certified
   Education Specialist

   eBay Marketing Specialist for Small
   Business Development Centers

   Owner: Auction Better Business
   Solution (Auction BBS)
   www.auctionbbs.com
   danse@media-net.net

The eBay Success Chronicles:

Secrets and Techniques eBay PowerSellers Use Every Day to Make Millions

By Angela C. Adams, B.A.

The eBay Success Chronicles: Secrets and Techniques eBay PowerSellers Use Every Day to Make Millions

Copyright © 2007 by Atlantic Publishing Group, Inc.
1210 SW 23rd Place • Ocala, Florida 34474 • 800-814-1132 • 352-622-5836–Fax
Web site: www.atlantic-pub.com • E-mail sales@atlantic-pub.com
SAN Number: 268-1250

ISBN-13: 978-0-910627-64-1   ISBN-10: 0-910627-64-9

Library of Congress Cataloging-in-Publication Data
Adams, Angela C., 1983-
  The eBay success chronicles : secrets and techniques ebay powersellers use every day to make millions / by Angela C. Adams.
      p. cm.
  Includes bibliographical references and index.
  ISBN-13: 978-0-910627-64-1 (alk. paper)
  ISBN-10: 0-910627-64-9
  1. eBay (Firm) 2. Internet auctions. I. Title.

  HF5478.A33 2006
  658.8'7--dc22

                              2006024269

EDITOR/ PROOFREADER: Marie Lujanac • mlujanac817@yahoo.com

ART DIRECTION & BOOK DESIGN: Meg Buchner • megadesn@mchsi.com

COVER DESIGN: Lisa Peterson • info@6sense.net

Printed in China

Table of Contents

CHAPTER 8: PowerSellers with Internet/ eBay Only Businesses   55

CHAPTER 9: How Selling on eBay Expands Brick-and-Mortar Businesses 197

CHAPTER 10: PowerSellers Who Use eBay In Conjunction with Their Brick-and-Mortar Businesses 201

CHAPTER 11: The New Wave—Trading Assistants 245

CHAPTER 12: PowerSellerTrading Assistants 249

CHAPTER 13: PowerSellers with Multiple Classifications 297

CHAPTER 14: Follow-up Interview with Dan Glasure   383

CHAPTER 15: The Future of PowerSelling   393

Charts and References   397

Index   405

This book is lovingly dedicated to my family.

To my mom, Mindy, who is no longer here, but always had faith in me and always knew that I would one day realize my dream of writing. I miss her every day, but know that if she was here she would be very proud of what I have accomplished.

To my dad, Stormy—I love you, <u>Dad</u>!

To my Nana, who has always been there for me and who I know I can always count on.

And to my sister, Rechelle, who even though we haven't always gotten along, will always be my big sister and very close to my heart.

Foreword

My first impression of eBay was probably very similar to that of thousands of new eBay buyers before me: "Wow! Great prices, huge selection, fast delivery, and all without the hassles of the mall."

After hundreds of successful purchases including razorblades, CDs, DVDs, books, tapes, running shoes, and even underwear (new), I noticed some eBay sellers had feedback scores in the hundreds, and even in the thousands. I became intrigued with the prospect of becoming an eBay Seller. Now at the time I had no idea how to sell, what to sell, when to sell, but that didn't seem all that important. (Does the old saying "ignorance is bliss" ring a bell?). I was simply interested in listing a few items on eBay to see how it all worked. So, I did.

I searched the house for what would be my "first" item listed (and hopefully sold) on eBay. Within 10 minutes my search was successful. In the back of a desk drawer I found the old 1985 Chicago Bears Super Bowl Champions Highlights VHS tape. Thanks to a trip to my local Wal-Mart (for a digital camera) I quickly cobbled together my eBay listing and digital photo for the 1985 Bears tape.

Just seven days (and three e-mail questions) later, I had my first successful eBay sale of $47.25. You'd think I won the lottery. It is not that the $47.25 was really going to change my life, but the idea that I could earn money listing and selling things from the comfort of my own home was exciting and quite empowering. That day I decided I would vigorously pursue this new world of eBay selling.

And vigorously pursue it I did. I started as thousands of new eBay sellers have done—selling my old "stuff" until all my "stuff" was gone. Then I did something very strange. I went and found more "stuff" at garage sales, resale shops, estate sales, army surplus stores, Goodwill, Salvation Army; you name it—I was there. And I sold all that "stuff."

Then one day I became intrigued with the logo next to many of the top eBay sellers' names—the eBay PowerSeller logo. I noticed that these sellers tended to have higher feedback scores, and they sold many repeat items to many repeat buyers. That became my next goal: to learn all I could about becoming an eBay PowerSeller. And learn I did!

Much of what I learned was the result of spending weeks and weeks of time sifting through literally thousands of eBay PowerSeller listings and countless books and tapes and magazine articles. (Yes, I even bought a few of those goofy $4 "drop shipper" lists.) I then started on a rather extensive and expensive period of "trial and error."

Today there is a better way to learn the strategies, tools, and principles employed by successful eBay PowerSellers. In this book, *The eBay Success Chronicles: Secrets and Techniques eBay PowerSellers Use Every Day to Make Millions*, Angela Adams has picked the brain of more than 60 successful eBay PowerSellers and handed you the keys to eBay selling success. If you are interested in getting started as an eBay seller or want to improve your eBay selling—I encourage you to read Angela Adams' *eBay Success Chronicles* from cover-to-cover for some of the best eBay selling ideas out there. I wish you tremendous eBay selling success.

— Jack Waddick

> *Jack Waddick does eBay full-time, is an eBay PowerSeller, travels the United States and Canada as an eBay University Instructor, is the #1 (of 970) rated U.S. Education Specialist Trained by eBay, one of ten U.S. eBay Business Consultants, and President of Oakview Training.*

There is so much more to selling on eBay, especially if you have made it your income-earning job and not just a hobby. You have to research and keep up with trends and other important factors. You have to market and cross-promote to get your items and your store to have your items noticed by as many people as possible. You have to follow up and learn to save money on the packing supplies you will undoubtedly use. You have to earn customer loyalty, to create a customer base—buyers who come again and again to see what you are offering.

Introduction

I thought selling on eBay was something to do in your spare time to get rid of all the extra clutter around the house. When I started this book, I did not realize people were making their livings through selling on eBay and was in for quite a surprise when I began getting responses from participants. They each answered questions about how they do the basics of eBay and how they feel about certain things when it comes to eBay. I was shocked to learn that each of these people was making almost as much, if not way more, than a normal entry-level position would offer! How exciting to know you have the power to make your own living at home during the hours you wish and with yourself as boss!

Another surprise for me was that I thought it seemed pretty easy to just get on eBay and list an item, sell it, and boom! You're all done. But there is so much more to selling on eBay, especially if you have made it your income-earning job and not just a hobby. You have to research and keep up with trends and other important factors. You have to market and cross-promote to your items and your store to have your items noticed by as many people as possible. You have to follow up and learn to save money on the packing supplies you will undoubtedly use. You have to earn customer loyalty, to create a customer base—buyers who come again and again to see what you are offering. And there is so much more to the business!

For this book, I interviewed 70 PowerSellers who make a living through eBay every day. They are interesting people, but they are exactly that: people. Each of the participants is a normal, hard-working, regular person who, through eBay, has become extraordinary. They have learned what works for them and how they can succeed through eBay in their own unique way. Whether it is selling items for others, making their own items, seeking out items through multiple avenues, or having a brick-and-mortar store where they already have an inventory stocked and ready for sale—they are doing it! The most exciting thing is: You can do it too!

I hope in reading these stories, you will see that eBay can be an amazing source of freedom. It can free you from a job outside the home, it can create a job for you to stay at home with children, and it can be the place where you sell those homemade items that you have always loved to create; it can be anything to you—even just being a hobby that is fun and a way to "get away" for a while from the demands of your everyday life!

I can't thank each of these participants enough for all of the time they put into helping me with this project. I hope you will learn something from their stories—I know I have!

part 1

The History

and Basics

of eBay

Build a platform—prepare for the unexpected...and you'll know you're successful when the platform you've built serves you in unexpected ways. That's certainly true of the lessons I've learned in the process of building eBay. Because in the deepest sense, eBay wasn't a hobby. And it wasn't a business. It was—and is—a community: an organic, evolving, self-organizing Web of individual relationships, formed around shared interests.

Pierre Omidyar
May 2002,
Commencement Speech
at Tufts University

chapter 1

In the Beginning

eBay, a name, even an icon of the driving train of commerce on the Internet.

On an average day, millions of items are listed on eBay with some individuals buying and selling thousands of items. Originally, eBay was primarily a site to auction off collectibles like trading cards, antiques, dolls, and housewares, but over the years it has exploded to practical items like used cars, clothing, books, CDs, and electronics.

People from all over the world buy and sell on eBay. Currently, eBay has local sites that serve Australia, Austria, Belgium, Canada, China, France, Germany, Hong Kong, India, Ireland, Italy, Malaysia, the Netherlands, New Zealand, Poland, the Philippines, Singapore, South Korea, Spain, Sweden, Switzerland, Taiwan, the United Kingdom, and the United States. In addition, eBay has a presence in Latin America through its investment in **MercadoLibre.com**.

Sellers can be a big business, a local store, or a teenager

unloading his old baseball cards.

At the top of the heap are the PowerSellers. They are the most active, often selling thousands, even hundreds of thousands of dollars worth of items each month. Buyers trust them. Sellers aspire to be like them.

So who are these PowerSellers, and what does it take to become one?

To find this out, you need to know about eBay. That is because eBay is more than just a commerce site. It has its own culture and its own language. Like the rest of the Internet, eBay is also growing, changing, and evolving in thousands of ways great and small. The evolution of eBay is something that would astonish a business school case study: it is largely an accidental company—started and grown by trial-and-error.

Working within this culture, adjusting to the ever-changing market place, and finding profitable niches are really what distinguish a PowerSeller.

The Birth of eBay

It has long been said that eBay founder Pierre Omidyar started eBay in 1995 so his girlfriend could have a way to trade Pez dispensers.

"Well, like every creation myth, there's always an element of truth," eBay Chairman Omidyar has said.

Omidyar worked for a small start-up company called General Magic in the early days of the Internet. He also ran a small consulting business named Echo Bay Technology in his spare time.

He started thinking that the 'Net could be used to create a perfect marketplace—where everyone was on equal footing and the market set the price. In other words, what would be the perfect free market? He thought that an auction format would become an excellent "market mechanism" for reaching the reasonable value of an item. It began as an entertaining, intellectual exercise because he really didn't have the time to develop it.

But Omidyar was always a curious person with an incisive mind. He spent a few months of his time off to develop some software. As an experiment, he introduced what he called AuctionWeb. He meant it to be placed as an adjunct feature to a Web site he'd developed for Echo Bay.

The first version of what would evolve into eBay went online in September 1995. He worked out of his apartment in the beginning. It trundled along, with Omidyar successively tinkering and upgrading the AuctionWeb.

It grew at astonishing rates despite feeble marketing efforts by its founder. Customers kept listing their items on AuctionWeb, with a buzzing number of buyers bidding and buying the items. Omidyar began to get a glimmer of the possibilities and decided to devote more time to Auction Web and his Echo Bay Web site.

This is when circumstances took a historic turn.

When he tried to register that site name in 1996, the name echobay.com was taken. Those were the early days of the

Internet when you had to fill out paper forms. Standing at the counter, Omidyar made a snap decision and decided to abbreviate Echo Bay. eBay.com was born.

And what about the Pez dispenser myth? Omidyar relates that about the time AuctionWeb started, he and his girlfriend, Pam Wesley, took a trip to Europe. While there, she bought a number of Pez dispensers. Back home, Pam started selling and trading them on AuctionWeb. It gave Omidyar a first hand look at the passion of collectors.

He later told that story to eBay's first public relations person, Mary Lou Song. She ran with the Pez story, and the myth was born about the origin of an absolute phenomenon. eBay has changed how people think about the junk they once might have sold at garage sales. In fact, the whimsy of the items people offered for sale on eBay is almost as legend as the site itself. There was the grilled-cheese sandwich with a toast pattern in the image of the Holy Mother that sold for $28,000. One man auctioned his forehead for advertising space for $37,375.

The Early Years

eBay's growth was stunning; Omidyar and his rapidly expanding team must have felt they had hold of a tiger's tail. Greater server power and new features were added on an almost daily basis. They landed an agreement with   to provide guaranteed payment for auction sales. The service, which quickly developed into eBay's PayPal, skyrocketed eBay business because of the ease and security for buyers and sellers to make and accept payments.

The Painful Early Years

The system could barely keep up with the demands placed on it. In 1996 and 1997 eBay users feared that it would crash each day. Two developments would change this.

First, measures were attempted to cut down on the demand for eBay—put on the brakes—to cut the strain on the system. Omidyar and his management team decided to raise auction rates from a dime to a quarter, and most drastically, to limit auctions to 10,000 new auctions each day.

Limiting auctions led to the rise of the PowerSeller. Since only 10,000 auctions were allowed, although many more demanded, there was a daily race by sellers to get their auctions listed before the 10,000 cutoff was reached.

Some sellers started developing their own software programs to allow them to upload their listings quickly so they could handle scores or even hundreds of auctions. Selling activity started to gravitate away from an every-person market to one dominated by several large sellers.

This also placed an unintended stress on the eBay system. As soon as the daily clock started ticking towards the 10,000 daily limit, the network was overcome with the new auctions from sellers racing to get in.

An overloaded network helped to lead to the second development, a doomsday event that rattled the very bones of the growing eBay monster.

June 10, 1999

This date is seared into the minds of each of the 400 eBay employees who worked there at the time. The ramshackle, slapped together, hodgepodge system crashed.

For 22 hours eBay was completely down in catastrophic failure.

It was a defining moment for eBay. First, each of eBay's employees hit call lists of users to apologize personally for the fiasco, an act that won raves from the users. Second, management plunged into the technical side of the company. They quickly ordered an overhaul of the old system to make it more robust, with more than adequate capacity and a better, more efficient design.

The Growing eBay

Since 1997 eBay has been the definition of an Internet business advancing into new and sometimes surprising markets. It has expanded into varied areas like real estate, medical equipment, and construction machinery. It sells billions of dollars of electronics. It is the world's biggest used car dealer.

It has also expanded into Europe and Asia, with even a little business going out to South America. eBay is in 33 international markets. In 2005, about 15 percent of its transactions involved a buyer and seller living in different countries. The number is expected to increase drastically in the next five years. Of eBay's 157 million registered users worldwide, 82 million are international and 75 million U.S. users.

Sellers have changed, too. Through the 1990s, eBay's sellers were mostly a motley collection of individuals. Now sellers range from individuals to major corporations. eBay's fast facts for 2005 stated that there were over 724,000 professional sellers in the United States who use eBay as the primary or secondary source of income, with another 1.5 million individuals who sell on eBay to supplement their incomes. It is one of the few places where someone operating off their coffee table can compete equally with an international corporation.

And those sellers are topped by about 100,000 PowerSellers. These top performers have many faces. Some are big businesses or a new marketing side of a brick-and-mortar shop. Some are housewives selling from their kitchen table. A surprising number are teenagers and college students blitzing staggering amounts of items from their bedrooms.

Some handle a closet full of items, and some have acres of warehouse space.

The common characteristic of PowerSellers, though, is adaptability. Business or individual, they've seen the world of eBay as it's grown. They've identified needs and found ways to fill those needs. Many PowerSellers are continually shifting operators. They find a niche and work that area as long as it is profitable. As soon as that need dries up, they are on the search for the next need they can fill.

One thing that has stayed constant is the way eBay management stays in contact with its buyers and sellers. Since June 10, 1999, eBay has been fanatical about following up on customer feedback. It is constantly bringing out new features and modifying old ones based on customer requests, the bedrock of the eBay culture.

It has also improved drastically in reliability. From the 1990s when daily system crashes were the norm, now the eBay platform is considered to be a model of reliability. Crashes are rare. In fact, the greatest challenge for eBay programmers is defending the site from a constant stream of would be hackers, spammers, and scammers.

The little auction site that started in Omidyar's apartment now has 135 MILLION customers. Quite a heady accomplishment for a ten-year period. And, yes, Pierre Omidyar did marry Pam Wesley, the Pez collector girlfriend from eBay's early days.

What's Next

Where does eBay go from here? More to the point, what about PowerSellers, those fabled heavyweights of the ranks of sellers?

chapter 2

Selling on eBay

eBay has been called the "World's Largest Garage Sale," a definition reflecting its most basic characteristic. eBay, stripped down to its barest essentials, is a single seller looking to sell one thing.

Most experienced PowerSellers follow a similar learning path to reach their final destination within the eBay hierarchy.

Almost all sellers start by offering old items they own. Have something you'd sell at a

yard sale? Sell it in eBay. It is a great way to cut down on the clutter of unused items you have. Better yet, it's the first few steps in familiarizing yourself on the process of listing and selling on eBay.

eBay offers a wide variety of educational tools, features, and services that enable members to buy and sell on the site quickly, safely, and conveniently. The site is filled with tutorials on how to use these services.

There are also programs to include online payments by PayPal, tips on safe trading, and the Developers Program for community members who would like to develop their own technology solutions.

Little Steps

Next, it is a simple matter to list your item. You post it on eBay and begin the wait. You feel a growing excitement as bids come in on your item and it sells. And there is nothing like the satisfaction of boxing up your item to ship t to your buyer.

You start listing more and more. More items sell. You realize it takes a long time to keep putting in listings the basic way. You start looking at auction management software like Blackthorne, Turbo Lister, and others to make listing and handling your auctions less time-consuming.

Once they've de-cluttered their homes, many sellers begin looking for other things to sell. Some start combing neighborhood yard sales or local auctions to find items to list. Some even start prowling eBay itself to purchase wholesale lots they can resell at their own auctions.

eBay soon changes from a hobby to a part-time business.

Bigger Steps

Originally, all sales on eBay were by Web auction. Over the years it has expanded to include "buy it now" and store-front sales. These alternative ways of selling make for faster transactions. Plus sellers have more control of the sales price.

However, as a safety measure for the marketplace, sellers are required to have minimum requirements for sales and customer satisfaction ratings to have Buy Now and store-front sales.

Sellers keep experimenting and becoming more sophisticated. They learn the need for establishing good practices to handle payments and shipping. They find what works for them and the products they sell.

On the Run

For many, a point comes when the seller discovers THE niche to fill and the source for the perfect set of items.

Most PowerSellers have a well-defined niche suited to their individual interests, abilities, or nature. Maybe it is selling hard-to-find motorcycle parts, or collectible Harley Davidson scarves. Whatever the product, if that niche is not overly crowded by seller-competitors, and you can fulfill orders reliably, you are on your way.

There are a few categories that PowerSellers fit into: having a brick-and-mortar store they use eBay to help supplement, having an Internet/eBay only business, and being a Trading Assistant. Many of the PowerSellers out there are able to fit into more than one of those categories. Many of them also take advantage of drop shipping as a method of selling items. Let's discuss this format and then jump into what it takes to become a PowerSeller, the qualifications, and benefits of doing so.

chapter 3

The "No Inventory" Solution: Drop Shipping

Some PowerSellers have their homes stuffed with products giving it that "eBay house" look. Others have rented thousands of square feet of warehouse space to store everything.

And some don't have anything. These PowerSellers use a form of selling called Drop Shipping.

Drop Shipping has been around for decades. With it you don't keep inventory. Instead, you reach an agreement with a supplier to ship your sold product directly to your buyer. In most cases, the buyer has no idea the item is not coming directly from you.

The Drop-Shipping Process

As with anything else, there are pros and cons of being a drop-ship seller. But first, a little bit about how it works.

Choose a Product to Sell

The very first step in any sales process is deciding what product to sell. Many factors should be considered before you make the decision, but for now, let's say that you've decided to sell digital cameras on eBay.

Locate a Supplier Who Will Drop-Ship for You

Using a research tool like Google or the Thomas Register, you can search for and find a company that will drop ship digital cameras for you, for example. If the company offers you a 35 percent markup over cost, which means that it will supply digital cameras to you for $100 each, then you should be able to retail them for $135 apiece. Make sure the drop shipper has a good stock of digital cameras on hand so you don't end up-selling a product that must be back-ordered.

Set up an Account with the Drop-Shipper

Now it's time to set up a reseller account with the company that will supply the digital cameras. This can often be done online or by phone, but some companies will require that you complete and return a reseller application to open an account.

List the Product for Sale on eBay

Now that you have your supplier lined up and you know that the product is in stock, it's time to list it. Remember that the drop shipper will charge shipping, so make sure to figure that into your sale.

The Product Sells

Great news—your digital camera has sold for $135, and your buyer pays!

Place the Order With the Drop Shipper

After your customer pays you, you contact the drop shipper to order the product on your customer's behalf. The drop shipper then ships the order to your customer under your company name and address.

Drop-Shipping Cons

Many people are afraid to use this method because of the horror stories that fill the Internet about unscrupulous drop shippers. These snakes take the money and don't fill the orders, merchandise items that are eternally back ordered, and so on. Some drop shippers are actually dishonest middlemen charging too much for items you can get cheaper elsewhere.

The worst problem with drop shipping is that you do not have control of shipping to your customer. You are entirely dependent on the reliability, or lack of it, of your supplier. You can have a shipping problem, have an upset buyer, and have absolutely nothing you can do to fix it except issue a refund, and take your lumps on feedback.

Drop-Shipping Advantages

There are also hundreds of honest drop shippers who can help you build a profitable eBay business. The benefits of a good drop-shipping relationship are many.

For a young, growing business, it can be a lifesaver that you don't have a lot of money tied up in inventory. Your money is free to go to much better place—your wallet!

Second, you have no money tied up in unsold items. There is nothing sadder than a pile of New Era Tiddlywinks you were convinced were going to be a hot item, only to find you couldn't give them away.

And third, you have no housing costs; no closets or garages stacked full of boxes, no self-storage rooms crammed with product.

Finally, if the line of products you are trying to sell isn't working, it is easy to shift gears and try out other items.

chapter 4

At the Very Top: PowerSellers

The busiest sellers can garner the title of PowerSeller. It is a title that is bestowed on you by eBay.

PowerSellers are eBay's top sellers who sustain a consistent, high volume of monthly sales and a high level of total feedback—with 98 percent or better positive rating by other eBay users.

The PowerSeller icon next to a member's user ID means that the seller meets the criteria for being a PowerSeller: consistent volume sales, 98 percent total positive feedback or better, eBay marketplace policy compliance, and an account in good financial standing.

As a buyer seeing this mark, you can be confident that you are transacting with an experienced eBay seller who has proven to be committed to customer satisfaction.

It is a brand that is truly a seal of approval. While there are no statistics eBay is willing to share, PowerSellers report that they typically see a surge of sales when they make PowerSeller status.

The Feedback Rating System

eBay strongly encourages all buyers and sellers to leave feedback after each transaction is complete so that other members may benefit from their experience.

A high feedback score and percentage is usually a good sign. It is a reflection of eBay's open ranking system. Every buyer and seller has a rating, based on the number of successful transactions they've completed and been rated.

Feedback represents a person's permanent reputation as a buyer or seller on eBay. It is made up of comments and ratings left by other eBay members during a transaction.

There are three types of feedback ratings: positive, neutral, and negative. The sum of these feedback ratings is shown as a number in parentheses next to every buyer and seller's User ID.

Each member may affect the score by only one point (positive or negative). However, a member may leave you one feedback rating and comment for each transaction with you.

A "Star" is awarded when feedback reaches 10 points (see the Star feedback chart on the next page). A ranking system correlates different colors and star designs to the number of the feedback.

Poor feedback ratings are a kiss of death to any seller or buyer, but especially for a PowerSeller. One important step in becoming a PowerSeller is understanding what buyers expect from a transaction and meeting or surpassing those expectations.

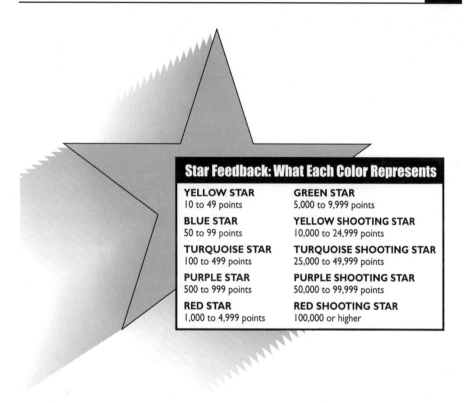

Star Feedback: What Each Color Represents

YELLOW STAR	GREEN STAR
10 to 49 points	5,000 to 9,999 points
BLUE STAR	**YELLOW SHOOTING STAR**
50 to 99 points	10,000 to 24,999 points
TURQUOISE STAR	**TURQUOISE SHOOTING STAR**
100 to 499 points	25,000 to 49,999 points
PURPLE STAR	**PURPLE SHOOTING STAR**
500 to 999 points	50,000 to 99,999 points
RED STAR	**RED SHOOTING STAR**
1,000 to 4,999 points	100,000 or higher

Compliance

It is important to note that there are problems in an open marketplace like eBay. There are sellers who overly hype poor or defective merchandise. Some will try to hide or overcharge shipping. Some will try to cut corners on packing materials. These shady sellers quickly get poor feedback.

Other buyers and sellers try to save fees and go behind eBay's back. They launch an auction, contact a buyer, then trade e-mails and arrange for the sale to happen outside the eBay system. A very few buyers try buying with fraudulent payment. Some sellers offer items they don't have. eBay has a large compliance and fraud section that quickly reacts to complaints.

Sellers soon learn to be accurate in their listings and clear about their shipping and return polices. PowerSellers, simply by the driving nature of their business, must be open and fair in their business dealings.

Why Become a PowerSeller?

There are exclusive benefits to the PowerSeller Program that celebrate success and help grow the business. These are just a few of those benefits.

- Membership is FREE: eBay automatically invites qualified sellers via e-mail

- Prioritized customer service: PowerSellers receive prioritized support by e-mail or telephone, depending on sales level

- Welcome kit: New PowerSellers receive a welcome package featuring an official certificate of achievement and essential advanced selling tips

- Networking: PowerSellers share selling strategies on an exclusive, PowerSeller-only discussion board

- Special offers: eBay works with many companies who only make certain promotions available to PowerSellers

chapter 5

PowerSeller Qualifications

PowerSellers reach this level by a combination of high volume sales and good customer service over time. Most take several months or years to qualify as PowerSellers. A very few qualify in as little as three months.

To qualify, members must:

- **Uphold the eBay community values**, including honesty, timeliness, and mutual respect

- **Average a minimum of $1000 in sales per month** for three consecutive months

- **Achieve an overall feedback rating of 100**, of which 98 percent or more is positive

- **Have been an active member for 90 days**

- **Have an account in good financial standing**

- **Not violate any severe policies in a 60-day period**

- **Not violate three or more of any of eBay's policies** in a 60-day period

- **Maintain a minimum of four average monthly listings** for the past three months

PowerSeller Levels

There are five tiers that distinguish PowerSellers, based on their average monthly sales total. Some benefits and services vary with each tier. eBay automatically calculates eligibility each month and notifies qualified sellers via e-mail.

PowerSeller Tier Sales Criteria

BRONZE	$1,000
SILVER	$3,000
GOLD	$10,000
PLATINUM	$25,000
TITANIUM	$150,000

Feedback

One key item PowerSellers must keep in mind is that the

98 percent or better positive feedback rating for PowerSeller program eligibility is calculated differently than the rest of eBay. The feedback percentage seen on the rest of the site is calculated based on feedback only from unique users. So if you have one person who has bought several items from you, all giving positive feedback, then that would only count as one positive feedback.

The PowerSeller feedback score is calculated based on total user feedback to reflect the fact that many PowerSellers have satisfied, repeat buyers. eBay calculates PowerSeller feedback by taking the total number of positive feedbacks and dividing them by the total number of feedbacks (both positive and negative).

Compliance with Marketplace Policies

A PowerSeller must comply with eBay marketplace rules and fair trading guidelines. All PowerSellers must not violate any severe policies and they must not violate three or more of any eBay policy in a 60-day period

PowerSeller program eligibility is reviewed every month. To remain PowerSellers, members must:

- **Uphold eBay community values**, including honesty, timeliness, and mutual respect

- **Maintain the minimum average monthly sales** amount for your PowerSeller level

- **Maintain a 98 percent positive** total feedback rating

- **Maintain an account in good financial standing**

- **Comply with all eBay listing and marketplace policies**; not violate any severe policies in a 60-day period and not violate three or more of any eBay policies in a 60-day period

Failure to comply with these requirements may result in the removal of a member's PowerSeller status.

Getting Better

To move up to the next PowerSeller level, you should:

- **Continue to comply with all of the PowerSeller program criteria**

- **Reach and maintain the next tier's minimum average** gross monthly sales for three straight months

eBay automatically e-mails and congratulates a PowerSeller upon attainment of the next tier. But once there, you aren't done yet. PowerSeller program eligibility is reviewed every month.

Staying a PowerSeller

To remain PowerSellers, members must:

- **Uphold eBay community values**, including honesty, timeliness, and mutual respect

- **Maintain the minimum average monthly sales** amount for your PowerSeller level

- **Maintain a 98 percent positive** total feedback rating

- **Maintain an account in good financial standing**

- **Comply with all eBay listing and marketplace policies** or violate any severe policies in a 60-day period and not violate three or more of any eBay policies in a 60-day period

If your account falls below the program criteria, you will automatically receive an alert e-mail from eBay explaining why you are in danger of being demoted from your PowerSeller status. You then have 30 days to bring your account back into compliance.

eBay does offer tips and education to help you maintain your PowerSeller status because eBay wants you to keep your status, if possible. However, after the 30-day grace period, if your account still falls below the criteria, your status as a PowerSeller ends.

This won't prevent you from achieving PowerSeller status again. A key exception to regaining status occurs if you violate any severe policies or if you violate three or more of any eBay policies within a 60-day period. In that case, you lose your PowerSeller status without notification. To regain your PowerSeller status, you must comply with eBay listing and marketplace policies over the next 60 days and maintain that compliance.

Those are the hoops a seller must jump through to reach PowerSeller status. Now, let's look at some things you get for your efforts.

chapter 6

How eBay Pampers PowerSellers

PowerSellers are tremendous engines of the transaction and listing fees eBay thrives on. eBay makes sure PowerSellers are happy with exceptional customer service and extra benefits.

PowerSeller Recognition

In many ways, simply the act of being recognized as a PowerSeller can be the greatest benefit there is, both for sales and ego satisfaction.

When that magical e-mail comes from eBay, you can look forward to a few special things right away:

- **Welcome kit for new members** featuring an official certificate of achievement from eBay and essential advanced selling tips

- **Personalized sales and feedback information** on program portal pages

- **PowerSeller icon next to user ID**

- **Use of PowerSeller logo** in item listings and on "About Me" pages

- **Unique PowerSeller logo merchandise** to wear and use or give to customers

- **PowerSeller logo letterhead** and business card templates for customer communications

The PowerSeller Community

Being a PowerSeller means you face a wide range of opportunities and challenges that most other PowerSellers have already experienced. It is easy to reach out and ask other PowerSellers, and advice is generally given freely.

Some areas to be familiar with:

- **Exclusive PowerSeller-only discussion board**

- **Monthly PowerUp! E-mail newsletter** featuring the latest program information, special promotions, and advanced selling education

- **Quarterly printed PowerUp! newsletter in the mail**

PowerSeller Exclusive Offers

eBay also keeps looking for ways to make the PowerSeller

status more appealing. A few of the typical exclusive offers include:

- **eBay Keyword Ads**—FREE banner ads worth up to $200/quarter

- **Health insurance solutions** for PowerSellers and their employees

- **Special invitations to participate in eBay events**

- **Additional special values from eBay** service providers

Priority Customer Support

One of the most important benefits is that eBay provides PowerSellers with priority customer support and technical assistance. If you are having problems with your account, a listing, or even problems with a buyer, eBay is quickly at hand.

All PowerSellers get top priority for e-mail support. Depending on your PowerSeller tier, you may also qualify for a live voice— a direct toll-free phone call away. At the top levels, a dedicated account manager is assigned to see to your needs. See the next page for a chart of Powerseller Tier Priority.

PowerSeller Tier Priority

	e-Support	Toll-Free Phone	Account Manager
BRONZE	✓		
SILVER	✓	✓	
GOLD	✓	✓	✓
PLATINUM	✓	✓	✓
TITANIUM	✓	✓	✓

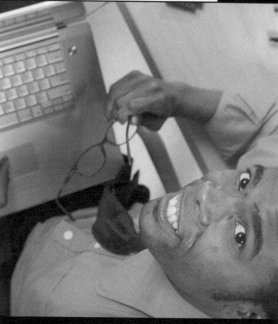

part 2

From the PowerSellers Themselves

"What we say here every day is that our success is really based on our members' success, our community's success. We've created an infrastructure and laid some basic ground rules to create this marketplace. But at eBay, all the buyers and all the sellers are just ordinary people. They're the ones who create the community that's successful. They're the ones who created the environment that is inviting to other people, to new people, and they're the ones who are really responsible for the success and continued growth of the service."

*Pierre Omidyar,
Government Technology,
February 1999*

chapter 7

The Internet Opportunity

eBay is the sole storefront for a growing number of entrepreneurs. The beauty of eBay is that it lets you get into e-commerce without having to go through the trouble and expense of setting up an e-commerce site of your own.

The most successful small businesses understand that only a limited number of people will buy their product or service. The task then becomes determining as closely as possible exactly who those people are and targeting the business's marketing efforts and dollars toward them.

A PowerSeller builds a better, stronger business by identifying and serving a particular customer group—their target market. So if you want to be a PowerSeller, one of your first duties is to refine your product or service so that you are NOT trying to be "all things to all people." Become a specialist!

eBay is also a great way to test a new product. It allows you to try marketing a new item, a craft, something you've made, or an item you've found that you think you can resell profitably.

You can do this with very minimal costs.

In many ways, eBay is a great equalizer. It offers you an opportunity to use your own intelligence, hard work, and desire to build a profitable business. Add to that the depth of tutorials available on eBay and associated chat sites, there is no end to the support and assistance a person has in growing a business.

No matter what you decide to sell, there are some basics all sellers must master. PowerSellers generally agree that there are several keys to making it big as an eBay PowerSeller.

A Picture IS Worth 1,000 Words

People want to see things before they buy them. For successful eBay selling, make sure professional-quality photographs accompany all products you list on eBay.

Do Your eBay Research

Before you list a particular product, spend some time researching similar products on eBay to help you gauge the interest for your product and to help you set a value on it. Some items may be listed under several categories but may sell much easier and for higher prices under others.

Learn All About Shipping

Shipping is under the control of the eBay seller, but some

methods of shipping are better than others. You want to find the best method of shipping for your product in terms of savings and reliability and then specify that shipping method in your eBay listing. And don't forget to include the shipping cost in your shipping information for potential buyers. There are more customer complaints over shipping problems than any other issue.

Learn to Write Good eBay Listings

For selling on eBay, you need a powerful eBay listing. And the trick to writing a strong eBay listing is to combine search-engine friendly phrasing with concrete details about the product in a way that will entice people to bid on your product. Take the time to craft your eBay listing just as you would any classified ad.

Make Payments Easy for Buyers

The more payment options you as an eBay seller can offer prospective bidders, the more bidders your product will attract and the more successful your selling on eBay will be. eBay has its PayPal system available to all, but there are many other payment options available. Research and find the best solutions for you.

Positive Feedback

Feedback really matters when you're selling on eBay. If you

have a consistent record of positive feedback, prospective buyers will both bid more often and be willing to pay higher prices. So you may want to hold back on placing higher priced products until you have established a successful track record as an eBay seller. Remember that reaching PowerSeller status is based both on selling amounts as well as a high feedback rating.

In our next chapter we will begin looking at specific case histories of successful eBay PowerSellers. We'll look at what they do, how they started, and explore their secrets of success. The first set of PowerSellers is those who have only Internet/ eBay Businesses.

chapter 8

PowerSellers with Internet/ eBay Only Businesses

This chapter profiles successful eBay PowerSellers. I have provided a wide sampling of product types and people of all ages from all over the United States.

Eran Dekel

Username:	decalofashion
Name:	Eran Dekel
E-mail:	info@decalofashion.com
Classification:	Internet/eBay Only Business
Current Tier:	Platinum PowerSeller
eBay Store:	DeCalo Fashion
eBay Store Location:	www.stores.ebay.com/decalofashion
Current Feedback Star:	Green
Projected 2006 Sales:	$1,000,000-plus

A Little Background

Eran Dekel has been a member of eBay since January 2003.

To be successful in business you have to be competitive, passionate, and have clear entrepreneurial vision. I graduated from Cooper Union, one of the toughest engineering schools in the country so competition, perseverance, and hard-work work were part of my everyday life. My engineering background has given me the analytic capabilities to crack the secrets of the eBay system and to create an efficient business model that enabled me to work on a part-time basis. We are lucky to be able to offer designer men's apparel and accessories at 40 to 80 percent below retail.

Eran Dekel—username decalofashion—is a part-time eBay seller. He began selling on eBay after his uncle, who owns a clothing store, asked him to help out by liquidating a few designer suits on the Internet.

> *I thought of eBay and when the first suit sold for a 300 percent profit, the Internet light went off in my head. I immediately saw the massive opportunity that the Internet presented for all types of businesses.*

Within three months of selling on eBay, Eran became a PowerSeller. He didn't even know what a PowerSeller was until he was informed he had earned the status of not only a PowerSeller but a Platinum one. He uses a combination of auctions and fixed-price store items to sell on eBay.

> *We use the "buy it now" option on all of our listings and occasionally sprinkle in a few $1 No Reserve auctions to attract buyers. Recently we have been rapidly expanding into other sales channels including our own Web site (**www. decalofashion.com**), Amazon, eBay Express, and more. We are focusing on new business opportunities and joint venture partnerships to catapult our business to the next level.*

Eran finds most of the items he sells from key vendors. He does not make any of the items he sells. He uses cross-promotions in his eBay listings and his Web site. He uses Channel Advisor to fulfill his multi-channel selling strategy.

> *E-commerce and eBay are different from anything else; you need to stay on the cutting edge. By surrounding ourselves with the best technology partners around, we were able to*

catapult our business to 100 percent annual growth.

Eran has found no real science to the importance of length-of-time and ending-time for an auction. He tries to spread his auctions evenly throughout the entire week.

We end most of our auctions between 8 p.m. and midnight but sprinkle a few during the day for maximum exposure.

When he hasn't heard from a buyer, his business will send automated reminders after three, five, and seven days of an auction's end. It will also automatically file an unpaid item dispute after 14 days have elapsed.

Non-paying bidders are a part of the business, and you have to be fully prepared for them.

Eran has found his policies, including his return policy, to be a positive part of his business.

The potential for success is within each individual. You can't be afraid to take risks or to try something new. You have to be flexible with your business and with your customers. For example, we nearly doubled our sales overnight when we introduced free shipping, 90-day money back guarantee, and a free silk tie with every suit purchase.

He finds international bidders to be great for business and said they actually make up 17 percent of his business! Because of the high costs of shipping large volumes of merchandise, whether international or domestic, Eran has the following advice for saving on those costs:

1. *We use a combination of UPS Ground and U.S. Postal Service Priority Mail to ship our items. UPS is more economical for heavier packages; U.S. Postal Service works*

better for lighter packages. We ship our international orders exclusively with U.S. Postal Service.

2. *We buy our boxes in bulk and at a heavy discount from a local vendor. U.S. Postal Service Priority Mail boxes are free, saving us a lot of money.*

3. *We work closely with our UPS and U.S. Postal Service account managers to negotiate volume discounts.*

4. *We seamlessly integrated our system with cutting edge technologies like Endicia and UPS World Ship to streamline our operations, speed up shipping, and ultimately increase our bottom line!*

Eran uses his "About Me" page to drive traffic to his Web site, **www.decalofashion.com**. To draw people into his eBay store, he heavily cross-promotes his store categories through his auctions listing template.

We also use a "Search by Size" algorithm to drive shoppers from our listings to our store.

Company Profile

Founded in 2003, DeCalo Fashion is eBay's leading menswear seller specializing in designer suits, jackets, slacks, shirts, neckwear, and more at 40 to 80 percent below retail price. DeCalo Fashion makes is easy for the fashion-oriented, value-conscious man to find the fabulous bargains on the products they love.

At DeCalo Fashion we want to offer the highest quality menswear at the fairest possible price while providing an exceptionally personalized, superior service that makes every customer feel as though they were shopping at a boutique from the comfort of their own home.

We stand behind the quality, authenticity, and value of all our products. Every single item comes with our 100 percent Satisfaction Guarantee and is backed by our 90-Day Hassle-Free Return Policy. DeCalo Fashion is proud to offer low flat-rate shipping on every order shipped and FREE domestic shipping on all orders over $75. Shopping on the Internet should not be expensive, and shipping costs should not stop you from buying at DeCalo Fashion.

At DeCalo Fashion, we believe that if we give our customers a great shopping experience, then growth in sales will eventually come on their own. So rather than focusing on maximizing profits, we focus on maximizing the service that we provide.

We are currently focusing on rapid expansion and new business opportunities. We have the knowledge and expertise to repeat our early success in any business niche. We plan on growing as fast as our financing will allow us to expand.

Contact Information for Eran Dekel
DeCalo Fashion
New York
www.decalofashion.com
www.stores.ebay.com/decalofashion
info@decalofashion.com
Toll-Free: 888-9DECALO (888-933-2256)

Geremy Gersh

Username:	ezauctioning
Name:	Geremy Gersh
E-mail:	geremy@ezauctioning.com
Classification:	Internet/ eBay Only Business
Current Tier:	Platinum PowerSeller
eBay Store:	ezAuctioning
eBay Store Location:	www.stores.ebay.com/ezAuctioning
Current Feedback Star:	Green
Projected 2006 Sales:	$1,000,000

Your eBay all-stars.

A Little Background

Geremy Gersh has been a member of eBay since July 2000.

Geremy Gersh—username ezauctioning—began selling on eBay because of the market growth potential. PowerSeller status caught up to him after only three months.

He is a full-time seller with about 40 sales a day—210 a week with an average starting price of $9.99. He said that the best way to get people to notice his listings is with good photos and a starting price of $9.99.

Geremy does not make any of the items he sells, but finds most of his items from consignments. He lists his items using auctions.

He uses cross-promotions and likes the listing software Liberty TA by Resaleworld. Geremy thinks that international bidders are good for business, but he does not believe drop shipping is a good method for selling items.

He does make use of a return policy which states:

> *We do our best to present accurate, detailed information about every item we sell. If you have any questions, please e-mail us at trading@ezauctioning.com before you place your bid.*

> *All items are sold "as is." We accept returns only if the item was not as described in the auction. Returns must be made within 10 days of auction close. Buyer is responsible for return shipping charges. Shipping and handling is not refunded in any case.*

Geremy said volume is the best way to save on shipping costs.

When he hasn't heard from a buyer, he "*works through eBay's Dispute Process.*"

He finds time and time-ending with an auction to be important, but "*by no means the most important.*"

Company Profile

ezAuctioning's mission is to create a scalable and efficient consignment service where individuals, businesses, and community organizations can drop-off higher value items for sale on eBay by experienced, knowledgeable staff at a fair price.

Contact Information for Geremy Gersh:
www.ezauctioning.com
geremy@ezauctioning.com
Phone: 703-778-6440 ext. 103

Shaun Smith

Username:	sunnking
Name:	Shaun Smith
Classification:	Internet/ eBay Only Business
Current Tier:	Platinum PowerSeller
eBay Store:	Sunnking
eBay Store Location:	www.stores.ebay.com/Sunnking
Current Feedback Star:	Shooting Yellow
Projected 2006 Sales:	$1,500,000

A Little Background

Sunnking has been an active seller on eBay since October 1998. Shaun Smith is the Vice President of Sales and Operations for Sunnking.

Shaun Smith—username sunnking—is a full-time eBay seller along with 14 other full-time employees of Sunnking (10 of whom are eBay ad writers).

The President of Sunnking, Inc., Duane Beckett, worked in the Scrap Metal Industry and was scrapping a large quantity of electronic equipment. As eBay was becoming more popular, it was the perfect marketplace for the valuable electronic equipment.

Shaun said that within three months (the shortest time possible), PowerSeller status caught up to Sunnking, Inc.

With just a few high value items, meeting the $1,000 per months is simple.

Using only the auction format currently, they sell around 800 items a week with a starting price of $9.99.

The reason is two-fold:

- *$.35 listing fee as opposed to a $.70 fee for a $10 starting price that really adds up for 800 auctions per week*

- *$9.99 results in a slight profit margin based on the work put into the auction.*

Shaun said that because 80 percent of all items purchased

on eBay are found through direct title searches, make sure to use all 55 characters allowed in the title. Here he has given a sample:

Brand, Model Number, Species (i.e. Printer or Laptop, or Hair Brush), and other key information.

Example:

IBM 600X ThinkPad PIII 500MHz 256MB Laptop 2645-KKU NR.

- *Brand – IBM*

- *Model – 600X & 2645-KKU*

- *Species – ThinkPad & Laptop*

- *Other – PIII 500MHz & 256MB*

Consider the following possible customers who will locate this item. A customer needing this specific unit for a manufacturing line replacement laptop will search for: IBM 2645-KKU, or IBM 600X. A customer who is thinking about buying a laptop and remembers the IBM brand searches for: IBM Laptop. A customer who wants a Pentium III laptop because they are one generation older than the Pentium 4 searches for: Pentium III laptop. These are just three examples with many more are possible. If the title were IBM Laptop instead, only one of the three customers would have found it.

Sunnking, Inc., gets the items they sell because they are an electronics recycling company.

As we provide our services to company in the Northeastern United States, we attempt to reuse/resell the product before recycling it.

To list their items, they hired a software company that created custom software for them. This software maximizes efficiency and productivity in the eBay department. They also use Blackthorne for post-sales management as well. They do minimal cross-promoting, using just what eBay does automatically and providing links to their store.

When it comes to the timing and time-ending of an auction, Shaun finds it very important.

> *Seven-day auctions are the most time an auction can run without adding another charge to the listing fee. Sunnking, Inc., does place major emphasis on the ending time of an auction, primarily because most bidding occurs in the final minutes or seconds.*

Most eBay buyers live in the United States or Canada, which means our auctions need to be scheduled to end at key times when customers across the country can be at their computers.

Prime Listing Times

- *3 p.m. EST- 5 p.m. EST (end of the work day on the East Coast), which is 12 p.m. PST – 2 p.m. EST (lunch time on the West Coast)*

- *9 p.m. EST – 11 p.m. EST, which is 6 p.m. PST – 8 p.m. PST. During these time frames are when customers are usually home from work.*

Also, no two auctions should end at the same time. Always leave at least one minute between ending times to allow for buyers interested in two auctions time to switch over and get that final bid in.

This issue of ending times in multiple listings is becoming less important with the recent development and expansion of the "snipe" bid which means the bidder pays a small fee to have a program externally place a bid for himself. By using a snipe program, bidders do not have to make sure they are at the computer, waiting for the final seconds to place a winning bid.

We have tested this issue by listing items that end in the middle of the night and the items do not sell for as much as the strategic listing time. In conclusion, not every eBay bidder is using snipe bidding yet and one less bid means a lower selling price.

Shaun recommends following eBay practice when a buyer is unresponsive: issue a second payment notice, and then a final payment notice, followed by a non-paying bidder alert. He said this routine gives the customer plenty of time to respond and doesn't tie down inventory for non-paying bidders. He does have a return policy that allows an item that was not described correctly to be returned for a full refund.

To save on shipping costs, Sunnking works exclusively with UPS. This is convenient for them as they do a daily pickup at the warehouse and they offer a percentage discount for major customers.

The marketplace for shipping and handling is pretty close and there is not much to save. Convenience wins out for Sunnking every time.

Shaun believes that international shippers are sometimes good for business

They do raise the overall selling price of product, but if they are unwilling to pay international shipping and handling cost after the auction ends, our bottom line is affected.

Although they have yet to try drop shipping, they are looking into it.

If the profit margin is substantial enough, it could be a successful business on eBay.

To drive people to their eBay store, Shaun said they provide links in their auctions and their store results are shown when a search is done. They also have a non-eBay site: **www. sunnking.com**.

A Final Piece of Advice

eBay auctions need to be as informative as possible. Include all information for the following issues:

- *customer questions*

- *payment terms and options*

- *S&H costs/terms*

- *warranty/return policy*

- *packing procedure*

The more information provided, the less work incurred after the fact.

Company Profile

Since 2000, Sunnking, Inc., has pressed forward with one goal in mind. Provide superior Asset Management/E-Scrap

Recycling services to the business world. Not only do we specialize in E-Scrap Recycling, we have the ability to find value in nearly all used equipment. By using on-line auction sites, and B2B networks we make maximum profit on equipment that may not be visible to others while recycling in an environmentally friendly manor.

We currently hold contracts with companies nationwide in order to recover top dollar on their assets.

Contact Information for Sunnking:

www.sunnking.com
Phone: 877-860-7866

Tim Miller

Username:	www.flatsigned.com
Name:	Tim Miller
E-mail:	TimMiller@FlatSigned.com
Classification:	Internet/ eBay Only Business
Current Tier:	Platinum PowerSeller
eBay Store:	www.flatsigned.com
eBay Store Location:	www.stores.ebay.com/ www-flatsigned-com
Current Feedback Star:	Green
Projected 2006 Sales:	$2,000,000

A Little Background

Tim Miller has been a member of eBay since August 1998.

Ten years ago I owed the IRS $25,000 in back taxes. To pay them I decided to put a few of my autographed books on Amazon.com. The prices attained were so high I discovered that I could replace my product from other brick-and-mortar stores and resell for higher prices. This became so successful, I financed my IRS debt with the IRS, paying their 25 percent interest while parlaying my auction earnings into buying more product to auction. My collection of autographed books went from about 100 to now 35,000 and my sales went from zero to $2,000,000 currently. When Amazon Auctions failed, I carried on this same method of business at eBay; hiring employees as the company grew. Now I publish Signed Limited Editions (President Gerald R. Ford, Buzz Aldrin, Val Kilmer, General Hal Moore) to sell as well.

*My Web sites are **www.flatsigned.com** and **www.flat-signedpress.com**, and the newest (not announced to the public yet) is **www.bookgradingservice.com**.*

Tim Miller—username www.flatsigned.com—began selling on eBay after Amazon Auctions stopped doing business. He is now a full-time seller with five full-time employees. Becoming a PowerSeller was not a goal he had set; it just happened after about six months.

In the beginning it actually meant something to be a "PowerSeller" but shortly thereafter, it meant and continues to be almost nothing to most sellers and buyers.

Using auctions, "buy it nows," and eBay storefront, Tim sells about 200 items a week.

The key for me is not quantity but higher end product.

His average starting price is $38.95, but he also uses reserves. Factoring in the reserve price, the average value jumps to about $1,000. He has found the best way to get people to notice his listings is through keywords, pay-per-click marketing, and building a larger customer base with free newsletters and outside advertising with Google, print ads, and even TV.

He finds most of his items from other sellers and he also publishes some of the books he sells. To sell his items, he uses Vendio software, which is now Dosadi. He also uses cross-promotion. He said the time to begin and time to end an auction is very important.

When he has not heard from a buyer, Tim will try and contact the buyer through the online channels provided by eBay and then by the phone number provided by eBay. He does have a return policy that gives the buyer 100-percent refund including all shipping costs both ways if he has made a mistake. If buyers make a mistake or just changes their mind there is a 20 percent re-stocking fee.

Tim believes the best way for the customer to save on shipping costs would be to bundle purchases and even ask for free shipping for large or quantity purchases. For the seller to save on shipping costs, he recommends negotiating fees with UPS, FedEx, and similar carriers, but also to be aware that only UPS really covers lost and damaged collectibles like books, baseball cards, autographs, and art.

Tim does believe international bidders are good for business, and he also believes that drop shipping is a good method for selling items. Tim has drop shipped both for other booksellers and for clients giving gifts of his books ever since he started his business. Providing these and all other requested services is how he has built up a high-end clientele who want to pay for these services. The convenience is worth the cost for those who are busy professionals. Drop shipping is rarely a problem, but Tim warns to be aware of credit card fraud especially from the South Pacific and the Middle East. In 10 years of business Tim has only experienced two fraudulent credit card situations.

> *Be fearful more of the wife or husband who spend large sums of money without telling their spouse. That can end up in credit card or PayPal charge backs as often as fraudulent credit card charges.*

To draw people to his eBay store, Tim uses e-mail campaigns, national advertising, and his Web site. He has a direct link to his Web site: **www.flatsigned.com** on his "About Me" page.

Tim Siegel

Username:	matrixmedical
Name:	Tim Siegel
E-mail:	tsiegel@matrixmedical.com
Web Site:	www.matrixmedical.com
Classification:	Internet/ eBay Only Business
Current Tier:	Platinum PowerSeller
Current Feedback Star:	Red
Projected 2006 Sales:	$700,000

A Little Background

Tim Siegel has been a member of eBay since January 1999.

Six years ago, Tim Siegel, 32, drove from Minnesota to Guatemala after hearing he could make money selling medical equipment down there. Tim had a degree in criminology that led him to a management position for a hospitality telemarketing company which allowed him to visit intriguing places like Guam and Malaysia. He decided to try to sell medical equipment when he heard he could make some money at it, all the while doing something he loves: traveling.

After a while, the 3,000-mile trip to Guatemala via truck or bus became exhausting for Tim. He was able to earn a lot of money for the medical equipment due to Guatemala's poor infrastructure and their willingness to pay top dollar for the equipment they needed. He said the Guatemalans would pay two to three times the amount for his equipment than those in the United States. But after five trips, he realized he was only breaking even. So, he washed his hands of it.

In 1999 he was given the idea to begin selling on eBay, and he went for it. After selling a fetal monitor for $500 that cost him only $250, he realized he would not be driving back to Guatemala again. Now Tim runs his eBay business, Matrix Medical, which sells all kinds of medical equipment—anything you might find in a hospital—to buyers from all over the world. This accounts for 95 percent of his business, with only 5 percent coming from sales of other merchandise.

Tim recently moved into a warehouse he purchased and has a full-time employee. Since selling on eBay, Tim said his confidence has risen. Being able to purchase items for a small amount and sell them for a large profit blows his mind. Although he is sure without eBay he would have been successful, he said it is still hard to say what might have happened on all those trips to Guatemala.

Tim Siegel—username matrixmedical—is a full-time eBay seller. Becoming a PowerSeller was not a goal, but it did catch up to him as his sales increased. It was about a year after he began selling on eBay that he earned the status. In 2005 his sales were just over $500,000. He projects they will be closer to $700,000 in 2006.

Tim sells about 40 items a week with his average listing starting price at "$300ish." He uses auctions and "buy it nows" on 90 percent of his items and said the best way to get his listings noticed is through the gallery photo. He uses Dream weaver to create his listings.

Tim gets most of the items he sells from hospitals. He does not make any of the items he sells and does not use cross-promotions.

He believes the time and time-ending of an auction is very important.

I end my auctions around 2 p.m. Central Time Zone during a work day as most people who should be working at that time are buying stuff on eBay.

When he hasn't heard from a buyer, Tim said his action depends on the buyer's feedback and the amount of time that elapses after the auction ends.

I would say it is best to file a non paying bidder.

Tim offers a 30-day warranty against mechanical defects for purchases in the lower 48 states, less the return shipping costs.

He believes international bidders are good for business. Tim said drop shipping is a good method for selling items only if you are lazy and want to cut your profits in half. He recommends not using UPS, but using FedEx to save on shipping costs.

They cost more than Fed Ex and are not as good as FedEx. Then use FedEx Ground and get an American Express Blue Card which gives you 5 percent off on Ground and 10 percent off on Express, and, I think, 15 percent on International Express.

Tim used to have an eBay store but closed it because it was not drawing any customers. He does have a Web site which he has linked to his "About Me" page per eBay's rules. His site is: **www.matrixmedical.net**.

Final Pieces of Advice

Start slow; sell something you have in your closet to get the hang of it. When you have a good feel for how the mechanics work, you can look into buying items and then reselling them. Don't get in over your head; in other words, make your first few purchases small as you don't want to break the bank on a mistake. That holds true for all purchases, regardless of your experience. I make money on just about everything I buy, but I have burned myself before. If you don't know what something is worth, don't buy it. You don't have to move on every opportunity that comes across your plate.

Protect your feedback. I offer warranties for the simple fact that if there is a problem, I am going to take it back anyway as my feedback would not be so clean if I sent people garbage and then said tough luck. Sometimes you run across a customer whom you cannot please; just have them send the item back and refund ALL of the money they sent you. Also, never leave feedback until it has been left for you. This way you can respond accordingly if someone leaves you unwarranted feedback. And remember, the first thing to do if you get negative feedback is to call the person on the phone using the phone number they have registered on eBay. If the number is not valid, the feedback can be removed based just on that.

I do not use reserves; it is a waste of money and wastes people's time. Just start it at your minimum and see what happens. I always use a "buy it now" if I am 100 percent sure that I know what it is worth. I have put "buy it now" prices that were much lower than an item sold for in the end, so be careful as you can burn yourself that way as well.

Make your item descriptions clear and simple with high quality photos. It takes just as long to take a good photo as a bad one. Buy a nice camera, light, and make a clean backdrop. Learn how to take clean photos with small file sizes as there are still cave-dwellers who use dial-up. And don't use music or other flakey, fancy things. You are simply trying to sell something, not entertain, so make it easy on the buyer.

Do not ship to Canada using FedEx or UPS. Use U.S. Postal Service so that the buyer cannot stick you with customs duties and taxes as they can with FedEx, UPS, and DHL. With FedEx, for example, the buyer can ignore the notices to pay the fees and after a few months you get the bill. This happens about 15 percent of the time when shipping to Canada.

Shipping internationally is very helpful depending on the product, but be careful with the shipping cost; don't underestimate and remember that the U.S. Postal Service has very strict size restrictions which vary from country to country. Shipping FedEx outside the United States and Canada is very expensive, but many people will pay as it is the only option.

Stay on top of your e-mail; don't take days to get back to people.

If you get a negative feedback before you have a good score, say 100-200, start over.

Accept PayPal on smaller ticket items. PayPal, or as I like to call it, PayPail, will cost you 1 percent more than if you just accept a credit card. And the buyer protection is the same, not to mention that the buyer will have much better customer service should a problem arise compared to PayPail. I only accepted checks and money orders until a year ago and never had a problem. Now I take credit cards and PayPail as you almost have to in order to compete. I am sure that I get higher bids when accepting PayPail, but is it really 2.5 percent more? I doubt it.

Gerard Bechard

Username:	gerardsbike
Name:	Gerard Bechard
E-mail:	gerard.bechard@verizon.net
Classification:	Internet/ eBay Only Business
Current Tier:	Gold/ Platinum PowerSeller
eBay Store:	Gerard's Bike Shop
eBay Store Location:	www.stores.ebay.com/Gerards-Bike-Shop
Current Feedback Star:	Shooting Yellow
Projected 2006 Sales:	$500,000-plus

A Little Background

Gerard Bechard has been a member of eBay since July 2000.

He has been the owner of Gerard's Bike Shop for 30 years. Once a brick-and-mortar location, it is now an Internet sales business that uses eBay exclusively for the marketing of his products. Currently in a transition phase of building and marketing a Trading Assistance aspect of the business which also includes training and consulting businesses on the start up of selling on eBay. His extensive background in manufacturing, construction, health care, retail, service, and a variety of specialties make him ideal for seeing the potential and working with just about any type of business to help it gain access to one of the largest outlets of merchandise—eBay. He has also had experience in helping clients set up eBay Trading Post (Drop Off Centers). He also complements his business as a eBay Educational Specialist.

Gerard Bechard—username gerardsbike—became a full-time eBay seller after his brick-and-mortar store was closed.

The choice was made for me. I was in the process of closing my bicycle retail and service location when one of my customers came in and gave me the idea to sell some of my outdated items on eBay. My first item literally was pulled back out of the trash barrel. It had been in my store for 18 years, and I couldn't have sold it for a $1 if I tried. That item ended up-selling for $76, $46 more than the price tag that was on it for 18 years. I was hooked. I transitioned my brick-and-mortar business to eBay and have never looked back.

Becoming a PowerSeller caught up to Gerard after just a short period of time. His status does fluctuate between gold and platinum because of the seasonal nature of his core cycling business.

When I started six years ago it was tougher to get to the first level PowerSeller status. There was a $20,000/month quota. I made that level in six months.

During seasonal times, Gerard sells around 400 items a week, whereas off season he sells around 150 items a week. He uses keywords and always includes a gallery image to get people to notice his listings. Some items he lists start at $.99, but most of his items start at $9.99.

Most start at $9.99 unless it is a questionable item that I don't want to let go too inexpensively by accident, or it is an item for a client who wants a sense of security and is not willing to take a gamble.

Although he does not make any of the items he sells, he has other avenues to find products to list.

I have some channels for distressed inventory that I have used in the past, but I have been making the transition and putting more effort into the Trading Assistant program.

Gerard does not use any other cross-promotion besides what eBay does with his listings.

I do have a marketing plan for promoting my Trading Assistant segment by using print ads that will also direct to my listings.

For listing software, Gerard prefers Turbo Lister 2. He used Vendio, eBay's Seller's Assistant Pro, and Blackthorne, but has found Turbo Lister 2 to be faster listing and easier to use.

Turbo Lister 2 is also what I set up for my clients who are starting their own eBay businesses. It's very easy to teach with a short learning curve.

He finds timing for an auction to be extremely important.

Most of my auctions are seven days with starting and ending times on a Sunday at 10 p.m. EST. If I have a particularly special item, I will run it as a 10-day auction with a start time of Thursday at 10 p.m. This gives it a trip through two weekends.

Gerard tries to send out one e-mail to a non-responsive buyer as a reminder.

I usually send one e-mail before starting the "non-paying bidder alert" process to see what the issue may be. There are quite a few times when they simply forgot or didn't know they won.

He does not have a return policy written out and no one has requested one from him.

Usually if there is a problem with an item or it's something that was not what someone expected, I will gladly take it back. If it was a defective item I will cover the return shipping cost also. I think people get a real sense of my business practice from viewing my feedback.

To save on shipping costs, Gerard tries to ship his one and two pound packages through Priority Mail with USPS.

Very fast service and the boxes are free of charge. Doesn't sound like much but supplies can add up considerably.

He said that international bidders are good depending on the items he is selling.

International shipping can be time-consuming with the forms and if the package is not sent with a premium service there is no availability of tracking. There are some items that I have that return 50 percent more in the international market than the domestic market.

Gerard has had some experience with drop shipping in the past.

But without some exclusivity of the product I found that there would be dozens of sellers on eBay in a price war, and no one was making any real money.

Gerard is in the process of completing a new Web site for his eBay Consulting and Trading Assistant business. He does not have any plan for driving people to his eBay store, but this site will have a link to his items on eBay.

It is basically there to give potential clients a sense of my experience. As far as an e-commerce type of site, there are no plans for one in the future. I don't see how you can be as cost effective as doing business on eBay directly.

Gerard markets most of his items with auctions and makes use of "buy it nows" as well.

I do place some items specifically in the storefront but there is usually not much action there.

Contact Information for Gerard Bechard:

Gerard Bechard

30 Westwood Ave

East Longmeadow, MA 01028

413-783-1644

www.protechia.com

eBay user ID: gerardsbike

Pro Tech Internet Auction Services

gerard.bechard@verizon.net

Charles & Mary Byrd

Username:	houstoncharlie2
Name:	Charles & Mary Byrd
E-mail:	charles@easyonlineselling.info
Classification:	Internet/ eBay Only Business
Current Tier:	Gold PowerSeller
eBay Store:	Texas LeatherCraft
eBay Store Location:	www.stores.ebay.com/ Texas-LeatherCraft
Current Feedback Star:	Green

A Little Background

The Byrds have been eBay members since April 2002.

Charles Byrd—username houstoncharlie2—started selling on eBay by accident.

> *My very first auction sold for $2000 and everyone involved came away from the deal happy. I had just bought a computer when a friend asked me if I thought I could sell a couple of burial plots for him on the Internet. He had bought four plots back in the 1960s for a $200 each and now only needed two. I had, of course, heard of eBay but had never been on the site. I told my friend I would give it a try. Three weeks later the cemetery lots were sold and so was I.*

He and his wife, Mary, sell on eBay full-time.

> *My day starts with answering e-mails and printing orders for the shipping department—my wife heads that—and the day ends with answering e-mails.*

Never setting PowerSeller status as a goal once he decided to start selling seriously on eBay, Charles said it only took him four or five months to reach the PowerSeller status.

> *When I first started, my main goal was to get a hundred feedbacks. I never envisioned being a PowerSeller let alone trying to make a living on eBay. It's funny how things can work out.*

The Byrds ship about 200 eBay orders a week. Their starting price for their auctions is usually a penny.

About the most common starting price that I have noticed on eBay is $.99. If you decide that you must have $25 for an item, start the bidding at $25 or set a $25 reserve price and start the bidding at a penny. A low starting price will attract more bidders in the early rounds and the more bids an item has, the more hits it will get in the later rounds. You have to be careful with setting a reserve, though. The bidder is not only bidding against other people but he is also bidding against your reserve price and doing so could be a deterrent to some people.

When it comes to getting bidders to notice their listings, they say the simplest thing that can be done is using the proper keywords in the title of the auction.

I see auction after auction where people use words like "Rare," "L@@K," and "Beautiful." Type the word "L@@K" into the eBay search box and it will pull up over 130,000 auctions for everything from potted plants to oil filters. The word "Beautiful" will bring up around 300,000 items but hopefully none for oil filters. Be specific when wording your title and you'll have a lot better chance of coming up in a search.

The Byrds do make some of their items, as long as time permits, and they hope to add a line or two of small leather goods to their business. Mostly, they distribute leathercraft supplies.

We occasionally will purchase items from crafters who are getting out of the business and wish to liquidate. We are always open to a deal if one comes up.

They make use of eBay's Turbo Lister software when listing their items for sale.

We use Turbo Lister mainly because it is free and we are familiar with it. We get calls from the major third party providers from time to time wanting our business, but so far we have turned them down. We try to cut costs where we can.

Charles and Mary also use eBay's built-in cross-promotion tools and find that it works well for them.

We try not to push things on people, but it doesn't hurt to show them a picture or two of our other listings.

Although Charles used to worry about the starting and ending times of his listings, he doesn't so much anymore.

I did not want auctions ending in the middle of the day when people were at work nor in the middle of the night when everyone was asleep and I still don't. But I just do not worry about it so much anymore. I do feel that an auction ending at 9 p.m. has a better chance of ending at a higher price than say one ending at 2 p.m. The problem is that 9 p.m. on the East Coast is not 9 p.m. on the West Coast. If you can target your customers by region, have your auctions end when everyone in that particular region is most likely to be at home and in front of a computer.

When dealing with buyers who are not communicating, the Byrds take the following approach:

Try to contact them via e-mail, and if they're not answering the e-mails there could be a perfectly innocent reason for it. Their computer might be down, their e-mail address could have changed, or they might be out of town. I once had trouble getting in touch with a winning bidder and later found out she had been in the hospital. I sure am glad I did not add a negative feedback to her troubles. Get their contact information from eBay and give them a call. Nine times out of ten the situation can be resolved with good communication. The worst thing you can do is to leave a negative feedback right away. After they get that negative, there really is no reason for them to try and work things out.

They do make use of a return policy as they feel it is very important to the success of business. They say their return policy of an unconditional 30-day money-back guarantee has been a deciding factor for many of their customers.

If you do not like it, just send it back, no questions asked.

The Byrds try to keep their shipping costs fair and accurate. They do not try to make profits from over-charging on shipping costs. Since they do not want to lose money from shipping costs either, they make use of the free packaging materials USPS gives with Priority Mail services. They have found it saves money and time. They do ship internationally.

We love our international customers. I have a big world map on my office wall with lines drawn from our location in Texas to the different countries we have shipped to. With the exception of Antarctica, we have shipped products to every continent on the planet. By golly we're global.

Although they do not currently drop ship, this is something they would consider.

I would love to find a couple of good drop shippers but if you are concerned with your feedback rating, a drop shipper can cause problems. I would need to have full faith in them before I could put my reputation in their hands.

Charles and Mary have a private Web site as well as their eBay store site. It is located at **www.texasleathercraft.com**. They do not link their Web site with any of their auctions, because of the rules eBay has created about such matters. When it comes to driving people to their eBay store, they have found search engines are the best solution for them.

Much of our store traffic comes from search engine results. Submit your store to the search engines, do data feeds, use the mailing list utility that eBay provides. Do anything you can think of to get your store URL in front of people.

The Byrds take advantage of all the selling formats: auctions, store-front, and "buy it nows."

Some people love the excitement of bidding while others would rather just purchase the item and go about their business.

A Final Piece of Advice

Answer all e-mails in a timely manner, be courteous with your customers at all times, and ship your orders as quickly as possible. If you hold to these three things you will not only be a success on eBay but have loads of fun as well.

Contact Information for Charles and Mary:
Byrd Custom Leather
PO Box 514
Porter, TX 77365
eBay ID: houstoncharlie2
PayPal ID: ebay@texasleathercraft.com
Website: www.TexasLeatherCraft.com
Call Toll-Free: 877-823-6207

Visit us on eBay at **http://stores.ebay.com/Texas-LeatherCraft.com**. For more great deals on leathercraft supplies, please check out our Web site **www.TexasLeatherCraft.com**. Check out our Leathercraft Blog for news and articles concerning leather and leathercraft: **www.texasleathercraft.com/blog**. Sign up for our free newsletter and receive great tips on leathercrafting as well as advance notice of upcoming specials!

Dana Zini

Username:	collectibledecorandmore
Name:	Dana Zini
E-mail:	dzini@collectibledecorandmore.com
Classification:	Internet/ eBay Only Business
Current Tier:	Gold PowerSeller
eBay Store:	Collectible Décor and More
eBay Store Location:	www.stores.ebay.com/Collectible-Decor-and-More
Current Feedback Star:	Red
Projected 2006 Sales:	$1,000,000

A Little Background

Dana Zini has been a member of eBay since December 2000.

Dana Zini—username collectibledecorandmore—is a full-time seller on eBay.

> *I was a buyer of primarily antique books and enjoyed my buying experience, and as I was shopping for books for myself I started shopping for books others may want to collect.*

Becoming a PowerSeller was a goal Dana had set for herself and it only took her a few months to achieve that goal.

> *With an average of 50 online sales through eBay every week and a total of 1000 a month through Web store sales, Dana said the best way to get people to notice her listings is through pictures. Her average starting price is about $24.99, and she markets her products mainly through auctions and her storefront listings.*

Though she does not make any of the items she sells, she finds most of her items through researching companies she likes that carry the lines she wishes to offer. She does not use any type of listing software. She does make use of cross-promotions with her listings.

Dana has a satisfaction guaranteed return policy, and a refund is provided less the cost of shipping and sellers fees (unless she notes otherwise).

> *All items returned for a refund must be in original packaging and shipped back within seven days from delivery, unless noted differently.*

She finds time and time-ending with an auction somewhat important. She does find international bidders good for business and drop shipping a good method for selling items. She uses drop shipping in her own store.

When she has trouble with a buyer, she finds e-mail communication to be the best approach to try to reach the person.

Her Web site **www.collectibledecorandmore.com** has a link to her listings on eBay. She uses this site to help drive people to her store on eBay.

Final Piece of Advice

Other information I think would be helpful: clearly noted return policy, damage/return policy noted, contact information, telephone number, and e-mail as well as multiple pictures and clear descriptions.

Company Profile

All of our products are offered at below the suggested retail pricing! We offer thousands of wholesale and discount priced accents for your home and garden, plus furniture, baby and nursery items, classic rockers and pedal cars, pet products, Christian and educational games and puzzles and some of the lowest prices on As Seen on TV products. We buy direct and sell direct from the warehouse to you! Here are just a few of the manufacturers we distribute for: Graco, Storkcraft, Kidkraft, As Seen On TV, Enesco Jim Shore Heartwood Creek, Enesco Kitchen Fairies, Gibson, Simply Home, Coke, Warner Brothers, John Deere, Petsafe, Manual Woodworkers and Weavers, Talicor Christian and

Educational Games, Coleman, Chicago Cutlery, Corning, Levels of Discovery, World Safari and Airflow. We hope you will enjoy browsing through our store of treasures. 100 percent satisfaction offered on all items; we want you to be happy with your purchase!

Please contact us for volume order discounts for weddings, corporate gifts, or resale. We provide drop shipping! If we don't have it, we would be happy to find it for you. Products are added daily so please check back often.

I can do all things through Christ who strengthens me. Philippians 4:13

Contact information for Collectible Décor and More:

www.collectibledecorandmore.com

orders@collectibledecorandmore.com

Heather Gillespie

Username:	3buttons*n*2bows
Name:	Heather Gillespie
E-mail:	custom_orders@3buttonsn2bows.com
Classification:	Internet/ eBay Only Business
Current Tier:	Gold PowerSeller
eBay Store:	3 Buttons N 2 Bows
eBay Store Location:	www.stores.ebay.com/3-Buttons-N-2-Bows
Current Feedback Star:	Green
Projected 2006 Sales:	$125,000

A Little Background

Heather Gillespie has been a member of eBay since October 2000.

3ButtonsN2Bows is named for my five children: three boys (buttons) and two girls (bows). We offer custom handmade decor to complement any child's room or nursery with a unique boutique touch. We specialize in fabric and wood items and enjoy creating custom items for your home. Our philosophy is that children should have fun, bright, and cheerful rooms to call their own, so we work hard to keep prices low and quality high.

How it all began: In 2003, I traded in a career outside the home to care for my twin girls. Following a respiratory syncytial virus diagnosis for both girls as well as low birth weight, it was clear to my family and to our pediatrician that my being at home was the only option. With a background in interior design and a love for crafting and sewing that dates back practically to the womb, a career in designing kids' room items was a natural fit. We have been blessed with a wonderful client base and great experiences on eBay, and now we are bringing our unique designs to our own Web site! We are grateful to all our customers for keeping it possible for me to be at home.

Heather Gillespie—username 3buttons*n*2bows—is a full-time eBay seller.

I had to quit my job outside the home when I gave birth to twin girls. With five children, working and paying childcare was not an option. I had sold some small things on eBay before so I was familiar with auctions; however, becoming a full-time seller was a whole new enterprise.

After only three months, Heather earned PowerSeller status.

It was never a goal. I just listed my auctions and the PowerSeller status came on its own. I never pay much attention to that title. The important thing for me is that my business benefits my family and satisfies my customers.

Making use of auctions, store-front, "buy it nows," and eBay Express, Heather sells an average of 250 to 300 items a week with an average starting price of $17.99. She gives a few ideas on how to entice people to notice your listings.

I think that clear photos and auction titles are the most important part of your business. Also, I include a small note about why I am a seller and I get many, many comments from buyers appreciating the personal touch.

Heather makes all of the items she sells. She does not use any type of software to list her items. She cross-promotes with other sellers. She doesn't believe the time and time-ending of an auction are at all important.

When she hasn't heard from buyers, Heather will always e-mail them once through eBay, and after three days she will send an Unpaid Item Reminder. She does have a return policy.

Returns are approved on a case-by-case basis. If the item is not what a customer expected, an exchange or full refund can be arranged. All returns are negotiated with the customer's satisfaction as the top priority.

To save on shipping costs, Heather will "combine shipping with $2 additional per item on top of the highest price items. eBay does this for me automatically."

When it comes to international bidders she said absolutely not.

There is too much hassle and unknowns with international shipping.

To drive people into her eBay store, Heather will use her auctions and eBay keywords. She also has a Web site: **www.3buttonsn2bows.com**. She has a link to that store on her "About Me" page.

A Final Piece of Advice

You have to limit yourself to what you can do well and do not underestimate the amount of time it takes to take photos, write descriptions, upload photos, answer e-mails, and ship your items. Doing a little well and making your customers happy is better than doing too much and having unhappy clients.

Jack Cheung

Username:	eBargainNow
Name:	Jack Cheung
E-mail:	mcc2047@yahoo.com
Web Site:	www.ebargainnow.com
Classification:	Internet/ eBay Only Business
Current Tier:	Gold PowerSeller
Current Feedback Star:	Red

eBargainNow Discount Laptops
eBargainNow.com

A Little Background

Jack Cheung has been a member of eBay since December 1998.

Jack Cheung obtained his MBA from New Jersey Institute of Technology. He has more than 10 years of experience in sales, marketing, and business management on some of America's leading consumer brands.

★

A part-time eBay seller, Jack Cheung—username eBargainNow—started selling on eBay for the extra income it provided. After only two months PowerSeller status caught up to Jack. He hadn't really planned it.

He has used auctions, a store-front, and fixed price as the areas he has marketed. With an average starting price usually

$.99, Jack sells about 15 items a day. He finds the best way to get people to notice his listings is by making sure the main keywords are in the title.

Although he wishes he could sell some homemade items, he currently does not. Jack finds most of his items by searching the Internet for deals and by customers calling him.

For listing software, Jack uses Mpire. He doesn't make use of cross-promotions. Time-ending with an auction is important to Jack as he has found that prices are lower on Friday and Saturday nights.

For non-responsive buyers, Jack does the following:

> *E-mail a few times, and then call after a week. Then file non payment on eBay.*

Jack has a return policy that gives 30 days for exchanges. To save on shipping, he buys stamps and postage right off eBay.

Jack does find drop shipping to be a good method for selling, but said that it is very hard to get good prices. He does allow international bidders and said they are good for business.

> *"...especially customers from Europe. They usually pay more than the domestic customers."*

Jack doesn't use an eBay store anymore, but when he did, he found he could drive customers to his listings there by using "buy keywords on eBay."

Contact Information for Jack Cheung:
eBargainNow
www.ebargainnow.com
E-mail: mcc2047@yahoo.com

Mike Boerschinger and Jeff Grissom

POWERSELLER PROFILE

Username:	Webauctionexpert
Name:	Mike Boerschinger and Jeff Grissom
E-mail:	mike@whatsitworthlive.com
	jeff@whatsitworthlive.com
Classification:	Internet/ eBay Only Business
Current Tier:	Gold PowerSeller
Business Name:	Web Auction Experts
Web Site:	www.Webauctionexperts.com
Current Feedback Star:	Red

Jeff Grissom

Mike Boerschinger

A Little Background

Mike Boerschinger and Jeff Grissom—username Webauctionexpert—have been members of eBay since December 1998. They run a part-time business on eBay, with full-time effort and time. They set becoming a PowerSeller as a goal for the status of the title as well as the extra perks (for example, the phone support). It took them four years to reach PowerSeller status.

Mike and Jeff make use of auctions and eBay Motors, while specializing mostly in "high ticket collectibles and cars." They sell about 20 to 30 items per week, and their starting price for their auctions is $1. They have found the following methods have worked to get people to notice their listings: keyword rich title and description, easy to follow, excellent photos, and a $1 starting price with reasonable reserve.

They do not make any of the items they sell. Most of their items come from wanted ads and consignments. To list their items, Mike and Jeff use Turbo Lister or "the old-fashioned way." On certain related items, they do use cross-promotions.

When it comes to the time of an auction and ending time, they find it to be very important.

> *The most effective are seven- or ten-day auctions, always ending at 6 p.m. PST on a Sunday.*

When they have trouble with a buyer they have yet to hear from, they will send out three e-mails to try to get the buyer's attention.

> *One reads "congratulations," one reads "I have not heard from you," and one reads "I need to re-list and request a refund of my eBay final value fees—hope to hear from you soon."*

They generally do not have a return policy. They sell their items "as is." However, they will take items back or issue a refund on occasion.

To save on shipping costs, Mike and Jeff recommend developing a relationship with a box- and packaging-wholesaler. They have found that as long as the international bidders pay, they are very good for business with very few problems. As for the drop shipping method, they do not care for it too much. As Mike stated:

I want control over what I sell and how it is packed.

Mike and Jeff are working on creating an eBay store, but they have a Web site: **www.Webauctionexperts.com** where you can find more information about what they do.

Company Information

*We have been very successful selling and consigning items on eBay, and the business has even started a radio show— check out www.whatsitworthlive.com. You can also look at some of our past auctions that are special at **www.Webauctionexperts.com**.*

Mike and Jeff feel that it takes more than an eBay account to sell successfully at or above market value. Creating the right environment to maximize value includes:

- *Access to global niche markets for specialty items*

- *Item valuation and online research*

- *High quality digital photography*

- *Item drop-off or pick-up services*

- *Secured and insured storage facilities*

- *Turn-key corporate training and liquidation services*

- *Diversified and market-tested selling strategies based*

on years of successful auctions

■ *Quick Cash—Web Auction Experts will buy your items at 50 percent of estimated value on-the-spot.*

■ *Want to sell it yourself? Enroll in a state of the art training session using official eBay curriculum. This training is a one-of-a-kind in the area.*

Contact Information for Mike Boerschinger and Jeff Grissom:

Mike Boerschinger

E-mail: mike@whatsitworthlive.com

Phone: 262-894-7348

Jeff Grissom

E-mail: jeff@whatsitworthlive.com

Phone: 414-507-4396

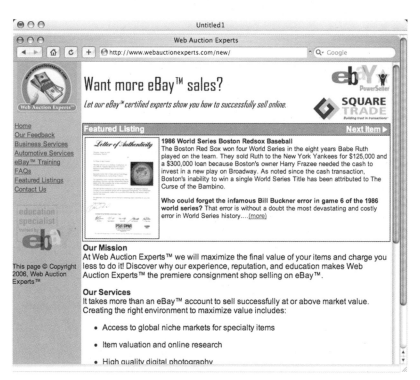

Catherine Allen

Username:	golfingaddict
Name:	Catherine Allen
E-mail:	golfingaddictsales@golfingaddict.com
Classification:	Internet/ eBay Only Business
Current Tier:	Silver PowerSeller
eBay Store:	Golfingaddict Sales
eBay Store Location:	www.stores.ebay.com/Golfingaddict-Sales
Current Feedback Star:	Green
Projected 2006 Sales:	$60,000

A Little Background

Catherine has been a member of eBay since September 1998.

My business name is Golfingaddict Sales. I originally started out selling occasionally in order to earn money to support my golf habit, but it turned into a nice "part-time job" that I can work when it is convenient to me. I sell a variety of things, but concentrate on school supplies, art glass, golf clubs, and stainless flatware.

I am an accomplished amateur golfer and have played

in tournaments around the country. I usually golf in the mornings before I start my eBay work.

Catherine Allen—username golfingaddict—was searching for extra holiday money when she discovered selling on eBay.

I was looking for a way to earn a little extra cash before the holidays and decided to sell a few Hallmark Ornaments on eBay. After a couple of weeks I realized the money was good and I enjoyed selling so I began to devote more time and effort into selling. Within a year I was selling on eBay "full time." I call it full-time, but in actuality it is probably considered part-time. My first love is my hobby (golf), and I spend a bit of time on eBay to support my golf habit.

Becoming a PowerSeller started out impossible and then turned into goals she would set for herself. It took her about eight months to become a PowerSeller.

Originally becoming a PowerSeller seemed to be impossible, as I was just in it to earn a little money, but once I started getting serious I began setting goals to reach certain PowerSeller levels.

Catherine sells around 100 items a week. She sells most items from her eBay store, so she sets the price she wants for the item. With true auctions, she will start them under $9.99 to save on the fees. She tries to keep her shipping costs low and make sure she has good pictures to add. She finds these are good ways to draw people to her listings.

The key thing, however, is to provide items that are not random and easy to find. I concentrate on the unique and rare items in order as people go searching on the Internet for things that they can't find locally.

She buys most of her items that she sells directly from the manufacturer or wholesaler and does not make any of her own items.

Catherine does not use any kind of listing software. She does use cross-promotions.

I run store promotion specials to attract buyers and to get people to buy more than one item.

When it comes to ending times, she goes with what works best for her.

I like to end things during the afternoons, but only because that is convenient to me.

Catherine doesn't have many problems with her buyers not contacting her.

I send a couple of reminders, but I don't have an issue with buyers who don't contact me. Providing them an easy way to pay and all the information they need to send payment seems to eliminate any issues.

She does not use the drop-shipping method. Because of her location and special shipping situation, she does not do any international shipping. She does have a return policy.

I offer a satisfaction guarantee and have a liberal return policy. Buyers can return any item to me for any reason.

Catherine sells mostly from her storefront. She does run auctions but very few of them. She has a Web site (**www.**

golfingaddict.com) that is linked to her eBay store homepage (**http://stores.ebay.com/Golfingaddict-Sales**).

A Final Piece of Advice

I think the key to being successful on eBay is treating people the way that you want to be treated. Buyers appreciate fair and reasonable shipping; they like to know that there is a return policy in case. They want their stuff fast and they want a fair and reasonable price. I try to be an average eBayer that gives above average customer service.

Greg Perry

Username:	bidmentor
Name:	Greg Perry
E-mail:	Perrys@BidMentor.com
Classification:	Internet/ eBay Only Business
Current Tier:	Silver PowerSeller
Current Feedback Star:	Red
Projected 2006 Sales:	$25,000-35,000

A Little Background

Greg Perry has been a member of eBay since April 1999.

Greg Perry is known as the earth's most prolific teacher on computers. He has written more than 75 computer books, all by major publishers, translated into all major languages, and sold in bookstores around the world.

Although his Windows, Microsoft Office, Digital Video, OpenOffice.org, and programming books have become bestsellers in the computer book world, his passion is eBay.

He and Jayne, his bride of 16 years, are PowerSellers. Greg is an eBay-certified eBay Education Specialist, and a columnist who writes about eBay.

His well-rounded writing career includes not only computer books but also countless computer-based articles as well as a best-selling book about managing rental properties and even a book about the government called Disabling America.

Jayne, his eBay cohort, entered the writing foray in 2006 with her first book that seems to sum up her life since 1999: I Married an eBay Maniac–One Couple's Journey to PowerSeller Status.

Greg Perry—username bidmentor—began selling on eBay because of the ease of entry into the marketplace.

I began in 1999 and thought I'd already waited too long to get into the foray. Now that Jayne and I are veteran eBayers, we know that eBay is still in its infancy.

Greg sells only part-time on eBay.

When it gets too time-intensive, we look for tools to speed things up such as Mpire.com, and we might hire part-time helpers.

After a year and a half of selling, Greg gained his PowerSeller status. The first two times he gained PowerSellers status, he lost it within the month because he did not maintain the minimum level of sales. Greg has not lost his status since becoming a PowerSeller for the third time. He is currently at the Silver tier.

Although we flirt with Gold about three months of the year, eBay is still just a sideline/hobby/business (pick one!) for us, and it's difficult to sell more than $10,000 a month to maintain the next level of Gold. But for part-timers, selling more than $3,000 monthly is certainly doable.

Mostly, Greg only takes advantage of the auction format for his listings.

Almost always we list in normal auctions. It's rare for a PowerSeller to sell in auctions only, and we do open an eBay store from time to time, but for us the cost isn't worth it. This is really an exception to what most should do, however. With rare books being our primary inventory item, each item is different and we have found they work best in auctions.

Greg and his wife, Jayne, mostly sell rare and used books. They usually start the auctions at $2.99 unless they know it will be a popular auction, and then they will start it out at a penny or $.99. They average about 100 items a week all dependent on their travel and their inventory.

If we're going to be out of town we'll drop that to as low as five and try to keep those e-Books and items we can drop ship so we can handle the shipments while on the road.

Greg has found the best way to get bidders to notice his listings is by keywords.

The BEST WAY, hands-down is to write keyword-intense titles. So many sellers spend time and effort on Google AdWords, eBay keywords, eBay store promotions, and so on—and those are great to do—without learning what it really means to write a keyword-rich title. You must flood your auction titles with keywords that most buyers will be searching for.

Having learned a lot of techniques that "so dramatically increase bids and/or profits," Greg has written several books about eBay and he will sell those sometimes in his auctions. He has never run out of inventory, had to advertise for more inventory, or looked for his inventory.

Our family and friends still rely on us solely. This means we have an eclectic base of auctions although a 10,000 rare book inventory of one friend is our cornerstone and why we sell mostly those. In the past two years we've sold all of those books we've physically been able to sell and we're only about halfway through it.

Because his auctions are each very different, Greg has looked at the different listing softwares, but mostly uses Mpire.

Keep in mind that our inventory is eclectic which means we often have only one of something and we might never have it again to list in the future. This poses a challenge because every auction listing has to be written uniquely and that's time-consuming. Many times we yearn for a more consistent product but we often hit a home run in unexpected profit that we wouldn't get from selling more of a commodity.

Therefore, our auction needs differ from a lot of PowerSellers who routinely sell the same inventory. We've looked at virtually all auction-related tools out there. Mpire.com works best for us because of its templates and layouts. They allow us to re-use saved pieces of auctions (such as shipping policies or payment policies) and that helps save us a tremendous amount of time. Other listing tools provide some similar features, but Mpire.com works best for our needs.

Greg does take advantage of eBay's cross-promotion tool.

Buyers of one kind of book see other books we're selling that would interest that buyer. eBay's cross-promotion tool takes more time than I wish it took to set these up, however. I'm unsure how they could speed it up but we wish there were a way.

He does not find the timing of an auction or the time-ending with an auction to be as important as it used to be for him.

Now that eBay is so massive, there seem to be millions of buyers and sellers on the site just about 24 hours a day. Friday and Saturday nights are still horrible for sellers, but great for buyers so always look for things on those days if you're in the market for something.

If he has not heard from a buyer after trying to contact them twice, Greg will make use of the non-paying bidder record.

That either gets their attention, or they ignore it and we get our fees back after the non-paying bidder process ends and we re-list the item.

Although he has a return policy, Greg said they sometimes forget to state it.

We should state it. Our return policy is that the item arrives in exactly the condition we described, or we refund 100 percent of the money.

Greg makes use of the USPS Media Mail service.

> *For us, Media Rate mail is a dream-come-true. Our buyers really appreciate the savings. It does mean we cannot use free Priority Mail boxes so we must find our own packaging. We also save a tremendous amount on insurance by using a private shipping insurer whose claim department is faster than USPS and far less costly.*

Greg does welcome international bidders and said they are very good for business. They make up about 20 percent of his income now. He also sometimes uses drop shipping as a method for selling some items.

> *About 10 percent of what we sell is drop shipped and that's inconsistent because sometimes we go months without selling a drop-shipped item.*

Although he does not always have an eBay store, he does have a few methods for drawing bidders into his store when he does have one.

> *We use Google AdWords, but we rely mostly on mentioning our eBay store in every auction and our "About Me" page. We don't always use an eBay store; it depends on our inventory.*

Greg does not use a traditional Web site that he links to his listings.

> *We do have a Web link that we call our "Auction Catalog." It presents a nice, gallery-and-title table of all our auctions. It's really just a saved eBay search that we've honed a little.*

> *It means that at any time, anyone can go here: **www. BidMentor.com** and see every item we have for sale. The*

*advantage of this is that we flood our e-mail signatures, Thank you e-mails, e-mails we send to bidders with questions, and so forth with, 'We love to reduce combined shipping charges if you win multiple items within the same week. To see our current Auction Catalog, click here: **www. BidMentor.com'**. This makes it very easy for us to entice bidders to look at our auctions some more, with the hope of saving on combined shipping costs. It's been far more effective than we ever expected.*

If any readers want to have me set one of those up for them, they can write me at NewCatalog@BidMentor.com and I'll create such a page for them free. They'll need to tell me their eBay ID (no password). I'll host their page and they can use it all they want. Their Auction Catalogs might be something like http://www.BidMentor.com/c/SellerID. I know that's long but there are some ways to shorten it that I'll share with them. There's no charge for this. I do it all the time.

A Final Piece of Advice

Anybody who sells anything who has not read one book or listened to one tape on Direct Marketing is leaving money on the table. Dan Kennedy and Jay Abraham are two writers/ speakers that every eBay seller should know about.

My wife wrote a chapter on how to implement direct marketing techniques in every auction in her book, I Married an eBay Maniac (Que Publishing, ISBN# 0789735628, May 2006). It's a chapter that will massively increase the bids and profits of anyone else.

I'll give you examples. She tells how a description should list benefits and not features. There's a huge difference! When you sell a Bluetooth-enabled phone, don't list Bluetooth-

Enabled; instead write, "No more fumbling for wires, just hold your phone close to your computer and let it suck in your Outlook names and phone numbers!" Read any Lands' End clothing catalog and even in their cheapest t-shirt descriptions, you are almost in love with the t-shirt before you've even touched it. Lands' End doesn't provide a boring list of features; instead they tell you the benefits of that double-stitched collar. Sell the sizzle and not the steak!

In her book, Jayne tells of one single sentence that will dramatically cause your auctions to rise to the top of your eBay category. I could tell you that one sentence here, but she would kill me. My point is not to entice you with it, but let you know that the sentence is common-sense although hardly anyone does it. Sellers don't do their homework and research. They don't understand simple direct marketing techniques such as proper headlines, up-sells, and writing an auction description that is so enticing, readers won't be able to help themselves. They will HAVE to place a bid.

Jack Waddick

Username:	direct210
Name:	Jack Waddick
E-mail:	jwaddick@oakviewtraining.com
Classification:	Internet/ eBay Only Business
Current Tier:	Silver PowerSeller
eBay Store:	Direct210
eBay Store Location:	www.stores.ebay.com/direct210
Current Feedback Star:	Red

POWERSELLER PROFILE

A Little Background

Jack Waddick has been a member of eBay since August 2003.

Jack Waddick does eBay full-time as an active eBay PowerSeller, eBay University Instructor, Education Specialist Trained by eBay, and eBay Business Consultant. His eBay classroom training schedule is available at **www.oakviewtraining.com**.

- *I am an active eBay PowerSeller (with more than 2300 successful transactions)*

- *Seller name: Direct210, feedback 1666*

- *As an eBay University Instructor, I travel the United States teaching eBay Basic & Advanced selling strategies*

- *As the #1 rated (of more than 950 in the United States) Education Specialist Trained by eBay, I teach eBay in the Chicago area*

- *As an eBay Business Consultant I work with small and large business owners across the United States to maximize their eBay selling efforts.*

Between his eBay selling, teaching, and business consulting, Jack Waddick—username direct210—makes eBay a full-time career.

> *I started on eBay buying a few things and wanted to try selling. In 2003, for my first item, I sold my old 1985 Chicago Bears Super Bowl Champs VHS video for $47.25 and I was hooked.*

After five months, Jack became a PowerSeller. He hadn't really planned or worked toward becoming one.

> *It just happened as I started selling more and more. I started "seeing" more and more items to sell as I started looking. I had 264 listings "live" at one time.*

Although his sales vary depending on his very busy travel schedule, Jack usually averages about 30 or 40 items sold a week. He uses a combination of eBay auctions, fixed price, eBay stores, and "buy it nows." When choosing his starting price, he always does research to determine the best price for his items.

> *I always do the research on an item before I set the start price to determine the best/competitive starting bid for the item. I start many items at $.99 each or $9.99. Always research first!*

He cannot stress enough what he finds gets his listings noticed the most.

> *Title Keywords, Title Keywords, Title Keywords. The 55 characters in the title are MOST important for buyers/bidders to find your listing. (No "Wow," "L@@k," or "Yippeee.")*

Jack does not make any of the items he sells, but he finds his items in different ways.

I started selling "stuff" from home, then garage sales, resale shops, thrift stores, and now I buy new product in quantity at retail (overstock, returns, clearance, and end-of-season) and sell it on eBay. I also buy some items on eBay and resell those on eBay for profit. Hint: misspellings.

Turbo Lister is Jack's choice for listing software. It is free to download and use.

Wonderful software. I also use eBay Selling Manager Pro software to manage my activity.

He does make use of cross-promotions and finds that it works very well for him.

I use my auction items to cross-promote my eBay store listing with words like "Don't want to bid and wait? See my eBay Store for a Great 'buy it now' Price."

Jack sells items just about always on a seven-day time frame.

I use seven-day listings 99 percent of the time, and I put up new listings between 12 noon CST and 8 p.m. CST seven days a week because many people wait to bid until the end of the listing and you want these bidders to be AWAKE. Sunday is a big traffic day, but I list things seven days a week.

He uses e-mail reminders to get the attention of unresponsive buyers.

After three days (then again at seven days) I send the buyer an e-mail invoice reminder. Sometimes people forget to pay.

No problem. I've only had three people not pay.

Although he doesn't have a return policy posted, Jack will always take a return if the customer desires it.

I don't argue with the customer.

When it comes to saving on shipping costs, Jack gives the following advice:

Buy a digital scale, weigh each item—never guess the weight. Quote flat shipping to U.S. 48 in each United States listing. Use calculated shipping for international listings. Use free corrugated boxes available at the grocery store for shipping. Use newspaper for packing/fill. Check/compare **USPS.com**, **UPS.com**, *and* **Fedex.com** *for the best rates. eBay sellers in the middle of the country have an advantage in quoting flat rate to U.S. 48.*

Jack does allow and welcome international bidders.

There are 26 eBay Web sites around the world. **eBay.com** *is the United States only. There are 25 more eBay sites for all the other countries served. All 26 sites are shown at the bottom of eBay.com home page. Fifty percent of eBay's total business is international. Don't ignore international.*

He has a little advice to offer for those who are considering drop shipping as a method of selling items.

Before getting set up with a drop shipper, do your homework to know whom you are dealing with. Check them out. Try a small order and see how they perform. Test them. See how it goes. It is your eBay feedback on the line so check their reputation before placing an order. There are many people calling themselves "drop shippers." Check them out. On the eBay Solutions Directory—see "Worldwide Brands." They research and rate many of the companies claiming to be drop shippers.

Jack not only has his eBay store (**www.stores.ebay.com/direct210**), but also has a Web site **www.oakviewtraining.com** that he uses to promote his eBay consulting business and eBay training classes. He uses the cross-promotion tools as mentioned earlier to draw people into his store.

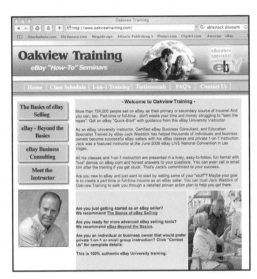

And now eBay is showing eBay store listings at the bottom of the page of any standard result page. That has meant more eBay store sales.

A Final Piece of Advice

Go slow. Don't try to do it all at once. List a few items. List a few more. Don't get overwhelmed. Take your time. Learn from others listings, DO your research on every item before listing it. Make some money and have some fun. And...Go to eBay LIVE!

Contact information for Jack Waddict:
www.oakviewtraining.com
Phone: 847-322-0088
E-mail jwaddick@oakviewtraining.com

John Anastasio

Username:	ClassicCarWiring
Name:	John Anastasio
E-mail:	info@classiccarwiring.com
Classification:	Internet/ eBay Only Business
Current Tier:	Silver PowerSeller
eBay Store:	Classic Car Wiring
eBay Store Location:	www.stores.ebay.com/Classic-Car-Wiring
Current Feedback Star:	Red
Projected 2006 Sales:	$45,000

A Little Background

John Anastasio has been a member of eBay since May 2001.

My name is John Anastasio. I own ClassicCarWiring, which is an auto restoration supplier. I am also an eBay PowerSeller under the same name and the local community "eBay" guy. In addition, I am an eBay Education Specialist and Trading Assistant. What started out as a hobby turned into a full-

*time career where I am in charge of all aspects of my life including my paycheck. eBay allowed me to market-test live sales for very low startup costs to see if their was a viable market to sell my items. My Web site is **www.ClassicCar-Wiring.com** and my e-mail address is info@classiccarwiring.com.*

John Anastasio—username classiccarwiring—is a full-time eBay seller. After about six months of selling seriously on eBay, "as opposed to just cleaning out the house," PowerSeller status caught up to him. He had set becoming one as a goal to eventually reach.

He sells an average of 35 to 45 items per week and his starting price really depends on each item. He said the best way he has found to get people to notice his listings is by providing proper titles and descriptions so that search results are maximized. He sells exclusively "buy it nows" on eBay Motors as his main business.

We create custom laminated wiring diagrams in full color for 30s, 40s, 50s, 60s, and early 70s American cars and trucks.

He makes the wiring diagrams himself and this is his main business, but on the side he also lists items he finds at flea markets and yard sales. For listing purposes, he does not use a specific software. He just keeps track of his expenses in a spreadsheet to "make sure it's worth it." When listing he also makes use of cross-promotions.

Listing to listing and all listings mention eBay stores.

All of John's sales are considered final and sold "as is." When he doesn't hear from buyers, he e-mails them using the eBay system and then tries e-mailing on his own.

John does not believe that timing of an auction and time-ending with an auction is as important as people once thought it was. He has never tried drop shipping as a method of selling items, but he does allow international bidders.

I have shipped worldwide with nary a problem.

John has the following advice for saving on shipping costs:

For lighter items use USPS (free supplies). Don't overcharge customers for shipping.

He has a Web site that is linked to his listings only for payment handling purposes **www.ClassicCarWiring.com**. John finds mentioning his store in all his listings is a good way to drive people in. He also recommends having the store name printed on any company literature and business cards.

A Final Piece of Advice

Be 100 percent honest and know what you are selling. If you can't answer a question, admit it. Keep listings to a minimum. You don't need dancing fairies, artwork, or music to sell an item. You have only a few seconds to lure the buyer in. Give clear, accurate descriptions with a minimum of clutter. I have as much fun going out looking for different things to sell as I do teaching others how to do it.

My eBay philosophy is to keep it as easy as possible. Unless the item calls for it, keep the descriptions clear and accurate. Take clear, focused pictures and keep the "fluff" to a minimum. If you are selling a pair of shoes, for example, you don't need animated GIFs and crazy color schemes. Size, condition, type, and any useful tidbits are enough. Clear instructions and prices for shipping, discounts, and returns are all that's needed at the bottom of a typical listing. A listing on eBay has the potential to be seen by tens of thousands of people from around the world. The goal is to give one of those pairs of eyes a reason to buy your item rather than another item.

Kurt Stoehr

Username:	hamstore
Name:	Kurt Stoehr
E-mail:	hamiltonstore@onewest.net
Classification:	Internet/ eBay Only Business
Current Tier:	Silver PowerSeller
Web Site:	www.hamiltonstore.com
Current Feedback Star:	Turquoise

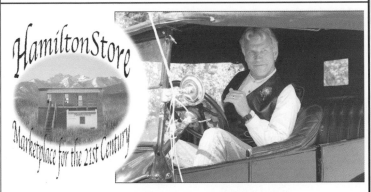

Kurt in a Model T he was selling in 2005

A Little Background

Kurt Stoehr has been a member of eBay since May 2002.

I am mid-50s, semi-retired from Silicon Valley (I don't miss it). I moved to Montana to marry my childhood sweetheart (true story). I started selling household goods on consignment and then got into vintage cars and then muscle cars. Now I'm listing real estate, cars, and antiques. I also teach eBay classes at local Adult Ed and am a sub at the local school. I've also become an eBay Certified Education Specialist which adds eBay support and authorized materials to my "Images to Invoices" seminars.

I've had to advertise very little, since my business is derived mostly from referrals and word of mouth. Every drive becomes a business-trip. I carry my cards and flyers which I post in places of business and on vehicles I see for sale. Many people give me a try. Garage sales are good sources, as are storage units which liquidate abandoned goods.

Kurt Stoehr—username hamstore—is a full-time eBay seller. He started out on eBay because of a lack of jobs in his area and his personal desire to be self-employed. In his second year of selling PowerSeller status caught up to him.

He now sells through auctions and eBay Motors with one or two sales a week. His average starting price varies and he said the best way to get people to notice his listings is through good images and ad copy.

Kurt finds most of the items he sells from "local folks" who see his flyers and will call him with items they want him to sell. He makes Hiking Staffs and Walking Sticks that he also sells through his eBay business. He does not use any kind of software to list his items because he works on a Mac G4 and most or all of the software is for Windows. He says the software is getting better for Mac users. ("They use either web- or java-based software which is then cross-platform"). He does cross-promote by putting his Web site URL in many of his listings (**www.hamiltonstore.com**).

Kurt has found a good time and time-ending of auctions that works well for him.

I like to try and do 10-day auctions starting on a Thursday so they end on a Sunday, about an hour or more before "60 Minutes" comes on TV.

He said the best approach to take when he doesn't hear from a buyer is to e-mail and phone them. He does have a return policy.

To save on shipping costs, Kurt uses USPS, UPS, and a local freight company. He said international bidders are good for business and they makes up 50 percent of his business. He does not believe drop shipping is good for selling items.

Contact Information for Kurt Stoehr:
Hamilton Store
Voice/ Fax: 406-363-1789
Cell: 406-369-0536
hamiltonstore@onewest.net
www.hamiltonstore.com

Lynn Dralle

Username:	TheQueenofAuctions
Name:	Lynn Dralle
E-mail:	Lynn@TheQueenofAuctions.com
Classification:	Internet/ eBay Only Business
Current Tier:	Silver PowerSeller
eBay Store:	The Queen of Auctions- All Aboardinc
eBay Store Location:	www.stores.ebay.com/The-Queen- of-Auctions-All-Aboardinc
Current Feedback Star:	Shooting Yellow
Projected 2006 Sales:	$100,000

A Little Background

Lynn Dralle has been a member of eBay since September 1998.

Lynn Dralle worked with her Grandmother, Cheryl Leaf, in her Washington state antiques and gift store since she was a young child. As an expert in the field of antiques and collectibles, and online auctions, Lynn has written many books designed to guide people through the lucrative world of Internet transactions.

More 100 Best Things I've Sold on eBay—Money Making Madness; 2006

The Unofficial Guide to Making Money on eBay; John Wiley & Sons, Inc., 2006

How to Sell Antiques and Collectibles on eBay...and Make a Fortune!; with Dennis Prince; McGraw Hill, 2005

The 100 Best Things I've Sold on eBay; 2004

I Sell on eBay Tracking Binder and I Buy on eBay Tracking Binder; 1999

She has been an eBay PowerSeller since 1998 and still sells on eBay full-time. She lives in Southern California with her seven-year-old princess/ballerina and ten-year-old all-star baseball player.

Lynn Dralle—username TheQueenofAuctions—is a full-time eBay seller. She actually only does half the work of her business—20 hours a week finding, photographing, and listing items—and her assistant, Maureen, does the rest—20 to 25 hours a week, answering questions, collecting payments, and shipping out the goods. She said they make a great team. Lynn never wanted to start selling on eBay. She avoided it as long as she could, but when her grandmother—whom she had been working with in the antique and gift store—got sick, she realized she needed to raise money quickly to pay for her care. She saw eBay as her answer.

To be honest with you, it was quite intimidating in 1998 when I first started buying on the site.

Lynn had not set becoming a PowerSeller as a goal, but after just three months of selling, she received the message that she had earned the status of PowerSeller. In 2005, her sales were at $90,000. She has always fluctuated between the Silver and Gold levels, while currently being at the Silver tier of the PowerSeller ladder.

I wish there was another level between the $3,000 Silver and $10,000 Gold. It is a huge gap and we are often selling at the $8,000 a month level, so an intermediate tier would be nice.

Lynn uses auction and store format to sell her items. She said her store is a very valuable piece of her business as she sells about $2,000 a month from items in her store. She sells between 100 and 150 items a week with most of her auctions starting at $9.99.

I have gone through many phases in my eBay career—starting everything where I thought it should sell (high prices like $99) and then I did a six-month stint with everything starting at $.99 cents. From a lot of trial and error—this is what really works for the types of items that I sell.

Lynn believes that keywords in the title of a listing are the best way to get people to notice that listing. She makes sure to use all 55 characters as often as possible and tries to write the best titles.

I also have a very loyal following that buys multiple items from me.

She finds most of the items she sells from garage, estate, and charity sales. She also finds some of her items from thrift stores. She also has a line of greeting cards that she designed for Sunrise/Hallmark/Interart for which she owns the designs, and she sells them on eBay. She does not use any type of software to list her items.

I find that the eBay SYI (sell your item) form works the best and quickest for me. I have tried many different listing software in the past and they were all more trouble than they were worth.

Lynn uses eBay's automated cross-promotion for similar items and sometimes she will also go in and choose the items she wants to cross-promote with a specific listing. She said this can be very time-consuming, though. When it comes to the timing and time-ending of an auction, she has the following advice:

I think that as long as it is within 7 a.m. to 7 p.m. Pacific time—you are safe. You just don't want your auctions to end in the middle of the night in the United States. Eighty percent of our customers are from the United States and Canada—so this is a big concern. With all the sniping software being used, time of day and day of week are getting less important.

When she hasn't heard from a buyer, Lynn will usually wait about two weeks and then use eBay to send the buyer a payment reminder. If she still does not hear, she will e-mail them personally. If a month goes by and she still hasn't heard, she will re-list the item and leave the non-responsive buyer negative feedback.

Most of the time when we go to leave the negative feedback, they have already been kicked off of eBay.

Although she does not list a specific return policy, Lynn does say she stands behind all her merchandise and that she wants her customers to be happy. She believes that listing a return policy "leaves the door open for 'buyers' remorse.'"

To save on shipping costs, Lynn quotes a flat shipping/ handling/insurance costs as she said it tends to help her bottom line.

We also use USPS for Flat Rate Priority shipping, and UPS daily pickup also lowers our rates. We always try to recycle shipping supplies and pick up free boxes all the time. We buy our packing tape and boxes from www.uline.com. They are quite reasonable if you live close to one of their locations. Otherwise, the freight can kill you.

Lynn believes international bidders are absolutely good for business. She has heard the horror stories that other sellers have had, but she has only had two bad experiences with international shipping.

If you want to have a well-rounded business that gets top dollar for your items, you must ship internationally.

She does not believe drop shipping is good for business because she said it puts you in direct competition with the other eBay sellers that are using the same source for merchandise.

You also can't personalize the experience with quick shipping, combined shipping, and a thank you note or article. However, if you can get an exclusive with a manufacturer—I think it can work.

To drive people to her eBay store, Lynn uses cross-promotion in every listing which she said helps. Every one of her listings has a banner which has links to her top five store categories. She also is able to draw customers into her store by mentioning that the buyer can save on shipping with multiple purchases. She also has a Web site which is linked to her "About Me" page: **www.thequeenofauctions.com**.

A Final Piece of Advice

eBay has changed my life. I went from working a 60-hour week in our family's brick-and-mortar antique store and never seeing my kids, to working from home and seeing too much of them! Just kidding. It has been an incredible change for us. I am a single mom and my kids know that they can come into my office anytime for any reason. They are little, seven and ten, and they love to help. I put them to work often, and my daughter loves going to garage sales with me. She has quite the eye and is even wearing a "Future eBay PowerSeller" shirt today! eBay is a great way to teach your family a great work ethic at a young age.

Contact Information for Lynn Dralle:

The Queen of Auctions

Lynn Dralle

Lynn@TheQueenofAuctions.com

She sells on eBay as TheQueenofAuctions

www.TheQueenofAuctions.com

Mark & Jan Tillema

Username:	thebiglittlestor
Name:	Mark & Jan Tillema
E-mail:	thebiglittlestore@ameritech.net
Classification:	Internet/ eBay Only Business
Current Tier:	Silver PowerSeller
eBay Store:	the.big.little.store
eBay Store Location:	www.stores.ebay.com/the-big-little-store
Current Feedback Star:	Purple
Projected 2006 Sales:	$30,000-50,000

A Little Background

Mark and Jan Tillema have been eBay members since October 1999.

At first it was just a few things a month, then after an eBay class in Chicago in 2004 we decided to try to make eBay a part-time job, with hopes of it someday becoming more of a full-time job.

We sell our own items that we no longer consider "treasures," also items for friends and family. Everyone knows we are eBay sellers. Whenever anyone asks where can I get this or that, we always say, "Have you checked on eBay?" Almost everything that we buy, from electronics and household items to books and even printers and peripherals for the computer, over the last several years have been purchased on eBay. It's not that we're addicted; it just really is cheaper if you are patient and search.

We do have hopes of being able to quit our day jobs to stay at home more with the kids. While we know that if you have a home business that you need to separate work and home, that is not our intention. We do not want to become a success and spend less time with them. As we say in our "About Me" page: We do want to stop working and play tea party (yes, they are girls); we do want to go to the park to swing and slide down the slides. If this means that we don't become a success, then so be it. When it comes to the business, the business comes in third. Faith, Family, and then the business.

This is also why we do not work on Sunday. We get up, have breakfast, go to church, and when we get home the rest of the day is family day. No business phone calls, no e-mails. This may seem a bit odd since we end most of our auctions on Sunday, but don't answer e-mails. Believe me, we thought of that, and though we have taken a chance, we can't tell you how many positive e-mails we have gotten on a Monday afternoon after explaining our position in a Monday morning response. Everything from: "We applaud what you are doing, and understand" to "Thank You for responding. I wish I would have been on eBay the day before. I understand completely and wish you much continued success with your eBay business."

"eBay is a fun place to buy and sell. You need to work at it, but it's worth it. Good Luck and above all HAVE FUN!"

Part-time eBay sellers, Mark and Jan Tillema—username thebiglittlestore—began selling on eBay to clean out some space in their home.

We had a room that was full of "treasures" and we wanted to reclaim one of our rooms, so we decided to sell a couple of things on eBay, and it went from there.

Until 2004, Mark and Jan did not sell but once in a while. After they began selling more aggressively that year, they earned their PowerSeller status. They didn't set earning the title as a goal until after attending an eBay class in Chicago that same year.

They try to sell around 15 to 30 items a week. To market their items, they use auctions, store-front, and "buy it nows." They have different starting prices depending on the items they are selling.

For something small $0.99, if it's something that we think should get a better price then $9.99. If you start the auction with too high a price then you risk no one bidding. It's better to have a reserve than to try to start an auction at $100. If we do have a reserve, we always include what that price is somewhere in our auction.

They suggest really focusing on putting the correct keywords in the titles of your auctions to get them noticed more.

And use as many keywords as you can, no one is going to search for the word "the" "or " "and" so don't put them in the title.

Mark and Jan do not make any of the items they sell; they purchase many of their items from wholesalers.

We got a federal and state tax ID after our eBay class. If you get a tax ID you will be able to purchase items that you wouldn't have been able to without one.

To list their items, they use the Turbo Lister software and they use the cross-promotional tools that eBay offers.

Mark and Jan say that the timing of an auction can be very important depending on what is being sold.

If you have something electronic, for instance, Sunday night would be best. Almost anyone who would bid on it will be home late on a Sunday evening. If you are selling something that a stay-at-home Mom may like, sometime around 2 p.m. on a weekday would be best. This would be right before kids come home from school or a baby/toddler would be napping and Mom would have a chance to check some things online.

They have a 100 percent money-back guarantee return policy in place. If they have trouble with a non-responsive buyer, Mark and Jan try e-mailing several times before having to get eBay to intervene.

But sometimes that is necessary.

To save on shipping costs, they suggest using boxes that USPS offers for free at USPS.com.

You sign up, order the boxes and forms that you want, and they send them right to your door at no cost.

Mark and Jan have yet to attempt drop shipping as a method for selling items. They do allow international bidders and believe they are good for business.

> We had a run where nine of ten sales were from England, France, Switzerland, New Zealand, and Australia. All the sales went off without a hitch.

To drive people into their store, Mark and Jan will offer some of the same products they have in their auctions in their stores. They also have a Web site linked to their store site: **www. thebiglittlestore.com**.

A Final Piece of Advice

> Everyone asks "What do I sell?" First sell some things around your house that you may not have sold on a garage sale. Then work up from there.

> First, you could sell what you know. If you have a hobby or there is something that you love to talk about, then maybe that is the way to go. If you are selling something and are asked a question, you will have an immediate answer, but if you are selling something you know little about, you may not even be able to answer the potential bidder's question.

> Second, sell what you see selling. It may take a few hours each night for several days, but look at completed items to see what has sold, then for a short time, you know that that will be something you can do too. However, success is generally short-lived. Once you see something selling well, even if you can get it cheap, someone else has seen that

also. You aren't going to be able to buy something for $15 and sell it for $100 long-term because before long someone else will see it who is willing to sell it for $80 or even $60. What sells for a good profit is always changing, so it will take work.

But in the end it's very gratifying to see those auctions end and the money adding up in your PayPal account.

Contact Information for Mark and Jan Tillema:

Mark & Jan Tillema
The Big Little Store
www.thebiglittlestore.com
219-741-9182

Marla Hughes

Username:	poodles*
Name:	Marla Hughes
E-mail:	poodlesauctions@hotmail.com
Classification:	Internet/ eBay Only Business
Current Tier:	Silver PowerSeller
eBay Store:	POODLES Fashions and Passions
eBay Store Location:	www.stores.ebay.com/POODLES-Fashions-and-Passions
Current Feedback Star:	Red

A Little Background

Marla Hughes has been a member of eBay since April 2003.

> *I have been successfully selling on eBay for more than three years. I specialize in selling high-quality clothing and accessories for men, women, and children. In addition, I also carry videos, DVDs, collectors' items, and seasonal merchandise for buyers' enjoyment and pleasure.*

> *I am an eBay trained and certified Education Specialist. I teach one-on-one individualized lessons to people who want to learn how to sell effectively and successfully on eBay.*

A part-time eBay seller, Marla Hughes—username poodles*—started selling on eBay to try to make extra money. She had enjoyed buying items and thought she would try her hand at it. She set becoming a PowerSeller as a goal and within about five months she reached that goal.

Her number of items sold per week or per day varies with the seasons. In the summer she sells anywhere from two to 20 items a week; during the fall she sells one to five items a day, and during the holidays she can sell anywhere from five to 12 items a day. Her starting price varies by item, anywhere from $9.99 to $99.99.

She lists items in auction format, store-front, "buy it nows," and fixed price. To get bidders to notice her listings she uses clear photos and writes very concise, excellent descriptions.

Marla does not make the items she sells, but she finds most of her items through wholesales, closeouts, and outlet stores. To list these items she uses Vendio software. She also uses cross-promotions for her store items.

When it comes to the timing of an auction, Marla has this to say about its importance:

Important, yes, but it also depends on the item(s) you are selling and whether you sell internationally.

When she hasn't heard from a buyer, Marla will send a polite e-mail to follow up with them. She does not accept returns unless the merchandise she has sold is defective.

To save on shipping costs, Marla recommends knowing the rates for UPS and USPS. She does accept international bidders and believes they are good for business. She does NOT use or support drop shippers in her eBay business.

Marla drives people to her store by placing links to her store in her auction listings.

Ronald C. Sharp

Username:	sharptradingcompany
Name:	Ronald C. Sharp
E-mail:	sales@sharptradingcompany.com
Classification:	Internet/ eBay Only Business
Current Tier:	Silver PowerSeller
eBay Store:	Sharp Trading Company
eBay Store Location:	www.stores.ebay.com/Sharp-Trading-Company
Current Feedback Star:	Shooting Yellow

A Little Background

Ronald C. Sharp has been a member of eBay since January 1999.

I am a Licensed Mental Health Professional, Webmaster. and CIO for several companies. My background includes psychiatric evaluation, substance abuse counseling, and school counseling.

I spent ten years in the enlisted and officer U.S. Marine Corps and have degrees and certifications in Counseling Psychology, Education, School Counseling, Communications, Chemical Dependency, and Psychiatric Assessment.

Ronald C. Sharp—username SharpTradingCompany—is a full-time eBay seller.

eBay gives me the financial freedom to provide counseling service to those who otherwise couldn't afford it. I do a little eBay work seven days a week. With Internet Cafes, hotspots, and cell phones with Internet access, I complete eBay responsibilities almost anywhere, any time.

Ron began selling on eBay with the intention of disposing of merchandise from his brick-and-mortar store that he had just closed. He planned to sell the items and then travel for a few years conducting research in psychology. His immediate success on eBay led him to stick with it for a little bit longer. That was five years ago. He had not set becoming a PowerSeller as a goal as his only goal was financial success. About one year after he started selling he received PowerSeller status, although he does say the status is not that relevant.

He uses mostly his store-front to sell his items.

From my time in the Marine Corps and law enforcement, having the right tool at the right time makes all the difference. We specialize in tools sought by law enforcement, firefighters, emergency response, adventure travelers, and U.S. Marines.

Ron sells anywhere from 75 to 100 items a week. His average starting price is only a penny, as he said, since he doesn't have a reserve; the one cent starting price usually is a big attention-grabber. He said the best way to get people to notice his listings is by having accurate titles, clear photos, complete descriptions, and an eye-friendly and inviting layout.

I once supervised publishing a weekly newspaper. Design layout for newspapers should draw the reader's eye through the entire page, not jumping from one spot to another. The same is true for eBay listings. Each element should draw the reader to the next in a natural flow. Reading any portion of your listing should be an invitation to read more.

Ron recommends that new sellers always start selling with items from their basements and attics.

Don't go buy a case of something hoping to rake in a bundle. In my hobby interests, I am always reading periodicals and attending related trade shows. I look for products I want and sell to those with like interests. You meet some great friends that way too. People drop out of eBay from burn-out. You can avoid burn-out by having a passion for your product type.

He makes a small percentage of the items he sells but most are manufactured. To list his items he uses Auction Wizard 2000 (**www.auctionwizard2000.com**). He said this program is rich with time-saving tools and has the best customer service he has ever encountered with a computer-related product. He does use cross-promotion on his items.

I invest in many offline and cross-media marketing resources: everything from business cards, e-mails, search engine submission, newsletters, discussion groups, blogs, eBay seller education workshops, and occasionally classified ads.

Ron believes the day and ending hour of an auction are crucial.

When to list depends on your client base and product

category. Middle America's nine to five workers tend to prefer shopping and browsing on Sunday evenings. Stay-at-home parents have a different free time. Those auctions should close in a time compatible with their free time. Time zone is also an important consideration. It's great to have an auction close at 9 p.m. to 10 p.m. on the West Coast, but not so on the East coast from midnight to 1 a.m.

Ron has a system in place for when he does not hear from a buyer. His first e-mail explains to the buyer that he or she should expect three e-mails from him. If the buyer does not receive all of them, then there is an e-mail problem. He will attempt the initial e-mail again, this time using eBay's system. If he still doesn't hear from a buyer he will use a backup e-mail account from Hotmail, Yahoo!, or G-mail.

Consider an approach of "Hey, we haven't heard from you, and wanted to make sure you got our e-mails. Can we help with anything?" With the tone of concern, wanting to help, and understanding avoids an adversarial relationship. Browse other eBay listings. It is shocking that listings include hostilities and threats like "We will leave negative if you don't pay immediately."

Ron has a return policy that is satisfaction guaranteed.

To save on shipping costs, Ron recommends comparing services. He said it is surprising, but FedEx does sometimes beat UPS. He also recommends paying attention to details like packing materials and box density.

There is a significant weight difference between packing with Styrofoam peanuts and newspaper. Consider cutting down a box that is significantly larger than the item shipped. An accurate postal scale is very important. When you print postage from home, a scale that is an ounce or two off adds up over time in voluntary donations made to USPS. Recycling shipping supplies can save over time and is eco-friendly. Visit your local electronics mega-store and ask if they have packing peanuts or bubble wrap they are disposing of.

Ron said that he has encountered few problems with international shipping, although he has had problems with PayPal's international policies. He does not drop ship.

eBay's policy is that you cannot sell anything you don't have in your possession. When you drop ship, someone else has the merchandise. As such, you forfeit your quality control over merchandise condition, quality of packing, shipping date, and if any third-party sales solicitations are added to the package. It is not uncommon for drop shippers to siphon off your new customers. They now have your customers' postal and e-mail addresses that can even be sold to additional parties or added to their own mailing lists. Drop shipping postal rates are usually higher than if you shipped yourself. We simply don't drop ship.

To drive people to his eBay store, Ron uses newsletters, great auction listing opportunities, search engine placement, and putting links everywhere possible that invite bidders to visit. He also has a "Web site presence" with his site, **www.sharptradingcompany.com**, that contributes to success on eBay.

A Final Piece of Advice

Sell like you want to buy. Any positive experience you have as a consumer should be implemented in your selling strategy. Most don't like reading long descriptions of how-

to-buy. Be brief and concise. Appreciate friendly and helpful sales people? Be the same to your buyers. eBay shoppers differ from mega-store shoppers. They want to be treated as individuals and have their trust earned. A natural trust often exists for brick-and-mortar businesses because consumers don't expect them to vanish the next day. eBay buyers' trust must be earned. Demonstrate that your business will be around well past receiving their purchase to resolve any problems. Also ensure that divulging their personal address and payment details with you is a safe choice.

Roy Yarris

Username:	themesnthings1
Name:	Roy Yarris
E-mail:	Themesnthings@cox.net
Classification:	Internet/ eBay Only Business
Current Tier:	Silver PowerSeller
eBay Store:	Themes N Things
eBay Store Location:	www.stores.ebay.com/ THEMES-N-THINGS
Current Feedback Star:	Red
Projected 2006 Sales:	$35,000-40,000

A Little Background

Roy Yarris has been a member of eBay since October 2000.

> *I started selling on eBay as a hobby, selling DVDs and other media. There were too many eBay sellers auctioning such items, so I realized that holiday or seasonal items do sell all year round. ThemesNThings started to offer some cool Halloween items just to see what would happen and was amazed at the demand for this season and so increased to all holiday and novelty items. In the last few years of selling, our customer base has grown rapidly. After becoming a Bronze PowerSeller, I took an online course offered by eBay and am now a certified Education Specialist trained by eBay. A few months later, we also became eBay Trading Assistants. We have reached our 1000 feedback and maintain a 99.9 percent feedback rating. We are also a Bonded eBay seller which really increased our sales. It does make eBay a safer place to shop.*

Roy Yarris—username themesnthings1—started selling on eBay as a hobby and then noticed he was developing a customer base. He decided to take his sales skills to the next level and began selling full time. After about six months, PowerSeller status caught up to him as his sales were beginning to increase.

Roy makes use of auctions, a storefront, and "buy it nows." He averages selling about 12 to 14 items a week depending on the holidays since seasonal items are his specialty. His average starting price for an auction is $1 with a reserve set. To make his listings unique and more likely to be noticed, he has a different Web design for each individual listing.

He does not make his own items that he sells, but he finds the items he does sell through private wholesale vendors. He does not use any type of listing software. He does make use of cross-promotions in his listings.

Roy finds the time and time-ending of an auction to be very important. He said Mondays are bad days to end an auction.

When he hasn't heard from a buyer, Roy will persist in communicating with them.

> *I have gone as far as calling before I took the next step of action. I try to be fair with everyone until I exhaust all means of communication.*

He does normally have a return policy, but it also depends on the item itself.

Roy does not believe drop shipping is a good method for selling items. He prefers to have his items physically in stock because the drop shipping pictures can be misleading. Although he believes that international shipping is good for business, he does not ship items overseas.

> *It takes much longer and costs more. You deal with customs taxes, and you cannot track items after shipping.*

To draw people to his store, Roy has found the eBay search engine to work well for cross-promoting.

Roy also has expanded to an online store to go along with his eBay store. The Web address is **www.themesnthings.net**.

A Final Piece of Advice

Do not try to make your profit in shipping charges. Don't start your auctions out at a very high price—you want to draw people to your auctions, not discourage them.

Stephen D. Ganus

Username:	eagleauctionsusa
Name:	Stephen D. Ganus
E-mail:	steve@eagleauctionsusa.com
Classification:	Internet/ eBay Only Business
Current Tier:	Silver PowerSeller
Web Site:	www.eagleauctionsusa.com
Current Feedback Star:	Purple
Projected 2006 Sales:	$60,000

Copyright EagleauctionsUSA 1999 - 2006 ©

A Little Background

Stephen Ganus has been a member of eBay since December 1999.

I have been an eBayer since December 1999 and started selling shortly after. I was, as many eBayers, a buyer first and soon discovered the attraction of selling and making a second income.

I became an Education Specialist trained by eBay in 2004

for the "Basics of eBay Selling" and in 2005 became certified to teach "Beyond the Basics" when eBay rolled the program out. I have a Five-Star Education Specialist rating (highest obtainable) and am one of only ten out of 52 certified Education Specialist in Texas.

I became a PowerSeller in 2004 when I took on the XM Satellite Radio Distributorship. I wasn't trying to become a PowerSeller but was just working on a little extra income to put away for retirement and rainy days. Since then my sales have increased and my 100 percent feedback rating seems to garnish me more business as referrals from satisfied customers have increased.

I am currently working on several "Deals" to expand my eBay business as I prepare for retirement from my 40-hour job in the next five or six years. As I expand with eBay and my e-commerce site I will go into a full-time eBay business in retirement.

I sell under eBay user ID of EagleAuctionsUSA so come see what I have to offer.

Stephen Ganus—username eagleauctionsusa—is a part-time eBay seller. He started selling on eBay for the extra income and to save up for retirement. He wasn't really planning on becoming a PowerSeller and said that the status just caught up with him after he signed a deal with a dealership. It took him about five years to earn the PowerSeller status.

Using mostly auctions and fixed price, Stephen sells about 30 items a week. He doesn't have a set average starting price; rather he does research on each item and starts it at the price that "reflects the market." To get people to notice his listings, he said the best way is using an "excellent gallery photo" and writing an "enticing item description."

Stephen does not make any of his own items and prefers not to disclose any information about where he finds the items he sells. To list his items, he uses Turbo Lister software. He also uses the automated cross-promotion that Selling Manager Pro offers.

Stephen finds the timing and time-ending of an auction to be very important.

> *You have to capture the market you are targeting when they are buying: Sundays for big ticket items as that is when married couples have time to decide. End auctions at a time when folks are most rushed to make a bid so they let the momentum carry them into bidding higher.*

When he hasn't heard from a buyer, he first requests their contact information from eBay and then waits 12 to 24 hours. If the buyer still hasn't e-mailed, then he will call them to see if he can work it out.

> *Sometimes folks have emergencies, and eBay is not at the top of their list to worry about.*

Stephen does offer a return policy that allows for returns on XM Products within 14 Days of purchase. Others are based on manufacturer warranty and return policy.

To save on shipping costs, he suggests getting all the boxes you can at the USPS or from eBay. He does believe international bidders are good for business and has been very successful himself with international clients. When it comes to drop shipping, Stephen just has one thought on that.

I have always said I would rather drop dead than drop ship!

Contact Information for Stephen D. Ganus:

EagleAuctionsUSA

http://mall.eagleauctionsusa.com

http://www.eagleauctionsusa.com

Phone: 832-465-7440

E-mail: steve@eagleauctionsusa.com

Susan Street

Username:	accessoriessusan
Name:	Susan Street
E-mail:	accessoriessusan@aol.com
Classification:	Internet/ eBay Only Business
Current Tier:	Silver PowerSeller
eBay Store:	AccessoriesSusan
eBay Store Location:	www.stores.ebay.com/AccessoriesSusan
Current Feedback Star:	Green
Projected 2006 Sales:	$250,000

A Little Background

Susan Street has been a member of eBay since April 2000.

After working in retail management positions for more than 20 years, I have combined my knowledge in all facets of running of a business with my love of creating jewelry. My designs have been sold in the best boutiques and department stores all over the world, worn in Miss America pageants, in Broadway plays, on runways, and many other places that would make a designer proud. However, my greatest joy comes from the wonderful feeling on lifelong friends I've made through my craft.

Susan Street—username accessoriessusan—is a full-time eBay seller.

My best friend, Laura, who was also a jewelry designer, came to visit me in New Orleans. I was no longer into the designing business but had a tremendous number of supplies. My friend was selling collectibles on eBay and suggested that I sell those supplies on eBay. After she showed me how to take photos and load them onto the eBay site, I was off and running.

After only eight months of selling on eBay, Susan was surprised and pleased when she was notified she was a PowerSeller. Now she sells 100 items through auctions and about 1,200 through her eBay store every week. She also often makes use of "buy it nows." Her auctions almost always start at only $.99. This is the best way she has found to get people to notice her listings:

I often list my most photogenic items with gallery photos, highlighted and with a border. Be sure to include the proper search words so that your items can be found by the people looking for your items.

Susan finds most of the items she sells from manufacturers in the United States.

I buy brass items manufactured in the United States and have them plated professionally. Since I was a designer for many years I have long-standing relationships with many manufacturers and importers.

She uses Marketworks.com (**www.marketworks.com**) to list her auctions and to track her sales. She also uses a store-front as well as her eBay store-front. She does not use any type of cross-promotions.

Susan's advice when it comes to the timing of an auction and time-ending of an auction is this:

It is a good idea to list items to end during a time when your bidder might be available to place bids and monitor the bidding. For example, if your customer base includes mothers with school-age children, they may be too busy to bid on your items ending at 3 p.m.

When she hasn't heard from a buyer, Susan suggests sending a friendly e-mail asking if they have sent their payment already, which perhaps I have missed. If they still do not respond, she said that a request for payment can be sent them with a notification that negative feedback will be left if they do not handle the matter.

Susan does have a return policy that states that if the customer is unhappy with the items they can return them for a full refund in their original condition and within a week of receipt.

She does not drop ship as she said she would not trust someone else to "deliver a good product in my name." She does believe international bidders are good for business and said that she has many who will shop with her weekly.

These customers have made my business much stronger.

To save on shipping costs, Susan recommends shopping for the lowest-cost shipping materials (she suggests **www. rmjdistributing.com**) and then combine customer's purchases from all of the sites you sell on.

To draw people into her store, Susan lists items with gallery photos and a border.

*This allows my listings to stand out from the others. My Web site (**www.accessoriessusan.com**) has a link to send customers to my eBay auctions.*

A Final Piece of Advice

Treat your business with respect; setting aside structured time each day to devote to your customers. Make certain you offer the best customer service possible. Answer e-mails professionally, using complete sentences. Be pleasant and helpful at all times. Do what you say you will do. Offer items you can speak intelligently about. Do the research so that you can describe your items correctly. Treat each customer as if he or she is the only one you have.

Company Profile

Since 1989 I've been a jewelry designer, so I have access to a large selection of component parts to create Victorian inspired jewelry and other projects.

Contact Information for Susan Street:
Phone and Fax: 423-929-7669
E-mail: accessoriessusan@aol.com

Tricia Hanley

Username:	pacificquest
Name:	Tricia Hanley
E-mail:	pacificquest@earthlink.net
Classification:	Internet/ eBay Only Business
Current Tier:	Silver PowerSeller
eBay Store:	Sell Online ART ANTIQUE Consignment
eBay Store Location:	www.stores.ebay.com/Sell-Online-ART-ANTIQUE-Consignment
Current Feedback Star:	Red
Projected 2006 Sales:	$36,000

A Little Background

Tricia Hanley has been a member of eBay since February 1999.

Hanley is a 40-plus "Sandwich Generation" stay-at-home mom. Being an eBay PowerSeller has afforded her the time to devote to her family and lie on her hammock. Hanley said, "There is no way to have it all, but all those little things in life like extra time and income sure make me feel as though I do have it all!"

Tricia Hanely—username pacificquest—began selling on eBay when her son was born. PowerSeller status caught up to her because she was selling on consignment and changing her items to expensive items only. The status came very soon after she began selling on consignment. She sells on eBay part time.

Tricia sells through auctions, "buy it nows," and the "make offer" formats. She sells fewer than 10 items a week, but her average starting price is $199.99. To get people to notice her listings she uses keyword-rich titles.

She finds her consignment items through word of mouth. She doesn't make any of her own items. To list the items she is selling, Tricia uses Turbo Lister. She cross-promotes her items with eBay's storefront.

Tricia thinks that the timing of an auction and the time-ending of an auction is very important. To save on shipping costs, she said weighing accurately and using Ground when possible are the best ways. She does believe international bidders are good for business.

When she hasn't heard from a buyer, Tricia will use eBay's contact member button. She has a three-day return policy.

Tricia has a Web site that she has linked to her "About Me" page. The site location is: www.pacificquest.us.

A Final Piece of Advice

Don't just enjoy buying stuff to sell on eBay, enjoy SELLING! You can get in over your head just buying stuff to sell on eBay. Make sure to do your research to find out what an item's current market value is, and list, list, list!

Contact Information for Tricia Hanley:
Pacificquest Auction Services LLC
Tricia Hanley Auctioneer
PO BOX 244
Keyport, WA 98345-0244
www.pacificquest.us
pacificquest@earthlink.net

Jessica Gottlieb

Username:	TheBetterBagLady
Name:	Jessica Gottlieb
E-mail:	ebay@thebetterbaglady.com
Classification:	Internet/ eBay Only Business
Current Tier:	Bronze/ Silver PowerSeller
eBay Store:	Tongue-In-Chic
eBay Store Location:	www.stores.ebay.com/Tongue-In-Chic
Current Feedback Star:	Purple

A Little Background

Jessica Gottlieb has been a member of eBay since June 2000.

I'm Jessica and my business is www.TheBetterBagLady. com. This will send you to my eBay store Tongue-In-Chic.

I started on eBay in the mid-90s and ultimately ended up making a business of it when Oprah put UGG Boots on her Favorite Things list and they sold out everywhere. Actually, there was just the perception that they sold out because I had hundreds of them here. At triple the money and only one set of pictures to take, a business was born.

Well, people finally figured out that UGGs are just plain UGGly so I had to find something else to sell. I still dabble in Chanel, Louis Vuitton and Hermes, but unfortunately there is so much counterfeiting that a lot of the profit is gone from that. I get a lot of great stuff from the television and movie studios. Right now I have Magnum P.I.'s old wardrobe.

Who knows what I'll sell next? I have helped dozens of people get their eBay business going and I like to tell them to keep it transparent. Everyone hates big government and big business because they believe that secrets are being kept. Publish as much as you can and people will see that you're honest.

Need more info? Call me 818-486-9363. I'm available for speaking engagements and fundraisers alike, as well as lectures or private consulting either in person or over the telephone. I am also currently giving seminars on starting your eBay business about once a month in and around Los Angeles.

Jessica Gottlieb—username TheBetterBagLady—is a part-time eBay seller. She sold random items from around her home until UGG came along.

I realized that I could triple my money selling UGG Boots so I became a seller.

After only three months, Jessica earned her PowerSeller status.

It just happened to me.

She now fluctuates between a Silver and Bronze tier depending on the time of year it is. She sells anywhere from one item a day to 20 items.

It all depends what I'm selling or if I'm even interested in working. I never work during the summer and I sell like crazy in November and December.

Jessica makes use of auctions, fixed price, and store-front to sell her products. She also uses cross-promotions with other sellers. She gets people to notice her listings with Featured Plus. Her starting price varies.

I like to start some items at $.99 but lately I've been starting men's shirts at $7.50. eBay has no averages. It's dishonest to say that eBay could ever have averages.

Sellers Sourcebook is her preferred listing software (**www. sellersourcebook.com**). Jessica does have a return policy depending on the item.

When she hasn't heard from a buyer, she e-mails first. She then tries to call and if that doesn't work, she files an unpaid item dispute.

Jessica said to save on shipping costs, make use of USPS and get all the supplies needed from them for free. She does not use drop shipping as she said, "You don't really know what the quality is of the item is or what the shipping is like." When it comes to international bidders, she said it all depends on the type of business it is.

There are as many business models as there are eBay sellers.

She finds the timing of the auction and the ending time to be very important.

She has a Web site that takes you straight to her eBay store (**www.TheBetterBagLady.com**) and draws people into her store, she said:

Just keep churning out the auctions.

Cathi Dillard

Username:	catsmagick
Name:	Cathi Dillard
E-mail:	catsmagicalshoppe@msn.com
Classification:	Internet/ eBay Only Business
Current Tier:	Bronze PowerSeller
eBay Store:	Cat's Magical Shopp
eBay Store Location:	www.stores.ebay.com/ catsmagicalshoppe
Current Feedback Star:	Red
Projected 2006 Sales:	$60,000-70,000

A Little Background

Cathi Dillard has been a member of eBay since May 2002.

I began with a dream that we could actually make a business of something I greatly enjoyed: "New Age" products. With an interest in Tarot and Alternative Religion books, we bought a small amount of inventory and started selling on eBay.

The first two years were such a learning experience. I discovered that large, bulky items were difficult and expensive to ship. I also discovered a most important lesson: just because I like it doesn't mean my customers would like it! I found a niche and settled into it very naturally. I started having repeat customers who often told me they came back for the customer service. I've stuck with a very strict policy of answering each and every e-mail and sending out any item purchased with 24 hours—often the same day if the purchase is early enough in the day.

When a customer wrote or called saying they had purchased something they didn't like or had buyers' remorse, I gladly took the product back. My philosophy has been "if the buyer isn't happy, they won't come back. If the buyer has an enjoyable experience, they will seek me out the next time." So far it has worked well for me.

I began to establish policies and clarify what this business meant to me. I try to use the Wiccan Reed: "An ye harm none, do what ye will." I am respectful of all who visit our eBay store, try to show kindness and tolerance, and have found it comes back to me ten-fold. Buyers are aware of what to expect when shopping at Cat's Magical Shoppe. They know they get a quality product at a fair price. They know that I'm accessible, reasonable, reliable, and friendly. When the buyers don't know what to expect, policies are not clear, and the seller doesn't return e-mail and phone calls, the buyer is turned off. Studies have shown that a consumer who has a negative experience will typically tell 10 others. I've tried extremely hard to make every experience at my eBay store a positive one, even if nothing is purchased.

That's probably the reason we have so many loyal customers: the buyers are intelligent and know when the bottom line is more important than they are. That is not the experience they have with me. When a potential customer asks my opinion of a product, I reply with an honest answer, even if it means losing the sale. I would rather lose a sale than have a buyer make a purchase they regret.

Maintaining 100 percent positive feedback has been another goal that so far we have achieved. I believe this is proof that my customer service policy is working and effective.

My long-term goal is to also have a brick and mortar store in addition to my eBay store. Unfortunately, the eBay store does not currently generate enough income to support me when combined with the necessary evil of health insurance that I'm offered at my "day job." But with or without a brick-and-mortar storefront, we'll keep the eBay store and continue our policy of dedication and fairness.

Cathi Dillard—username catsmagick—decided to begin selling on eBay after her company downsized.

I was working as an accountant for a small chain of retail stores when I was notified that I was going to be laid off due to "corporate downsizing." I decided to look at it as an opportunity to do something I liked.

She manages a full-time job as well as doing eBay full-time.

I work a full-time job; however, eBay is a full-time job as well. Part of our strategy is honest and fast customer service. This means monitoring e-mails continually throughout the day, and we promise a turn-around of 24 hours or less.

It took Cathi about two years to gain her PowerSeller status. She is now at the bronze tier. Although she never thought she would sell enough to reach the silver tier, she is almost to that point.

It was definitely not a goal. I began by selling things that I was interested in and enjoy and wasn't really interested in making this a career. It was, at that time, more of a hobby.

With the weekends being a heavier time for selling, her sales are around 10-30 items, whereas during the week sales are around three to eight items a day. She said Friday and Saturday nights are her heaviest. Cathi does tend to use the "buy it now" feature more than regular auctions.

With an auction, I tend to start with the minimum I would accept. As all of our items are new (we don't sell used), we typically double an item's purchase price. We use auctions when the item probably won't bring double an item, and use the auction to "test" the market price. Sometimes we're surprised by the results! Our items do not do well in the beginning at .01 market.

Cathi has found the key to what makes buyers notice her listings.

We don't use many of the tools eBay offers, mostly due to the pricing. We have lots of repeat and word-of-mouth customers. Noted customer service and 100 percent positive feedback entice buyers more than anything else.

She sells only new items that she finds from various wholesale distributors and manufacturers as brick-and-mortar stores do.

We subscribe to trade publications that offer us information on the vendors that operate in our genre, New Age.

Cathi does not use any type of listing software. She does use cross-promotion.

We use eBay's cross-promotion of our own items as well as cross-promoting another eBay stores that sell a service complementary to ours.

She finds the time and more specifically the time-ending for an auction to be very important.

If we use an auction, we make sure the auction ends Friday, Saturday, or Sunday. Buyers typically are working and concerned with their personal lives throughout the week and don't want to have to worry about when an auction is going to end.

Cathi has a process she goes through when she hasn't heard from a buyer of one of her listings.

> *We begin the process by sending a polite reminder e-mail. If that does not generate a response, we then send an e-mail offering our support if the buyer is experiencing a personal or financial problem. This usually generates a response, but if not, we send a final e-mail warning the buyer that, as much as we dislike doing so, we will have to notify eBay that they are a non-paying bidder. As a last resort, we file a non-paying bidder report to recover the fees incurred with the sale. I think that it is important to note here that we do not leave negative feedback. In the interest of "good karma" we leave positive feedback or nothing at all.*

She does have a return policy in which she will accept any item back for any reason within seven days of receipt.

> *If a customer is returning an item because of buyers' remorse or any other reason other than an error or damage on our part, the buyer incurs the return postage expense and usually a small restocking fee.*

For saving on shipping costs, Cathi said it is critical to find wholesale shipping supplies since this is what consumes much of her cash flow. For customers, their best saving for shipping costs would be to combine items. She does not use the drop-shipping method.

> *We advertise as selling Fair Trade, organic, or ecologically-friendly items, and we want to ensure that is true by hands-on. We maintain an inventory of all the items we sell. I've also heard of not so good experiences from other eBayers who have tried drop shipping.*

When it comes to international bidders, they are welcome at this time.

> *While we currently offer world-wide sales, we have been considering limiting our area to the United States, Canada, and Mexico. There isn't currently a reliable method of tracking international orders for confirmation of delivery.*

Cathi only makes use of her eBay store. She had a private Web site during the first year she had an eBay store, but found it to be too much. Since eBay offered her more exposure, she chose to stick with it and let go of the other one. Her store mostly uses eBay Keywords to draw potential buyers in.

> *We just recently upgraded our store from "basic" to "featured" providing more exposure. We also try to change the look of the storefront periodically and frequently update and add to the keyword list to try to pull in buyers who haven't visited before.*

The areas she markets are:

> *Mostly our eBay storefront and "Buy it Now," with maybe 5 percent of our items using an auction.*

A Final Piece of Advice

> *I think the most important thing is to find a niche that is not saturated. I was lucky to be interested in New Age products. Other New Age eBay stores tend to be either handmade items, or specialize in one or two things: books, tarot, or candles, for example.*

> *The second thing is to find a gimmick or something that sets you apart from other stores. We send a few sticks of incense*

along with every order we ship out. We've found that buyers not only enjoy the sticks themselves, but are also grateful that a seller is really interested in earning their trust and business.

Contact information for Cathi Dillard:

www.stores.ebay.com/catsmagicalshoppe

catsmagicalshoppe@msn.com

Dawn Ortiz

Username:	mistymae
Name:	Dawn Ortiz
E-mail:	dawn@scraphappens.com
	mistymae1@aol.com
Classification:	Internet/ eBay Only Business
Current Tier:	Bronze PowerSeller
eBay Store:	Because Scrap Happens
eBay Store Location:	www.becausescraphappens.com
Current Feedback Star:	Red

Scrap Happens
www.scraphappens.com
Great scrapbooking products at affordable prices

A Little Background

Dawn Ortiz has been a member of eBay since November 1999.

I'm a WAHM (work at home mom) of two wonderful children. I "retired" from my full-time career, after working in radio for more than 20 years (I started young!) to stay home and raise my children. eBay has made it possible for me to do this and continue to earn money for my family.

My goal as an eBay seller and business owner is to offer great paper-crafting products at affordable prices, as well as extend superior customer service. I usually ship within two business days of receiving payment, and I personally respond to all e-mails and answer all questions as best I can.

One of the most enjoyable parts of my job is meeting people all over the country and all over the world. I invite you to stop by and check out my Web site and/or eBay store soon. I look forward to meeting you!

A part-time eBay seller, Dawn Ortiz—username mistymae—decided to start selling on eBay because she wanted to stay home after having her first child. She hopes to go to full-time selling once her children are older.

It was 1999 and I just had my first baby. I returned to work full-time as planned but I just wasn't happy. I wanted to stay home and be a full-time mom. I knew that our family could probably "get by" on my husband's income, but if we had another source of income to fall back on, I'd be more secure in my decision to stay home. I started small. I listed auctions once a week, twice a week on occasion.

About two years after she started selling on eBay, Dawn became a PowerSeller. She didn't really have becoming a PowerSeller as a goal.

I remember the day I received the e-mail from eBay. I thought it was one of those "phishing" e-mails. I didn't believe it at first! When it finally hit me, I was so thrilled.

She makes use of the following markets: Auctions, "buy it nows," Store-front, and Best Offers.

For Dawn, an average starting price for her items is anywhere from $3 to $4.50. She has about 80 to 100 auctions listed a week, with 80 to 90 store items listed a week. She said the best way to get people to notice her listings is with a "catchy title and nice pictures."

Although she does not currently make any of the items she sells, she did in the past. Dawn finds most of the items she sells through wholesale vendors.

Turbo Lister is Dawn's choice for listing software. For cross-promoting, she doesn't really do anything but what eBay already does for her.

I let eBay's system take care of that for me. It seems to do a great job!

Dawn finds that time and time-ending with her auctions is very important.

As a seller, you have to find the right time of day to end your auctions based on the buyers you're trying to target.

When she hasn't heard from a buyer, Dawn sends out a personalized e-mail hoping to hear back.

If there's still no response, a reminder from eBay's unpaid item system might help.

Although she doesn't actually have a return policy listed with her auctions, Dawn does try to correct any problems with a buyer.

I want my customers to be happy so they'll purchase from me again. I don't have a return policy listed in my auctions (it's on my list of things to do!), but I will try to fix any problem that a customer has with my item or items.

Dawn has a method in place to help her save on shipping costs as well as offering a way for her customers to save:

I save on shipping costs by purchasing my shipping supplies from other eBay sellers. I use USPS and offer my customers insurance if they want to purchase it.

My customers save on shipping if they purchase multiple items from me. I offer great combined shipping rates, as long as they make one combined payment (to save me on PayPal fees).

International eBayers are absolutely welcome to bid on her items.

I just started shipping to Europe, Australia, and Canada and have definitely seen a difference already.

Drop shipping is not something Dawn participates in.

Personally, drop shipping is not for me. I'm a "control"-type person, so I like my products in-house where I can see them.

Besides her eBay store (**www.becausescraphappens.com**), Dawn also makes use of a Web site outside of eBay (**www. scraphappens.com**) that is linked back to her listings. She has found a few ways to drive people into her eBay store.

I have a link in each auction description, a cute name and logo, and I purchased a Web site URL that is directed to my eBay store (**www.becausescraphappens.com**).

A Final Piece of Advice

I can't stress enough: communicate with your buyers and ship as fast as possible. If you keep your customers happy, they'll think of you for their next purchase.

The best advice I can offer is "Don't give up!" If you have the desire and drive to be an eBay seller, you can do it. It may take months to get your business off the ground, but I'm proof that it can happen!

Contact Information for Dawn Ortiz:
Dawn Ortiz, mistymae
Web site: www.scraphappens.com
eBay store: www.becausescraphappens.com
Located in Riverside, California
E-mail: dawn@scraphappens.com or mistymae1@aol.com
Phone: 951-688-7831

Jana Molinaro

Username:	serendipity_gift_boutique
Name:	Jana Molinaro
E-mail:	info@serendipitygiftboutique.com
Classification:	Internet/ eBay Only Business
Current Tier:	Bronze PowerSeller
eBay Store:	Serendipity Gift Boutique
eBay Store Location:	www.serendipitycollection.com
Current Feedback Star:	Purple

A Little Background

Jana Molinaro has been a member of eBay since January 2004.

My name is Jana and I am the owner of Serendipity Gift Boutique. I have been married to a wonderful man, named Gary, for 27 years and we have four beautiful children: Vanessa, Amber, Lauren, and Steven; two grandchildren: Matthew and Eden, two loveable dogs: Roxie and Julio, and a singing parakeet: Polly.

For a number of years, I worked in the family building business and loved the contact with the customers and delivering a product I could be proud of. After moving from beautiful Ellicott City, Maryland, to the charming, small, quaint town of Littlestown, Pennsylvania, I decided to strike out on my own, with the support of my family, and sell my passion. I have always loved unique gifts, inspired by my beautiful mother, and I wanted to introduce others to my love of beautiful, unusual items for the home, including collectibles, one of a kind pieces of art and unique everyday items. I try to carry products that will enhance your home; some conversation pieces, some fun items that will make you smile, some that will possibly increase in value and some things that are meant to be passed down from generation to generation, all in a variety of prices and all below retail. It also feels good to be my own boss and know I am making a little money to boot.

I thought about opening a brick-and-mortar store and still might, in addition to my eBay store, but I wanted to share my love with as many people as possible, and eBay provides that venue.

I am still learning the ins and outs of eBay sales and am learning new things everyday. A couple things I have learned is that there are unbelievable bargains to be found on eBay and that there are many reputable sellers on eBay. I have been fortunate to become friends with many of them. You'll find my Sellers Potpourri page is full of ethical eBay sellers, all of whom care about providing quality products at a fair price, with an emphasis on customer service.

After being approached to sell on eBay by a girlfriend Jana Molinaro—username serendipity_gift_boutique—thought it would be fun and decided to give it a try. After only three months, she became a PowerSeller. Having not even known there was such as a thing as being a PowerSeller, it came as a surprise to her. She is now a full-time eBay seller.

Jana sells about 25-30 items a week with an average starting price being hard to determine because of the wide range of items she lists. She uses her store and "buy it nows." She has two big things she believes gets her listings noticed.

A Good Title is an absolute MUST. Do not use words like CUTE, L@@K. Use appropriate keywords and use every character eBay allows. For auctions, I use a subtitle sometimes and sometimes a border, especially if there are many items up for auction in my particular category and my particular item. I also capitalize one word in the title. My products are all new, so I always use the word NEW. If it is a No Reserve auction I always use NR, If I have something unusual, I use the word UNUSUAL. If I have used all the keywords that pertain and I still have characters left to use, I will use a word like beautiful or a phrase like subtle shading or some such emotional word or phrase.

Good pictures are also a MUST. Take time with your pictures. Get a good setting for the picture. Use good lighting, preferably natural light. Crop the picture so that you can clearly see the item. If it is glass, consider putting white paper inside the glass. Experiment and read about backgrounds. Mostly white is best, but sometimes it is better to use a color. If it is jewelry, sometimes black is the best. Get a good camera, and you might want to invest in a light box.

Jana does make some of her own products as well as getting the rest from the manufacturers. She uses Selling Manager Pro for her inventory control and re-listing. She also makes use of cross-promotions.

> *I cross-promote with ten other sellers and in various Web rings and selling associations.*

Although timing of an auction and time-ending of an auction used to be very important to Jana, it's a little less important as she has gotten herself established.

> *I always ended my auctions on Sunday nights (6 p.m. PST) when people are home. By ending on a Sunday night your auction has more visibility over the weekend when people are really looking. Your item is moving up in visibility as it is coming to an end: it is on the first page of the auctions. People say that there are different good ending times depending on the items one sells and to whom one is selling. For instance, I've heard that if you are selling to women, you should end your listings at noon PST during the week, but the best bet I have found is to end on Sunday night.*

Using her TOS (Terms of Service), Jana sends out a friendly reminder to an unpaid buyer after three days.

> *...then another at the ninth day after a sale. My TOS say that I must hear from them by three days regarding payment and payment must be received by ten days. Only once did I have to open a UPI and that ended with a mutual agreement. Be friendly and professional in corresponding with a buyer who doesn't respond.*

Jana does have a seven-day, money-back return policy in place.

To save on shipping costs, she has found a way that works best for her and offers that advice here.

Use appropriate but lightweight packing materials and package your product before you put it up for sale, so you know exactly what it weighs.

Having heard many stories of unreliable drop shippers, Jana has not made use of that form of selling. She does absolutely believe that international bidders are good for business.

I love my international buyers. I did not start out selling internationally, however. I needed to feel comfortable with selling first and selling in the United States only. There are certain rules that apply when selling internationally. For instance, some countries have bans on certain products; you cannot sell leather goods to Italy, for example.

Although she has another Web site she makes use of, it is really only to provide her more "Web presence;" it has some of her products listed. To drive people to her eBay store, Jana has found keywords to be a big factor.

I use eBay keywords (META tags), eBay Keyword campaigns, store pages to describe my products fully and use various keywords. I am a member of various Web rings, and I cross-promote with other sellers.

A Final Piece of Advice

As with anything else, as you pick up momentum, you pick up more momentum, but there are some things you can do to start the momentum.

1. *Taking a class at eBay University is an excellent way to start.*

2. *Once on eBay, look for eBay discussion boards. I got into a Selling Basics group that was private and where you*

need an invitation. That is not a problem. Just e-mail the Group Leader and request an invitation. You can start out hovering, but participate on the boards. You will get to know people and learn all kinds of new things. Networking is one of the keys on eBay. I made friends who made logos for me, buttons for my store, gave me great sources for products, ideas on how to expand my product lines, helped me with HTML, helped me set up my shipping costs. Read, read, read all you can and I just cannot stress enough the need to network, network, network.

3. *Especially in the beginning, make use of all the free marketing that you can find. Join Web rings, put keywords in your titles and descriptions.*

4. *I began as I meant to go on. I spent the money initially to use eBay's listing designer and the Gallery image. I wanted to give a nice presentation. There is so much competition on eBay, you have to use every available means to make people remember you and want to buy from you.*

5. *After you are a seller, continue to buy regularly on eBay to see how other sellers handle their businesses and presentation and how they handle problems.*

6. *Write an eBay Guide about something that might be helpful to others, such as info about one of your products or some aspect of eBay. It gives you credibility and is indexed by search engines.*

7. *Always be professional in your correspondence with buyers and, if you are upset, wait until you have cooled down to respond.*

8. *Network, network, network!*

One last piece of information I can give you is to remember if you open an eBay store, you must use the auction format to drive traffic to your store. Have at least ten auctions going at any one time.

Company Profile

Serendipity Gift Boutique: "Where the Unexpected is Always Expected" –Unique gifts & collectibles featuring MaggiB, Ganz, Turov, The Teapottery, Tony Carter, and Royal Doulton figurines! We carry teapots, ceramics, tea, vintage items, Webkinz, Burton & Burton, Harney & Sons tea, Kimberly Shaw Tea Cards, and Marye-Kelley decoupage! We have a fabulous and eclectic array of gifts. There's a little something wonderful here for everybody!

Mardi Timm

Username:	justcuriosities
Name:	Mardi Timm
E-mail:	mardi@wi.rr.com
Classification:	Internet/ eBay Only Business
Current Tier:	Bronze PowerSeller
eBay Store:	Just Curiosities
eBay Store Location:	www.stores.ebay.com/ Just-Curiosities
Current Feedback Star:	Red
Projected 2006 Sales:	$15,000

A Little Background

Mardi Timm has been a member of eBay since March 1998.

In the last eight years, Mardi's passion for eBay has never wavered. She is an active buyer, seller, and eBay educator in her area. Mardi has had many interesting experiences on eBay. The most memorable thing she ever bought was an original Whoopee Cushion from the early 1930s. The most memorable listing she ever did was on April 2, 2005: she presented a seminar with another Education Specialist, Monica Doyle, and at the end of the seminar they listed the only remaining Frank Lloyd Wright hotel on eBay for $10 Million.

Mardi became a PowerSeller two and a half years ago when she decided to make eBay her full-time job. She is a Bronze PowerSeller and will eventually grow to Silver level, but right now she is splitting her time between selling and training. Mardi is a Certified Education Specialist trained by eBay.

No matter how busy she gets, Mardi will always continue to buy and sell.

> *I love to dig through our stuff, find things of value to sell, and then research them to see if my instincts are correct. My daughter has also become a successful eBay seller and buyer, too, and she assists me if I need help. It's a family affair!*

Mardi Timm—username justcuriosities—sells on eBay full time. She splits her time between her selling and her education functions. She teaches people how to sell and consults with businesses and individuals who want to begin selling on eBay.

Mardi got started selling on eBay when she realized that not only could she be doing a lot of buying through eBay, she could also being selling there as well.

I started out by selling some postcards that I had bought from an estate sale. I paid only $.50 for all three postcards and netted more than $86 on them. I was totally hooked.

Mardi started out just wanting to sell some of the collections her mother had left her when she passed away. Once she made up her mind that she wanted to become a PowerSeller, the status came within two months.

Currently she is selling between 15 and 20 items a week using auctions, a few "buy it nows," and her store. Her starting price is based on research of her items.

I have settled on a starting price that makes people feel as though they will be happy with the item they bought and that they got it for a good price. Everyone must thoroughly check out their market in order to determine a good starting price for their items.

Mardi recommends that when a seller is trying to get buyers to notice their listings they should be sure to have a good title.

Using only keywords and a gallery picture are the best tools to get people to notice. Once they go inside then you must have a precise, honest description and lots of excellent pictures.

To find her items she sells, Mardi goes to rummage sales, flea markets, and even her own basement! Since she inherited so many collections from her mother, she said it should keep her very busy for years to come with that stock alone. She also sells items for other people. This allows her to gain experience selling items she isn't very familiar with. To list all these items, Mardi makes use of two different software listing programs.

I am learning to use Blackthorne. I like it. It is easy to use and keeps track of everything. It is also nice that it resides on my computer so it can be on my laptop and travel with me. I also love using Turbo Lister. The new version is awesome and very easy to use.

Mardi finds cross-promotions to be a very valuable tool for both vertical and horizontal selling. She always uses cross-promotion and with her store she is able to cross-promote 12 items at a time!

She believes the timing of an auction can be important depending on what is being sold.

I believe it can be a critical element in sales. For instance, if I were selling adult video games, I would probably have them end in the wee hours of the morning. I certainly would not have them end at 8 or 9 a.m. Most of the people who play those video games are in their late teens or early 20s and they are college students. These people are usually up at 1, 2 or even 3 a.m. This is the time to get their attention. It is always important to know your market and know when they are shopping.

When she hasn't heard from a buyer, Mardi will always make an attempt to contact them. She said e-mailing and even making a phone call is necessary at times to make sure you are putting forth an effort.

I believe people are good and they sometimes make a mistake, so I like to help them out. Other times, something has happened and they cannot respond. That happens, too. In that case my effort is helping them by discovering the problem and helping them solve it.

Mardi only accepts returns when she is the one who made the error by describing the item incorrectly. In eight years she has only had one return!

To save on shipping costs, Mardi recommends recycling your packaging materials—only if they are clean, of course. Other advice for saving on shipping costs:

- *Use USPS free boxes.*

- *Have USPS pick up your domestic packages, saving you gas money by not having to drive to the post office. Keep in mind this will not work for international shipments but will you save you on the domestic ones.*

- *See if any stores will save their peanuts and give or sell them to you at a reasonable cost.*

Mardi believes that international bidders are good for business. In fact, she said she would lose about one quarter of her business if not selling internationally.

The world is getting very small and the market is moving outwards from the United States. It is imperative that people sell internationally if they are going to grow their business.

She prefers not to use the drop-shipping method for selling any items. She does not drop ship because of her concern that her seller's image is then no longer in her own hands.

Drop shippers' practices directly affect my business. For

instance, if they take longer than I would to ship, my customer might leave me negative feedback or complain to eBay or PayPal. I have no control over how a drop shipper does business so I choose not to use them.

That said I have known people who have used drop shippers very successfully. I believe that the most important thing to do is to know your drop shipper. If you can hook up with someone locally or within a reasonable distance, you can visit their facility and form a relationship; that would be the ideal situation.

Mardi links her education Web site to her "About Me" page. She also uses cross-promotions and has a link on her Web site (**www.youcansell2.com**) to drive people to her eBay store.

A Final Piece of Advice

I think the most important thing you can do in an eBay business is to be honest and give your buyer the benefit of the doubt. If you are honest and open, you will do well. Know your product, do tons of research on and off eBay to determine your price point, and include many pictures. Make your auctions look as though a person around the world can virtually pick up your item and turn it around, just like they could in a store. That is what sells!

Dr. Marguerite Swope

Username:	mhswope
Name:	Dr. Marguerite Swope
E-mail:	mhswope@gmail.com
Classification:	Internet/ eBay Only Business
Current Tier:	Bronze PowerSeller
Web Site:	QuickSellOnline.com
Current Feedback Star:	Red
Projected 2006 Sales:	$18,000

QuickSellOnline.com
Everything eBay

A Little Background

Marguerite Swope has been a member of eBay since March 2000.

Dr. Marguerite Swope took early retirement from the Computer Science faculty at Penn State in 2000. After selling some of her books on eBay, she was hooked and quickly became a PowerSeller. Now she has six years' selling experience, more than 4000 feedbacks (100 percent positive) and in 2005 was chosen to be an eBay University instructor. She is an eBay Trading Assistant and Certified Education Specialist and Business Consultant trained by eBay and has an eBay consulting business. In addition to teaching for Pennsylvania SBDCs, she has taught hands-on seminars at the South Hills School of Business and Technology in State College, Pennsylvania.

A part-time eBay seller, Dr. Marguerite Swope—username mhswope—began selling on eBay after buying something that didn't work and then selling it.

> *Then I sold more, and more. It wasn't really a decision. I just realized how easy it was.*

PowerSeller status caught up to her. She has been selling on eBay for more than six years and has held the PowerSeller title for most of that time. She uses auctions and an eBay Store to sell her items.

Because this is only a part-time venture for Marguerite, she can sell anywhere from just a few items a week to 30 items. Her average starting price is $9.99 and she has found a good way to get people to notice her listings.

> *Have a good title with searchable keywords. Sell brand name items. Use a gallery photo and use a subtitle either to tell more about your item or to advertise your other items, unless you want to spend $19.95 to feature your item.*

Marguerite finds most of the items she sells through this account at thrift stores. She has a supplemental account she has a store-front with. This is her DaisyThreads eBay ID and in this eBay Store all you will find are her handmade items.

To list her items she uses Turbo Lister. She also does cross-promoting.

In my store, I heavily cross-promote.

Although she has no statistical data about the ending time and day of her auctions, she said,

I like to end my auctions at night and choose Sunday, Monday, Tuesday, or Wednesday. I think those are good evenings.

When she hasn't heard from a buyer, she sends out several e-mail notices and an invoice.

After seven days I file an unpaid item strike. That often gets their attention.

When it comes to return policies, Marguerite has one for both of her IDs with a little difference between them. For her DaisyThreads account, it is a no-questions asked policy. With her mhswope account, she only grants a return if she has misrepresented the item.

Marguerite ships all of her items through Priority Mail. She allows international bidders to her listings and believes they are good for business. She would not personally use drop shipping as a method for selling, but she has heard of people who have been able to use it successfully.

To drive people to her store, she uses her auctions, search engines, and referrals.

A Final Piece of Advice

Just use good basics—good titles, thorough, honest descriptions, very good photos, and honest policies. State things positively rather than negatively—be friendly. And trust in the goodness of people.

Additional Company Information

In addition to her main eBay ID (mhswope), she also has a line of clothing and scarves she designs and sews (or knits). She sells these in her eBay Store under the ID DaisyThreads and in craft fairs around Pennsylvania.

Michael Dutton

Username:	mdutton
Name:	Michael Dutton
E-mail:	micronets@sbcglobal.net
Classification:	Internet/ eBay Only Business
Current Tier:	Bronze PowerSeller
Current Feedback Star:	Purple
Projected 2006 Sales:	$35,000

A Little Background

Michael Dutton has been a member of eBay since August 1998.

Michael Dutton—username mdutton—started selling on eBay because it was the market for selling the items he liked to buy: "That is, anything that I think has a market that sellers are ignoring." He didn't set becoming a PowerSeller as a goal, but after a year of selling he achieved the title and he is "loath to relinquish it."

He does eBay part-time, selling anywhere from less than 10 to 60 items a week.

> *Most of the items I sell I buy at tag sales and the vagaries of my source leads to the variation.*

Michael has come up with a strategy that he finds works well when pricing his items.

> *I like to start at $.99 if I feel there will be two likely bidders. If the item is such that only one person may be bidding (blown glass bowls are such an item) I will list it at my minimum selling price. The reason for this is that everyone loves a bargain and if you think you might get it for under a dollar you will more likely raise the bid once someone else bid on "your" item. This strategy has allowed my items to be among the highest priced of their kind.*

To get people to notice his listings, he offers the advice of using the keywords you, as a buyer, would look for when searching for an item.

You need to have directed words in the listing. If possible, use the make, model, color, size, and any other detail a buyer is looking for. Only after that should you list condition. Always use a gallery photo. Have as many photos of the item as you can in every listing. Many of my listings have 12 photos.

Michael does not make any of his own items, rather he finds most of his items as tag sales and in consignment shops. Sometimes he will also purchase an eBay item and "produce a better listing, selling it, most often at a nice profit." To list his items he makes use of Selling Manager Pro and is also looking into using Vendio. He does use cross-promotions, especially if he is selling a collection.

When it comes to the time and time-ending of an auction, Michael said it is absolutely important.

If your item is special, you want it to end on a Sunday evening PST. I have made money buying items ending on Sunday morning and selling that same item so it ends on a Sunday evening. When you have time to search out items, so do most of your buyers.

When a buyer doesn't respond, he will send a second notice and then use eBay's non paying bidder program and re-list the item for sale. His return policy varies from item to item.

Musical instruments and cameras I always give a week to inspect the item.

Michael uses USPS to ship just about all of his items.

I have tried UPS and DHL with less than satisfactory results. UPS breaks about one out of seven items shipped and DHL has over billed me. I am currently in a heated dispute with DHL over $200 of phantom charges.

Michael has never tried drop shipping because he said that would be leaving his reputation in someone else's hands. "Not a good idea." He finds international bidders good for business.

Whenever a bidder asks what shipping will to be to, say, Australia, I always post the answer in the listing. If someone else is considering paying an extra $10 in shipping, that makes U.S. buyers see they will need to bid another $10 just to get the item. Selling on eBay is mostly psychology. Understand that and you will succeed.

A Final Piece of Advice

Think like a buyer. Look at listings and examine what makes them attractive or unclear. One of my favorites is a watch that was photographed from across the room—and only one bad photo at that. That item was resold at a very good profit.

Rich Siok

Username:	appealingsigns
Name:	Rich Siok
E-mail:	sales@appealingsigns.com
Classification:	Internet/ eBay Only Business
Current Tier:	Bronze PowerSeller
eBay Store:	Appealing Signs
eBay Store Location:	www.stores.ebay.com/ Appealing-Signs
Current Feedback Star:	Red
Projected 2006 Sales:	$20,000

A Little Background

*My wife, Nila, and I operate a family-owned, one-stop sign shop. We specialize in custom banners, vehicle magnetics, vinyl window lettering, vinyl vehicle lettering, ready-to-apply vinyl graphics, and of course, our novelty signs in plastic and aluminum. We have partnered with some of the best sign shops in the country. If a customer calls with questions we will take the time to get them the correct answers. We are very involved in various community/business organizations, including our local Elk Grove Chamber of Commerce. I am currently a board member and past chairman from 2004. Nila is very involved in the Community Character Coalition— spreading good character through schools, community, and business. Donating time back to the community has really brought a great satisfaction in our lives. What goes around comes around is very true in our lives. We love our business and the creativity it allows us. We have had so much fun selling and buying on eBay. eBay customers are great! And from our customers' feedback, they like dealing with us too. Please come visit us at: **www.appealingsigns.com**.*

Rich Siok—username appealing signs—is a full-time eBay seller. He started selling on eBay to help with his regular sign business during its slower times. As he got busier and began selling more on eBay, becoming a PowerSeller became a goal. After six months it caught up to him and he is now a bronze-tiered PowerSeller.

Selling in just about all the formats available to him on eBay, Rich sells about 10 to 20 items a week with an average starting price of $16.95. He has found the best way to get people to notice his listings has been through the specials he runs.

Because he is in the sign business, all the items he sells are custom-made signs. He also sells some items that he finds from antique stores or estate sales. To list these items he uses Auctiva listing software. To cross-promote, he will occasionally run a "buy this, get that free or half price" deal.

Timing of an auction varies for him. He tries to end an auction every day if at all possible.

I use different times of the day for ending auctions. Believe it or not lunch time can be good.

When he hasn't heard from a buyer, Rich will continue sending reminder e-mails for two or three weeks. After that he will report the unpaid item to eBay.

I must say, this does not happen often.

He has a 100 percent satisfaction guaranteed return policy.

We want our customers to be happy and to come back and tell their friends.

Rich has found the best way to save on shipping costs has been to take advantage of USPS since they offer free Priority boxes and labels.

I can order all my boxes online. I can also print my own labels using PayPal at the office so this saves a lot of time. I also have the USPS to pick up my boxes that are ready to ship.

Rich has done a great deal of research lately as he has been considering entering into drop shipping as a way of selling items. He has been trying to find the right people to work with and he said he will see what happens soon! When it comes to shipping internationally, Rich ships only to Canada.

The shipping costs seem high overseas. It is too costly for a product that only costs $17 to $25.

To draw people into his eBay store, Rich has uses two methods.

I always have auction items running. We also use Auctiva which is an awesome way to have people view all your items that you are selling.

A Final Piece of Advice

Our company has great succss with eBay. My wife and I are Education Specialists trained by eBay. We teach others "The safe and right way to sell on eBay." I encourage everyone to get some training. eBay takes time to learn. Do everything one step at a time. Hook up with a mentor. This is a great group of people to buy and sell to. Listen to Griff on wsradio.

Where else can you make money while you're sleeping?

Steven Gartner

Username:	celebglasses
Name:	Steven Gartner
E-mail:	stevengart@yahoo.com
Classification:	Internet/ eBay Only Business
Current Tier:	Bronze PowerSeller
eBay Store:	Celebrity Glasses
eBay Store Location:	www.stores.ebay.com/ Celebrity-Glasses
Current Feedback Star:	Red
Projected 2006 Sales:	$40,000

A Little Background

Steven Gartner has been a member of eBay since October 2002.

Steven Gartner—username celebglasses—is a full-time eBay seller. He began selling on eBay as a natural extension to his already-in-place e-commerce site (www.celebrityglasses. com). Selling on eBay allowed him extra exposure and free marketing for his e-commerce site—"a win-win situation." He set becoming a PowerSeller as a goal. He was close for a few months so he increased his volume of selling and it happened for him. It took him about five months to reach the status.

I would have reached it much sooner but I had to learn the ins and outs of eBay beforehand.

Steven markets through auctions (10 percent) and then the rest are "buy it now" via his eBay store. Although his volume changes all the time, he can sell as little as just a few items a day to several hundred if selling wholesale, his normal number of items sold per week is anywhere from 10 to 25 auctions. For his store, his average starting price is generally $9.99. When he lists his items as auctions, they will start at $5 to $6 for a seven-day auction and $10 for three- and five-day auctions.

I change the prices all the time for auction listings because it is very interesting to see the outcome which is always different, yet exciting.

To get people to notice a listing, Steven said the best way is use of eye-grabbing photos, using the gallery feature and having a great listing template.

Of course, using the correct key words will make you or break you.

Steven finds most of the items he sells through different contacts.

I was fortunate to have numerous contacts with wholesalers who supply my products before I even decided to sell on eBay. This is usually the biggest hurdle for most people to get started; that is having the connections, resources, and contacts for items to sell.

To list his items, Steven uses Auctiva and the new Turbo Lister. He knows there are others, but has not had the chance to look them over yet. He said he prefers to keep costs to a bare minimum. Using Auctiva and eBay's software, he is able to cross-promote in his listings. He also mentions his e-commerce site on his "About Me" page.

Steven has found through experience and studying other sellers the best time to end an auction is in the evening around 6 to 8 p.m. PST.

> *I have ended auctions a bit earlier and later than this and have had success as well, but the main tip is to end your listings in the evening. It used to be the thought that ending your listings on Sunday evenings was the best but I have had much success with end days being beginning or midweek as well.*

He will send out several e-mails to a non-responsive buyer via eBay's process and his own. If he still hasn't heard from a buyer within seven days, he will use eBay's unpaid item report process which he said works quite well.

> *At one point I thought about calling buyers via the telephone; however, by discussing this with other sellers via the message boards I realized this was not such a productive idea.*

Steven only gives a refund or return if the item was misrepresented or damaged during the shipping process.

He said the best way to save on shipping costs is to try to obtain the materials needed for shipping for free or a discounted price.

There are a lot of extra hidden costs that will increase the actual shipping for us sellers. One good way to get back some of those extra costs is to charge a handling fee or a flat rate charge for shipping. I charge a flat rate of $6 which includes all the extras that go with my actual shipping such as the crush proof boxes, sunglass pouch, packing slip, bubble wrap, packaging tape, and gas to drive to the post office.

Steven believes international bidders are great for business. He gets a large portion of his business from overseas customers, especially from the United Kingdom, Canada, and Australia.

Shipping time is slower but people overseas generally buy more items and/or are great repeat customers. So far I have shipped to places such as Australia, Japan, Saudi Arabia, Malaysia, and Turkey. I have many customers in Canada and the United Kingdom who regularly buy from me.

Although he has not had experience with drop shipping, he has been informed by other sellers who do use drop shipping as a method for selling items that it can be a very risky source.

Usually the product line the drop shipper carries is so oversaturated already on eBay that the profit margin will be very low for the buyer. The other complaint has been that the in-stock availability of products sold is most often not available when they do sell.

Right now, Steven uses his auctions to drive buyers to his store. Although he has thought about buying keywords, he has yet to try it. He did make use of a site called **ioffer.com** which drove customers to his eBay store.

A Final Piece of Advice

My advice to someone wanting to become a small-time seller or a full-fledged PowerSeller is to study how eBay operates before you start. Starting on eBay as a buyer first to become familiar with that process. Start selling by listing household items and once you get your foot in the door you can then consider selling on a more frequent basis. Another suggestion is to study other sellers. You can learn much about others and your competition by seeing what they do. There is so much to learn and figure out, but you will really only learn by doing.

Contact Information for Steven Gartner:

Company Name: CelebrityGlasses.com

Web site: www.CelebrityGlasses.com

E-mail: admin@celebrityglasses.com

Phone: 425-830-3695

chapter 9

How Selling on eBay Expands Brick-and-Mortar Businesses

Remember 1994? The Internet was going to be the great business equalizer. Anyone could build a Web site and compete with the "big guys."

Didn't happen. In fact, many brick-and-mortar businesses are doing quite well. And they are doing well on eBay.

Brick-and-mortar is the term associated with the types of physical businesses you see as you drive down your street. It's the donut shop, the hardware, and video stores. The thought was that e-commerce merchants had too great an economic advantage over their brick-and-mortar competitors. Online merchants didn't have to own expensive retail space. They weren't forced to keep cash intensive inventories and didn't have the same expensive sales and advertising costs. They could offer products much more cheaply than any "real" businesses could hope to compete with.

But many brick-and-mortar businesses didn't see a threat. They saw an opportunity. Traditional brick-and-mortar, multi-channel, and catalog businesses embraced the Internet, some more than others.

The local bakery didn't have to worry about some online confectioner undercutting their business. Instead, the bakery could develop new products to sell themselves on the Internet. They could expand their expertise and customer base without opening a new store. They can wait on customers at the front door while shipping cheesecakes out the back.

Do traditional businesses that use eBay have an edge over pure-play Internet businesses? A brick-and-mortar merchant very possibly has a killer advantage if we consider buyer behavior.

The key is many businesses have found that, unlike their Internet-only competitors, they have direct contact with their customers. They talk to them every day. They know their needs and wants. They know what makes them happy.

So if a brick-and-mortar business reaches out online, they have a thorough understanding of their customer. That is customer and product knowledge few Internet-only businesses can match.

No matter how hard a pure-play Internet marketer tries to improve sales, the brick-and-mortar store has a huge advantage. Several groups, including The Kelsey Group, Overture, and SuperPages.com, have released studies that suggest a lot of searches by potential buyers are simply research. People surf the Internet to become informed before going to a local business to buy. Offering items on eBay can actually increase sales at the store.

Want more proof? Many "Pure Internet" businesses are opening stores and mailing catalogs. They want the killer advantage of online presence combined with the ability to drive customers to brick-and-mortar stores.

Another benefit of selling on the Internet is the increase in the amount of product they need. Greater numbers generally means lower overall costs due to high volume, and that brings down the cost for supplying the brick-and-mortar customers. It decreases prices and increases profits for both sides of the business.

What a deal!

Also, since traditional businesses often have a good mix of products to sell, they have an advantage of keeping repeat business. You can sell a cheesecake this week. When the holidays arrive you can send them an "Exclusive Offer" for some cookies or fruitcake.

And finally, a brick-and-mortar business normally has relationships with suppliers, accounting systems set up, and a lot of the basic operations any business needs to operate and flourish. It is a gentler learning curve to get started.

Following are a number of PowerSellers who use eBay in conjunction with their brick-and-mortar businesses.

chapter 10

PowerSellers Who Use eBay In Conjunction with Their Brick-and-Mortar Businesses

Following are a number of PowerSellers who use eBay in conjunction with their brick-and-mortar businesses.

ExpressDrop Chicago

Username:	expressdropchicago
Names:	Amy Mayer, Michael Mayer, Ellen Navarro, and Timothy Bruno
E-mail:	info@expressdrop.com
Classification:	Brick-and-Mortar Store Using eBay
Current Tier:	Platinum PowerSeller
eBay Store:	ExpressDrop Chicago
eBay Store Location:	www.stores.ebay.com/ExpressDrop-Chicago
Current Feedback Star:	Green
Projected 2006 Sales:	$1.4 Million

EXPRESSDROP We sell for you on eBay.

A Little Background

Amy Mayer, Michael Mayer, Ellen Navarro, and Timothy Bruno have been members of eBay since February 1999.

ExpressDrop Inc., Chicago's first and most experienced eBay drop-off store, was founded in January 2004 by partners Amy Mayer, Michael Mayer, Ellen Navarro, and Timothy Bruno. Each of the principals brought their own area of expertise to the table to form the core of ExpressDrop.

After reading an October 2003 article on AuctionDrop and QuikDrop in *The New York Times*, Michael Mayer, Amy Mayer, Timothy Bruno, and Ellen Navarro could not help but be convinced of the necessity for this type of business in the Chicago area. As stores with a similar concept began to rise in popularity, ExpressDrop was born, not only to add this service to the Chicago marketplace, but also to provide the customer-service and customer-education oriented facets lacking in the eBay drop-off store industry.

Amy Mayer, Michael Mayer, Ellen Navarro, and Timothy Bruno—username expressdropchicago—are full-time eBay sellers. After hearing about the concept of drop-off centers, they were "immediately convinced" this type of service was needed in their Chicago area.

Not only does it offer an easy and convenient way for anyone to list items on eBay, but it offers individuals the chance to have items professionally listed and backed by a large company which is likely to lead to higher bidding.

They set reaching PowerSeller status as a goal and within two months of high-volume selling, they achieved their goal.

Becoming a PowerSeller was a goal because it is a status that eBay buyers look for and trust. The PowerSeller label signifies a seller that has a standing history with eBay and a list of successful transactions behind them.

The team will list anywhere from 250 to 600 items in a normal week with the wide range dependent upon the time of year. They prefer to start off their auction items at $19.99 with no reserve. When they do "buy it nows," they tend to vary the price of the item based on its brand as well as "its past success on eBay." They make use of all areas of eBay for selling, including auctions, "buy it nows," and storefront. To get people to notice their listings they follow the research of similar items sold previously on eBay.

We rely heavily on research of similar completed items that sold successfully to help us to determine the keywords that will bring the most potential bidders to our auctions. By having as many searchable words in the titles as possible, we attract more bidders and the auction prices end higher.

Because they sell items on consignment, they find most of their items from their customer drop-offs or by collecting them.

We retrieve or are shipped masses of inventory at a time from the corporate clients that we seek out. We sell overstock for our corporate ("retail") clients.

To list their items, this group makes use of eBay's software, Blackthorne, as well as proprietary software. They also use Yahoo! and Google search terms to cross-promote their items.

They are very careful about the timing of their auctions.

We pay close attention to the times that auctions end as we want as many potential bidders to be awake and able to bid on our items as possible. We are careful not to post too early in the morning because the time difference on the West Coast, and we do not allow auctions to end on holidays when less people are available to bid.

ExpressDrop does have a return policy that states items can be returned within seven days of the close of the auction if the item has not met the listed specifications. When they haven't heard from a buyer, they will attempt to contact the winner at least twice by way of e-mails and possibly even through the telephone before resorting to contacting eBay to file a non-paying bidder dispute.

We have found that patience and dealing directly with buyers instead of using eBay as a middleman is typically the most successful and least threatening.

The team does not use drop shipping. They do believe international bidders are good for their business.

For many items international bidders are critical to a good sale; however, you must be well-informed of overseas shipping costs and policies so that this information can be passed on to potential buyers prior to the end of an auction.

Because ExpressDrop is a high-volume seller, they receive a discount through UPS for shipping. They have found for them and for anyone who is a high-volume seller, that this is the best way to save on shipping costs. Because of the discount they are able to pass that savings down to their customers.

If you are not a high-volume seller, the best place to start cutting costs related to shipping is to use free supplies offered by UPS and USPS to those that use their services for shipping.

They also have a Web site besides their eBay store site: **www. expressdrop.com**.

Contact Information for ExpressDrop:

ExpressDrop has three locations in the Chicago area. The addresses and contact information for each is listed below.

ExpressDrop
1900 W. Belmont Ave.
Chicago, IL 60657
Phone: 773-975-7355

ExpressDrop West Loop
346 N. Justine St.
Suite 201
Chicago, IL 60607
Phone: 312-421-5293

ExpressDrop Wilmette
Eden's Plaza
3232 Lake Ave.
Wilmette, IL 60091
Phone: 847-256-7355

Dan Glasure

Username:	dans.train.depot
E-mail:	dan@danstraindepot.com
Classification:	Internet/ eBay Only Business & Brick-and-Mortar Store Using eBay
Current Tier:	Platinum PowerSeller
eBay Store:	Dan's Train Depot
eBay Store Location:	www.stores.ebay.com/Dans-Train-Depot
Current Feedback Star:	Shooting Yellow
Projected 2006 Sales:	$2.4 Million

A Little Background

Dan Glasure has been a member of eBay since January 1999.

> *I actually started on eBay selling comic books and then Legos, but my real interest was model trains. My father and I had a chance to purchase a very large train collection. He put a second mortgage on his house to finance it. We sold it all on eBay, started buying more collections across the country, and the rest, as they say, is history!*

> *We have been selling on eBay for six years now, and we are currently one of the biggest sellers in the entire Toys and Hobbies category. We rank among the most successful sellers in terms of product sales and customer satisfaction on eBay.*

Dan Glasure—username dans.train.depot—is a full-time eBay seller. His business, Dan's Train Depot, currently has seven employees. About seven years ago Dan wanted to begin making some extra money, so he started selling on eBay. By the time eBay instituted the PowerSeller program he was already qualified and was awarded the status. In 2005, Dan's eBay business yielded him $2.4 million in sales. He projects the same amount of sales for 2006.

Dan sells anywhere from 300 to 500 items a week, with the price now dependent upon the item itself (he used to start all items at $.99). Besides spending money on advertising, trade shows, and other areas of marketing, Dan also has found the loyal following the company has built up means that his eBay store is the easiest way to get people to notice his listings. It is easier to sort the items in the eBay store format. He also uses auction listings.

He finds most of his items from estate sales, large collections, and store buy-outs, to name just a few. Dan uses Blackthorne Pro to list these items. He also makes use of cross-promotions when selling his items. He believes the timing of the auction is very important. He offers a satisfaction guaranteed return policy.

Dan jokes that when he hasn't heard from a buyer he will "contact someone in their town to rough them up a little bit!" He was just kidding of course, and when he hasn't heard from a buyer he will generally send a few notices to remind them and only file a non-paying bidder alert if it is necessary.

Dan absolutely said NO to drop shipping as a method of selling items. He does believe that international bidders are good for business. To save on shipping costs, he recommends buyers combine auctions.

He does not have a Web site linked to his auction listings, as that is against eBay policies, but he does send them to his "About Me" page, and from there he sends them to his Web site. To draw people in to his eBay store, Dan said they have a link on every one of their auction pages as well as advertising in trade magazines. He also directs people to his eBay store from his Web site. His two Web sites are: Danstraindepot.com and Brasstrains.com.

See Chapter 14 for an in-depth interview with Dan Glasure.

Jennifer Riojas Mogan

User Name:	eAuctionGurus
Name:	Jennifer Riojas Mogan
E-mail:	TheGuru@eAuctionGurus.com
Classification:	Brick-and-Mortar Store Using eBay
Current Tier:	Gold PowerSeller
eBay Store:	eAuction Gurus
eBay Store Location:	www.stores.ebay.com/eAuction-Gurus
Current Feedback Star:	Red

A Little Background

Jennifer Riojas Mogan has been a member of eBay since February 2000.

Growing up, taking care of siblings, and daily chores—education was pushed aside. Despite the fact that Jennifer had no university education, she was determined to make something of herself.

While raising her own children after an abusive marriage, she decided to return to school. Being a single mother, working long hours, and attending the local junior college were heavy burdens to carry. Jennifer made the decision to attend an accelerated accounting course through another local college named Humphreys. There she received a certificate in accounting.

Jennifer had an opportunity come along through the college administrator. She was offered a job at Gould Medical Foundation as an administrative assistant for the medical director of the facility. Jennifer worked under the direction of the medical director and the managed care director. Soon Jennifer was training peers at the Utilization Management Department. She was also working in the accounting department, splitting her workdays between the few departments, using her computer skills and accounting skills. Within a year she graduated to the accounting department where she worked for two years.

Two years into her accounting position at Gould Medical Foundation, Sutter Hospital bought Gould Medical Foundation. The word "downsizing" was buzzing around the office. Her boss spoke to her about the downsizing issue. He explained that either her partner or she would have to go. Her partner was older and had been in her job for several years. However, Jennifer had computer skills, and the times were changing. He indicated Jennifer might be the one to stay. Since her partner was the breadwinner of her family and in her 50s, Jennifer immediately started job searching.

Jennifer quickly received a job at Pacific Pre Cut in Tracy, California. She would work as the human resource director. Jennifer, for the first time, would have her own office and desk. She was amazed at where she had come; she was determined to do more and to continue to climb.

One morning on the way to work, Jennifer was in a terrible car accident that left her unable to continue to work. She was relatively new at her job: it had only been six months. The road to recovery was rehabilitation, doctors' visits, treatments, and hardships.

Feeling restless while unable to work, Jennifer knew there was something she could do. One day, her new husband came home talking about eBay. He said it is a place where you can sell on the Internet and make money. They had no idea what it was, so they researched it on the Internet.

That was more than six years ago and her success has been phenomenal. eBay was the answer to a prayer and the beginning of a new success for Jennifer and her family.

With no university education and only the basic school courses, Jennifer was determined to make something of herself. She has done that but feels this is only the beginning.

She climbed the eBay rungs and has earned eBay titles along the way. She is a PowerSeller, eBay Registered Trading Assistant, and an Education Specialist trained by eBay.

She has been requested to do many speaking engagements for companies like the National Black Masters Business Association, where she received an all-expense lavish paid trip for herself and her husband. She has also received another paid trip to eBay Live! 2006 in Las Vegas to stay at the Grand Luxor by Mpire (an excellent listing and managing tool). She has also been asked to put her two cents' worth into a few books, such as this one. Who would have thought all this would be available through eBay?

A full-time (and more!) seller on eBay, Jennifer Riojas Mogan— username eAuctionGurus—started selling on eBay to gain independence and income. She set becoming a PowerSeller as a goal and after just months, she realized her goal.

Jennifer sells several items a day with an average starting price of $.99 for her auctions. Auctions are her primary form of selling on eBay. She finds people notice her listings mostly because of her great titles. She also uses several eBay services to boost sales such as Cross-Promotion service, Second Chance Offer service, and anything else offered.

Jennifer's husband invents items to sell on eBay for her. He is currently working on an invention for eBay now. Mostly people bring items to her through her Trading Assistant business, which is why the brick and mortar became so important. To list and manage her items she uses Mpire.

Only the best will do.

Timing of an auction and the ending-time are things she attends to carefully.

Very important if you want top dollar for your item!

When buyers haven't paid her, she attempts to e-mail them.

Then wait two or three days and e-mail them a non-paying bidder notice through eBay's system—that gets them motivated!

She has a return policy that includes a satisfaction-guaranteed policy. If a buyer is not completely satisfied with the purchase, she offers a money-back guarantee. Buyers need to feel secure when making a purchase. She has only had to use the refund policy a couple of times over the past six and half years.

She does accept international bidders and finds them to be absolutely good for business. She does not use drop shipping as a method for selling items. She will not rely on someone else to keep her good name untarnished. Besides, she has not heard of many drop-shipping success stories. To save on shipping costs she suggests the following:

Gather your own packing supplies from gift shops (peanuts, bubble wrap, and boxes) and also use the Flat Rate shipping supplies from USPS.

She does have a Web site linked to her auctions (**www.eAuctionGurus.com**) and she finds she is able to drive people to her store through auctions ("auctions, auctions, auctions").

A Final Piece of Advice

eBay is a great place to make extra money. It can seem overwhelming at first; however, it is a repetitive act. You will get the hang of it if you choose to stick with it. There are many tools available to make the listing and managing process less burdensome and easier to manage. If you are having trouble with the eBay process, I suggest you look up your local eBay Education Specialist on the www.PowerU.net

site. Education Specialists are trained to walk you through the process one-on-one until you get the process down. In your own living room if you so choose!

Jennifer Riojas Mogan's Seminar Profile

Jennifer has worked as an eBay seller for more than six years. Jennifer's titles include: PowerSeller status, eBay Registered Trading Assistant, and Education Specialist Trained by eBay.

Jennifer leads eBay training in seminar format all over Central California and has consulted privately for several individuals and companies.

Jennifer's passion is to assure, pursue, coach, and assist in the process of individuals becoming successful on eBay.

As a successful eBay seller, Jennifer has the experience and the knowledge to help others achieve success. She offers training classes as well as individual consulting. She has an office in Lodi, California, where the group classes are held. If you are interested in additional information, contact Jennifer at eAuction Gurus.

Contact Information for Jennifer Riojas Mogan:

Jennifer Riojas Mogan

eAuction Gurus

110 S. Cherokee Lane

Lodi, CA 95240

Phone: 209-518-8590

www.eAuctionGurus.com

TheGuru@eAuctionGurus.com

Chris Crepeau

User Name:	michauctionsales
Name:	Chris Crepeau
E-mail:	Chris@MichiganAuctionSales.com
Classification:	Brick-and-Mortar Store Using eBay
Current Tier:	Silver PowerSeller
eBay Store:	Michigan Auction Sales
eBay Store Location:	www.stores.ebay.com/Michigan-Auction-Sales
Current Feedback Star:	Red
Projected 2006 Sales:	$475,000

A Little Background

Chris Crepeau has been a member of eBay since August 1997.

Chris is a Missouri Auction School Graduate, an active member of the National Auctioneers Association (**www.auctioneers. org**), an eBay mentor with the Disabled Online Users Association (**www.doua.org**), member of the Michigan State Auctioneers Association (**www.msaa.org**), eBay Education Specialist, member of the Professional eBay Sellers Alliance (one of the largest selling groups on eBay and formerly the eBay Elite), a Silver PowerSeller, an eBay Trading Assistant, an eBay Motors Dealer's Assistant trained by eBay, a CAGA Certified Appraiser, State of Michigan licensed real estate sales person, and State of Michigan licensed Automobile broker.

Michigan Auction Sales is based in Lansing. Our goal is to take all the hassles, inconveniences, and wasted time out of selling an automobile or any other item, while maximizing the financial return for our clients. We handle all aspects of each sale, from pre-sale inspections, to advertising, marketing, and even legal transfer of ownership.

Chris Crepeau—username michauctionsales—is a sometimes part-time, sometimes full-time eBay seller. He began selling on eBay because of his live auction business.

As a live auctioneer, I am always looking for ways to reach more potential bidders. Since my business is in a somewhat economically depressed area, we often see items go for more on eBay than they would at one of our live auctions.

Becoming a PowerSeller was not a goal for Chris, yet after several years of selling, he became one. He believes it was during the first year of the program that he became a PowerSeller.

We didn't even realize that the PowerSeller status existed at the time until eBay notified us that we had achieved it. Once we were PowerSellers, we always thought it was nice when we'd jump to the Titanium level after selling a high dollar asset. We are currently back to Silver, but most recently, we were Titanium PowerSellers.

Chris sells about 40-100 items a week. Most of the items are smaller, but sometimes the sales include items such as boats, RVs, cars, trucks, and heavy equipment. He finds most people notice his listings because he categorizes the items correctly and starts his auctions with no reserve and a $.01 starting bid. The average starting price for his items is anywhere from $.01 to $.99.

> *Sometimes if the demand is low, we will put a higher bid, but mostly no-reserve $.01 sales. If you research the item and conclude that the demand is there, you will do well.*

Although he does not make his own items to sell, Chris has sold handmade items for others. He said the market for these types of items does vary. He gets his items from different places.

> *They are mostly consignments from other private individuals, banks, businesses, and government agencies. Auctions and Estate Sales are excellent places to buy items for resale on eBay!*

Chris uses the Selling Manager Pro listing software. He also has a Web site besides his eBay store located at **www.MichiganAuctionSales.com**. For cross-promotion, he sometimes advertises his eBay auctions in a local newspaper and at his live auctions. He's found the best way to drive people to his store listings is through his other listings.

Time, more specifically time-ending, is very important to Chris in the case of a high-dollar item.

> *Think like your buyer and try to plan your auction accordingly. I've seen Sunday evenings the most profitable night to end an auction. However, if you are selling a piece of business*

equipment, having the auction end during business hours is better.

Chris uses the method below when he hasn't heard from a buyer.

Contact them by e-mail with a friendly reminder, wait a few days if no response, give them a friendly phone call. If no progress, consider re-listing the item.

They do not accept returns except in the case of inadvertent misrepresentation. Chris uses UPS to save on shipping costs.

Get an account set up with UPS and have a daily pick-up. This will reduce your shipping costs. Reuse and recycle all boxes and packaging materials.

Drop shipping is something Chris said would be good for others to use. He does not use this method himself. He does allow international bidders but warns sellers to be wary.

Just be careful about lost packages in some of the countries having unscrupulous mail carriers.

We sell in our eBay store, eBay Motors, and use "buy it nows." Mostly, we do our listings in the auction format.

A Final Piece of Advice

PayPal is no pal of mine! Be cautious that you buy ONLY from PayPal protected buyers and ship to confirmed addresses within the United States when accepting PayPal. Accept PayPal at your own risk from buyers outside of the United States. There are many buyers who know how to work the system and will. They can get you to send the item and then get your money yanked back from you by PayPal. Do not accept PayPal for anything that cannot be shipped: automobiles, pickups, deposits. They can get charged back to you with ease by an unscrupulous buyer.

Contact Information for Chris Crepeau:
Michigan Auction Sales, LLC
5312 South Pennsylvania Ave
Lansing, MI 48911
Phone: 517-322-3090
www.MichiganAuctionSales.com

Jennifer Guenther

User Name:	enkorestuff
Name:	Jennifer Guenther
E-mail:	enkorekids@enkorekids.com
Classification:	Brick-and-Mortar Store Using eBay
Current Tier:	Silver PowerSeller
eBay Store:	Enkore Stuff
eBay Store Location:	www.stores.ebay.com/Enkore-Stuff
Current Feedback Star:	Red

The Enkore Kids Family: Pictured from left to right are: Richard, Mary Ann, Heather (holding baby Madelyn), Becky, Jennifer, and Kevin (holding Elizabeth).

POWERSELLER PROFILE

A Little Background

Jennifer Guenther has been a member of eBay since March 2001.

We've been eBay PowerSellers for three years and primarily list recycled kids' stuff for our customers, but we also sell some new items. Our eBay ID is EnkoreStuff, a name that allows us to encompass not only our usual kid-related items, but also the occasional power tool or golf club set my husband may want to list.

In addition to operating our brick-and-mortar store and listing items on eBay, I am also an eBay Certified Instructor for the eBay Basics Course and Beyond the Basics course, and I teach four classes a year at the Frederick Community College.

Running her brick-and-mortar store full-time and eBay part-time, Jennifer Guenther—username enkorestuff—started selling on eBay as an expansion to her store.

I decided to sell on eBay as another outlet for selling children's items that came in daily to our resale store, Enkore Kids. It allowed us to accept more items and help local families recycle their kids' stuff.

Jennifer had set becoming a PowerSeller as a goal that she wanted to reach; it took her the minimum time allowed to attain that goal.

From the time I started listing our overflow store items on eBay, I became a PowerSeller within three months.

Although the number of items she sells during the year tends to vary (around Christmas she can sell around 40-50 items a day), she finds that her average of 20-30 items per week is still very profitable. Her listings generally start at only $.99, but with a reserve price set—she does disclose her reserve price so that her customers realize it is reasonable—and a "buy it now" in place to "encourage quick bidding or buying." To get people to notice her listings, Jennifer uses the following technique.

> *I use a consistent template and offer store credit through* **MyStoreCredit.com** *to help bring repeat business. I also use eBay keywords and market my listings to my brick-and-mortar customers.*

She does not make any of the items she sells, but she finds her items through her customers.

> *We sell some new items which do very well around Christmas time, but our regular items are used and brought to us by our customers.*

Jennifer uses Turbo Lister software and cross-promotions.

> *Because I have the eBay store, I have 12 other listings that show at the bottom of all my listings.*

She has a tip to offer when it comes to the timing and time-ending with an auction.

> *It's important to know your customer demographics and your competition to determine when to end an auction and how long you should list the item. Be sure to know what will be going on at the ending time of your auction. You need to be sure your listing doesn't end when some other event may be taking your customer's attention (such as the SuperBowl).*

When she hasn't heard from a buyer, she uses Selling Manager Pro to send an automated invoice and reminder e-mails.

If I have still not heard from them, I'll call if they have left a phone number, but if all else fails, I use eBay's Non Paying Bidder Dispute process to contact them. Often e-mail is filtered out with spam filters so although they may not have received any e-mails, when I use the dispute process and file a claim through eBay, the buyer will know immediately the next time they log on to eBay and nine times out of ten a buyer who didn't respond to my e-mails (most of the time because they didn't get them) will pay after I file with eBay. The key is to give the buyer the benefit of the doubt and be professional and understand that life happens: they may not have received the e-mails, or something more important may be taking their time.

Jennifer does have a return policy but has found that few people have ever taken advantage of it.

I do allow a no-questions-asked return policy for my items, though I do not cover or refund the cost of shipping unless there was a mistake I made in the listing.

To save on shipping costs, Jennifer uses Priority for her items that weigh less than four pounds and UPS for all of her heavier items. She said that if you are going to be doing a lot of shipping, it is good to set up a daily pick-up account with UPS. This will save money on the UPS charges.

Jennifer finds international bidders to be good for business.

Though you are more likely to sell lightweight items or items that fit in the Global Priority Mail flat-rate envelopes, be sure to know the costs and ensure they are covered in your flat-

rate shipping or use the shipping calculator to avoid having to answer repeated questions about shipping costs.

She does not use drop shipping as a method for selling her items.

I distrust using a third party to fulfill my orders. Most drop shippers I've looked into say shipping will be done within two weeks, but most customers expect faster shipping than that.

Jennifer does not have an outside Web site linked to her listings, but she finds that eBay keywords, auctions, or fixed-price items bring attention to her store listings.

A Final Piece of Advice

Look to your interests and area of expertise to determine what your product line should be on eBay. You'll be a more trustworthy seller if you can offer good, sound advice on the items you are selling and you'll have more fun if you like what you're writing about and shipping. However, start small! Don't spend a lot of time and energy (and money!) listing hundreds of items. Do your research (use completed auctions—a free search for two weeks of data from eBay or subscribe to a research site for up to 90 days of research data) before you list a single item. Know your competition: the more there is, the slimmer your margins will be. Once you've found an item, if it's a new product line, don't buy a large amount from a wholesaler before you test it out in case your research doesn't pay off. Once you've found a product, don't rest, as the market place won't keep a single item or line profitable for long!

Company Profile

Enkore Kids is a resale shop that specializes in "previously-loved" kids' clothing, developmental toys, and related equipment for newborns to age eight. We also carry select new items from such vendors as Baby Einstein, Melissa & Doug, Robeez®, Ergo Baby Carriers, Clean Shoppers, and others.

Contact Information for Enkore Kids:
Westview Promenade in Frederick, Maryland
www.enkorekids.com
E-mail: enkorekids@enkorekids.com
Phone: 301-668-0837

Ken Siegel

User Name:	scorebid
Name:	Ken Siegel
E-mail:	scorebid@qwest.net
Classification:	Brick-and-Mortar Store Using eBay
Current Tier:	Silver PowerSeller
eBay Store:	Siegel's Diamond and Gold Outlet
eBay Store Location:	www.stores.ebay.com/Siegels-Diamond-and-Gold-Outlet
Current Feedback Star:	Red
Projected 2006 Sales:	$300,000

A Little Background

Ken Siegel has been a member of eBay since August 1999.

A full-time eBay seller, Ken Siegel—username scorebid—began selling on eBay because of the market potential.

It gave us the instant access to millions of potential buyers with limited advertising expenses. We get many unusual items in our store from people who need cash, but our in-store items sometimes have limited appeal.

After a couple of years of just testing the waters of eBay to see what the benefits and liabilities would be, Ken became a PowerSeller.

After we saw the benefits, we realized it was necessary to be more qualified to become a PowerSeller and Trading Assistant.

He markets in almost every area possible on eBay, especially auctions with many being seven-day, no reserve; "buy it nows" for items with relatively stable values, and store-front. Listing about 30 to 40 items a day, Ken said his average starting price is $.99.

The best way to lure potential buyers is with a very low starting price on a popular or hard-to-find item.

Although he does not make any of the items he sells, Ken does sell items that others have specially made. He finds his items from many different venues.

We have an established jewelry and loan business. Customers need to sell items for quick cash, or some customers can wait 20 days and sell an item on eBay for consignment. We also work with several 501(c)(3) organizations and offer services to their foundations' supporters.

To list his items, Ken uses Kyozou, a major third party vendor.

It is very expensive software but it allows us to operate both an e-commerce store and e-consignment within one software package with many security controls that most of the other software packages didn't offer.

To cross-promote on eBay, Ken has a scroll at the bottom of the screen in all his auctions.

And we use Sellers Voice to advertise the auction and promote other ongoing auctions.

Timing of an auction and when it will end are very important information, according to Ken.

If your item is one that someone in the United States is most likely to buy, then you need to end the auction at a time when most of the interested people will normally be at home.

When he hasn't heard from buyers, Ken attempts to contact them a few times after the end of the sale.

Sometimes the buyer forgets that he or she has bid on an item or goes out of town before the sale ends. We have seen a little of everything over the years and buyers sometimes get "buyers' remorse." About the only thing you can do is apply for a refund from eBay and re-list the item if the second chance offer doesn't go through.

Ken does have a return policy that allows a three-day approval period to all of his buyers.

Although he has heard that some buyers do very well with drop shipping, the business is not yet ready to "enter that arena." Most of the time, he does find international buyers to be good for business.

Smaller items that can be easily shipped overseas lend themselves to international shipping. Larger items that are worth more than $500 also offer good areas of opportunity.

For his buyers to save on shipping costs, Ken recommends combining a few items at one time.

Some sellers won't offer combined shipping, and I think that hurts the selling price as that is usually reflected. We normally offer options of USPS or UPS, but DHL can be lower priced at times.

Ken does have a Web site that is linked to his eBay store: **www. scorebid.com**, and he finds that he can drive people into his store in multiple ways.

We use a variety of advertising with radio, TV, and newspaper. Some direct mail work well.

A Final Piece of Advice

The number one buying advice is making sure the person on the other end is a "normal," honest person. If the person doesn't have much positive feedback, ask them a question or get a phone number so you can talk with this person directly. Remember, if it sounds too good to be true then it probably is. On the selling end, research the market for your item, take quality photos, start your price as low as possible, and give your customers some sort of buyer assurance. Make sure you ship with excellent packaging material and respond to questions on a timely manner.

Company Profile

ScoreBid is an e-commerce and eBay Trading Assistant company formed by Siegel's Jewelry & Loan to handle Internet trading primarily. ScoreBid gives customers the option of consigning primarily jewelry, small antiques, coins, trading cards, sterling flatware, dishes, or memorabilia in our retail store or use eBay to sell any of their valuable goods that they no longer need.

Contact Information for Ken Siegel:

103 3rd Ave SE

Cedar Rapids, IA

Phone: 319-366-1554

www.scorebid.com

scorebid@qwest.net

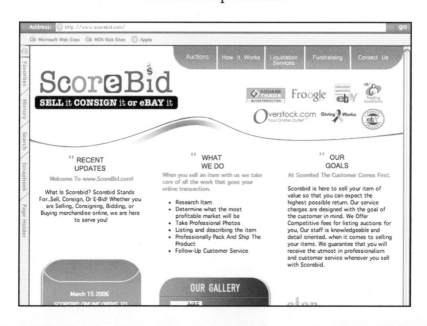

Erin Dixon

User Name:	hatterassurfer
Name:	Erin Dixon
E-mail:	xnailery@aol.com
Classification:	Brick-and-Mortar Store Using eBay
Current Tier:	Bronze/ Silver PowerSeller
eBay Store:	Hatteras Surfer Shop
eBay Store Location:	www.stores.ebay.com/Hatteras-Surfer-Shop
Current Feedback Star:	Green

A Little Background

Erin Dixon has been a member of eBay since April 2003.

One of my favorite places on earth is Hatteras Island, North Carolina, hence, the eBay ID "HatterasSurfer." We have built our love of the earth and ocean into our philosophy of recycling during the shipping process, encouraging customers to recycle the packaging materials as well. We can scoot off to the island in our recreational vehicle and never be out of customer contact. We can pad back and forth from the ocean and still get customer orders out. What a great alternative to the hustle and bustle of the ordinary workplace. eBay has allowed us to expand and contract our business to suit our needs and all the while maintaining PowerSeller status. Heck, it's been so much fun it doesn't qualify as work.

A part-time eBay seller, Erin Dixon started selling on eBay to help her brick-and-mortar store.

eBay offers a selling environment that is supportive and relatively safe. All of the information you need is right at your fingertips and other sellers are eager to share and help you navigate the eBay selling platform. It seemed like a natural extension of my brick-and-mortar salon and retail business. The eBay support-staff were there at each step. They have helped me get products, structure listings and avoid fraud. I wish I had that type of support when I opened my business 20 years ago. Plus the general public knows eBay is the place to go to find anything!

Although she didn't really know what a PowerSeller was when she became one, Erin received the status after less than a year of selling.

eBay was quick to educate me. Becoming a PowerSeller is much like a snowball—once you get rolling you pick up momentum and gather more mass. It was so easy. Sure, I had to dedicate more storage space and I had to find more items, but it was fun. Just being a PowerSeller has increased sales and credibility with potential customers. We love the PowerSeller-only events at eBay Live! Networking with other PowerSellers helps us keep up-to-date and competitive while keeping our expenses low.

Her PowerSeller status actually fluctuates between Silver and Bronze status.

I can earn what I need and still have time for family and friends. In the beginning I was caught up in the sell, sell, sell mode. Now I try to maximize my income, while reducing effort. I stick with perennial best sellers and wholesale off items that move slowly. If a category gets oversold, I move on to newer items. The truth is you can make as much money as you want on eBay. But you have to watch your profit margins and keep supply and shipping costs down or it will be short-lived. It's all about the profits you can put in your pocket.

Erin sells anywhere from 60 to 200 items a week with her average starting price at $7.99. Some of the ways she gets people to notice her listings is by using clear, focused gallery pictures and accurate keywords—which she said will create the biggest draw.

If my competition is using all caps—I avoid using all caps. Developing a standard terms of sale section will help reduce after-sale problems. Spell out everything for the customer ahead of time. Specify shipping costs or use a shipping calculator in each listing. Keep the tone friendly and upbeat, avoiding threats and negative words. Offer as many forms of payment as possible. If there are limitations or restrictions, explain them up front.

She uses Selling Manager Pro to manage her listings.

We have had some growing pains and it has helped us keep track of increasing inventory and communications so that our customers get their products without a hitch.

Erin has a tendency to carry items she uses herself and most of her items are new. She also attends merchandise shows a few times a year.

> *If I stumble on a product I just can't live without, I will contact the manufacturer to find a distributor and set up a resale account. Most are fairly accommodating; after all, they want to sell goods. Running a legitimate business with all of the related licenses ensures our ability to find new, quality items. Manufacturers and distributors will avoid anyone without a retail resale tax Id number. I now ask distributors if they have a problem with my carrying their items on eBay. When they understand that I won't devalue the product or represent it in a negative light, they are usually agreeable to the idea.*

She also makes some of the items she sells.

> *I do have a line of cushion nail files custom-made to sell. Did I tell you I own a salon? I started having nail files manufactured so that I could get the perfect nail file. Before I knew it, I was selling them to others on eBay. I started out selling packs of a dozen; now I sell them by the hundreds because so many people like them.*

Erin uses cross-promotion all over in her listings.

> *Individual listings are linked with other items the client might like. E-mails contain specials and a link to my eBay store. Sending shoppers directly into my eBay store has cut my listing expenses which is really important since the starting price of my items is so low. You have to sell a greater number of lower priced items and make far more shoppers happy as opposed to a few high priced items.*

Timing is an important aspect to an auction. She said that tracking the best time of day for auction listings to end could mean the difference between no sales and high sales.

Know your customer. If the item is for small children, most likely this person doesn't stay up all night, so 3 a.m. would not be a good ending time. My highest successful ending time is between 7 p.m. and 11:30 p.m. EST. I still have auctions ending at other times, but unless a pattern emerges where items are selling more at that time, I won't list duplicates or multiple items.

Erin finds sending out reminder e-mails and calling tends to be the best approach when dealing with an uncommunicative buyer. Using the contact member feature from eBay, she is able to get the buyers' phone numbers to give them a call.

Most members are just as busy as we are. They forget, the computer breaks, or they can have medical issues. Working with clients on issues they may have increases return sales. I am never rude or hasty. Your communication style has much to do with your success rate. If I have sent several e-mails through the eBay system with no reply, I try to send one through my e-mail provider, making sure to use a detailed subject line and friendly tone. After all, they came to me to purchase. The customer has a lot of choices on eBay and they vote with their wallet. A negative experience ensures they will go elsewhere next time.

When it comes to returns, Erin does not have many problems. She just asks that her customers read the listings carefully before bidding.

It is easier and less expensive to make a client happy than to lose a client. A happy client might tell one person; an unhappy client will tell everyone they know. It goes without saying that if I make a mistake, it is my responsibility to fix it.

Erin has found a way to save on shipping costs by recycling her packing peanuts and using clean, sturdy boxes.

We do not recycle boxes that have distributor info or logos on them. Hey, why give away where we get our items? We have the best postal workers here in Virginia. I simply notify them that I have a pick up and I can focus my attention on other things, rather than standing in line at the post office. I am happy to say that in the last five years only one parcel has gone missing. Most of our items are small, light, and easy to ship in a bubble mailer. Printing postage through PayPal has cut out processing time and allows us to track shipments through the Selling Manager Pro service. We love Priority Mail and all of the free shipping supplies that come with it. On the occasion where we ship an item not allowed in the postal system, we use UPS.

She also believes international shippers are good for business. She said they are great for the American economy.

They bring revenue into our communities that would otherwise just not be there. We do run into problems on occasion when bidders do not understand why certain items cannot be exported or why shipping time is longer. That is when good communication is an asset. Spelling each detail out in the listing avoids any misunderstandings, such as how to deal with customs and who pays any associated fees. It is tremendously important to know what items may be exported. Some products have different versions for sale in each country and a company will stop selling to you if they find out you are "diverting" their product to an unapproved country. If you don't have time to research the export laws for your items, it is best to avoid export.

Erin no longer uses drop shipping in her business. Without being able to guarantee the actions of others, she has found the best idea is to list only the items she has in stock and available since doing so allows her to pack up and ship the item that day.

Drop shipping is an area that is still changing. Again, good communication may thwart any problems encountered. Every concept has its growing pains. We haven't ruled out drop shipping altogether. We are just waiting for some of the bugs to be worked out before using it on eBay. We continue to have relationships with several drop shippers. We use them in our other venues/Web sites. eBay demands better customer service and tighter shipping schedules than any other selling venue.

To drive people to her store, Erin uses a few different methods.

*We use an e-mail signature that contains our eBay store URL. We also encourage clients to visit the store by including pens, magnets, business cards, and brochures in shipments that we send out. These items can also be found in our bricks-and-mortar store for even more cross-promotion. We use **constantcontact.com** for our e-mail promotions.*

Erin uses auctions, "buy it nows" and her store to sell her items.

I have a domain name that I forward right into my eBay store, and it is included in e-mails and business cards that are enclosed with each order.

She sells part-time on eBay.

I feel a little guilty when I tell people that I only do this part-time. It is so easy that I don't have to spend a ton of time on it. I can even run it from my RV while on the road traveling and going on buying trips.

A Final Piece of Advice

I run a successful salon and I am a professional freelance writer and speaker, as well as an eBay PowerSeller. The thing these all have in common is communication. Good, clear communication makes the difference between a sale (and possible repeat customer) and no sale. Describing an item so that even if no picture were available, the customer could see it clearly, aids in selling products. Every little detail: size, color, smell, uses, how-to, longevity, cleaning, history, and more! My career outside of eBay has helped the eBay business.

I have an assistant who helps with the marketing and collating of materials, leaving me free to write listings. We travel to eBay events together and take classes.

Company Profile

The HatterasSurfer shop is operated year round and stocks and eclectic mix of items. We are friendly, fast, and fun. Grab a Jolly Roger Flag for your inner pirate or some colorful caps for your furry companion's nails. Fashion sunglasses, health and beauty, and the slightly irreverent can all be found in the HatterasSurfer eBay store. No matter what you choose, you can count on us to fill your order fast and promptly ship it to your mailbox. Have a question? E-mail us and we'll do our best to get you an answer. Quick PayPal checkout means you can hit the beach or surf instead of chasing down a money order.

Yes, we ship many packages. You can rest assured we do everything possible to reduce the impact on the environment. Do your part by recycling packing peanuts and boxes through your local packing store or your favorite local eBay seller.

Contact Information for Erin Dixon:

Erin Dixon
Chief Sorter-of-Stuff
www.HatterasSurferShop.com
Nail Care Services
PO Box 1189, Newport News, VA 23601
nailcareservices@aol.com

Danielle Loukataris

User Name:	divinefinds
Name:	Danielle Loukataris
E-mail:	shop@divinefinds.com
Classification:	Brick-and-Mortar Store Using eBay
Current Tier:	Bronze PowerSeller
eBay Store:	Divine Finds
Store Location:	www.divinefinds.com
Current Feedback Star:	Turquoise
Projected 2006 Sales:	$15,000

A Little Background

Danielle Loukataris has been a member of eBay since February 2001.

My business is Vintage Fashions; I strictly sell high-end pre-80s items that include handbags, jewelry, clothing, and other accessories. I pride myself with understanding each item and hand selecting the best pieces I can find with little or no flaws. I sell online, out of my storefront in Buffalo, New York, at the Manhattan Vintage Clothing Show three times a year, expanded to international shows, and of course on eBay!

A part-time seller on eBay, Danielle Loukataris—username divinefinds—started selling on eBay at first just out of curiosity.

...but also to make extra money of course! I was a stay-at-home Mom and God bless my babies, but I was also a bit bored after a while of not working or having time to have a steady part-time job with real hours. It just didn't work out for me.

Becoming a PowerSeller was a surprise to Danielle.

It is based on the amount of money you sell a month–not how much you sell. I always thought it was the other way around. So after I sold my cousin's Harley I was invited to become a PowerSeller! That eBay Motor sale put me in the running along with some other things I had recently sold.

Her PowerSeller tier is tough to determine because she is in danger of losing her status.

I only have about a 108 feedback score so I am struggling to keep my status. I use eBay for really great items and when I can find the time between my boutique and teaching others how to sell, too. I also have become an Education Specialist and am finding it fun to teach others how to make money!

Danielle doesn't really have the time right now to sell as many items as she wishes she could. But when she does list items, they are usually at a starting price of $29.99.

I am now training someone else how to list items for me. My new boutique is just under a year old and I have an online site that also needs my time. Basically, I'm growing faster than ever and am just getting a handle on it all!

She finds that photos are definitely the best way to get her listings noticed.

Use every character they allow and don't use words that won't be picked up by the search engines–those are in place to help you. I have shown others how c.1985 is not going to be picked up as easily as 1985 or using just 80s will get more hits. Research is also part of seeing what others did to bring the hits in. But photos are really the key. Photos really are your way of getting noticed. Spend more time on a great photo instead of unsearchable words like L@@K HERE. That would take two clicks. A great gallery photo is what is going to get a faster click and let's face it–we're lazy and in a hurry! It's so worth the $.35!

Although Danielle does not make any of her items she sells (yet!), she finds her items through different avenues.

They come through my door sometimes unexpectedly for a consignment, but I mainly buy outright by appointments set up through my store-front and buy directly from the original owners.

She does not use any type of listing software, but Danielle does make use of cross-promotions.

When it comes to the time and time-ending of an auction, Danielle used to find it very important.

...start on a Thursday for a ten-day auction with it ending

on a Sunday is still a nice way to get noticed and most likely the best time for people to frequent eBay—a weekend. This way it goes through two weekends. But time is weird now because I welcome the international buyers. Just remember everything is PST, so I post a lot of things early evening so both coasts can have a chance to enjoy the day and check later in the evening. People still like to watch the end of the auction and bid at the last second.

When she hasn't heard from a buyer, Danielle will use all the tools eBay allows for disputing. She continues to contact the buyer and make her requests using these tools.

And most importantly state your terms firmly in writing allowing buyers to know that you will not tolerate payment past a time period from sale end or a warning will be sent after that time has passed. Every once in a while you will get someone with a sob story that's probably true. Try to be patient but firm on your terms—remember leaving bad feedback may result in bad feedback for you as well.

Danielle does have a return policy that she uses by discretion.

If it is something I never want to see again—no way! But when I'm using eBay to direct others to my Web site, I use the same policy as I have in my store and online. I am confident about the items I sell.

Her return policy states that buyers are to contact her within 24 hours by e-mail or phone. She has to receive the purchase within five days in the same condition. The rest of her return policy can be seen on her Web site under her shipping and returns tab.

Danielle has found the best way to save on shipping costs is by using USPS.com to order free boxes.

And PayPal to click right from the buyer's payment now too! It's really as easy as click and ship—drop off without staying in line or have it picked up and you always receive a free delivery confirmation!

She does not make use of drop shipping as she does not prefer to rely on other people. She does believe international bidders are good for business.

Absolutely, the dollar is dying! I'll ship anywhere—eBay statistics show that almost half the market is overseas. If you don't sell to international bidders you just cut your market in half—that is NOT good business, and PayPal makes it simple to do conversions with so many different currencies instantaneously.

Danielle does not have an eBay store, but makes use of a Web site which is linked to her listings **www.divinefinds.com**. She has tried all the different avenues of eBay selling—"buy it nows," auctions, and eBay Motors—except the storefront. She said she might when she's sure she will be able to keep up with the postings.

A Final Piece of Advice

eBay was a huge stepping-stone for me to the online market and showed me that my product was desirable. Once you master it, it can be very lucrative. Treating it like a business will show results. They make it so easy now; I am constantly learning what's new. I taught myself by clicking on more and more links to learn how eBay worked, but the desire to make money and get out of a very controlling relationship was also an issue. It was my pocket money and I learned I was pretty good at what I was doing. It led to a Web site, a store-front, and a divorce! I am now supporting my family on my own and every time the cash flow slows down I say to myself, "I'd better list something on eBay!" When I see an item in my inventory that has been around for years I think—Put it on eBay and get rid of it! And when I find something collectible I say to myself, "Oh, I can't wait to put this on eBay!"

Contact Information for Danielle Loukataris:

Divine Finds

www.divinefinds.com

Phone: 716-332-2807

220 Lexington Avenue, Buffalo, NY

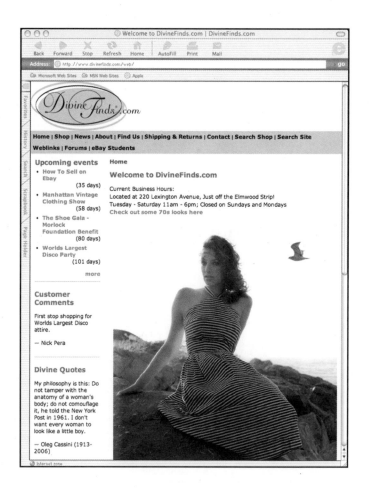

chapter 11

The New Wave— Trading Assistants

In recent years a new type of PowerSeller has developed—the Trading Assistant. Realizing that many would-be eBay sellers are too intimidated to do it themselves, eBay-savvy marketers are helping out, making profits along the way.

If you're an experienced eBay seller and want to help other people sell their items, you can be listed in eBay's Trading Assistants Directory. Being listed in the directory is free advertising of your services to people looking to sell their items on eBay

Trading Assistant Requirements

To be listed in the directory, you must meet the following requirements:

- You've sold at least 10 items during the past three months.

- You have a feedback score of 100 or higher.

- 97 percent or more of your feedback is positive.

- Your eBay account is in good standing.

If you meet these requirements, you can create a profile in the Trading Assistants Directory. You'll be able to describe your specialties, fees, terms, contact information, and drop-in hours at your location. Your profile will appear in search results when people look for Trading Assistants in your immediate area.

You can create more than one profile in the directory. For example, if you have several drop-off locations, you might create a profile for each location.

Selling items on eBay for other people is essentially the same as selling your own items. All normal trading rules apply. As the official seller on eBay, you are responsible for accurately describing the item.

You list the item, communicate with buyers, manage the listing, receive the winning buyer's payment, ensure the item reaches the buyer, give and receive feedback. You are also ultimately responsible for paying eBay's selling fees, even if you choose to pass the expense on to the client as part of your overall fee to them. This is something you should discuss with the client in advance.

Of course, when you are a Trading Assistant you are not an eBay employee. And while there are rules covering your operation, you have to work out rules, fees, and policies with your client.

Once an item sells and is paid for, you can send the sale money (minus your fees) to the client.

Many areas, especially larger metropolitan areas are quickly becoming dotted with "eBay Drop-off Stores." These are drop-off points for potential clients to get their items to eBay PowerSellers. While many Trading Assistants are working out of storefronts, others simply go to the home or work of the client and pick up the item there.

The following chapter is dedicated to eBay Registered Trading Assistants.

chapter 12

PowerSeller Trading Assistants

The following pages are filled with eBay sellers who are Registered Trading Assistants—they sell your items for you on eBay so you don't have to!

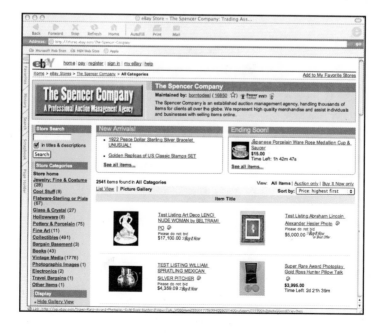

Christopher Spencer

Username:	borntodeal
Name:	Christopher Spencer
E-mail:	spencer@borntodeal.com
Classification:	Trading Assistant (with eBay Drop-Off Store)
Current Tier:	Platinum PowerSeller
eBay Store:	The Spencer Company
eBay Store Location:	www.stores.ebay.com/The-Spencer-Company
Current Feedback Star:	Shooting Yellow
Projected 2006 Sales:	$700,000

The Spencer Company
818.567.4000 www.borntodeal.com

Christopher, left, is conducting research on an antique woodworking plow-style plane on the eBay Web site.

A Little Background

Christopher Spencer has been a member of eBay since June 1999.

Christopher Spencer is an eBay Shooting Star, eBay PowerSeller, eBay Trading Assistant and author of *The eBay Entrepreneur: The Definitive Guide to Starting Your Own eBay Trading Assistant Business* (Kaplan Publishing, available September 2006). He runs a successful auction management business in Los Angeles, California. He has been featured in *Time Magazine*, *The Los Angeles Times* and has appeared on television and radio and in numerous magazines, newspapers and Web sites. He has listed more than 160,000 items on eBay since 1998 and he presently lives in Burbank, California. He travels the world educating entrepreneurs on the finer points of using the eBay trading community. He quit a nine-to-five job to sell on eBay full-time and now he is a lead instructor with eBay University and also a reservist in the U.S. Navy. He takes great pride in mentoring other eBay entrepreneurs and showing them how to make eBay a cash machine. Christopher has also achieved the status of Certified eBay Educational Specialist trained by eBay to instruct the general public on how to use the eBay site.

Christopher is a full-time eBay seller. He also is an author (*The eBay Entrepreneur: The Definitive Guide to Starting Your Own eBay Trading Assistant Business*, Kaplan Publishing, available September 2006), a Certified Education Specialist, and an official eBay University Instructor.

In 1998, I was working a full-time job when a friend of mine in the antiques business gave me a few items to sell on eBay. They were WWII medals. They received such high prices that he gave me sixty more items to sell. After I sold those items, he wanted me to sell for him on a regular basis. The hobby started to become a business. I enjoyed doing it and quit my full-time job in 2000 to sell on eBay full-time.

Already having reached the PowerSeller requirements before the program even started, Christopher became one as soon as the program began. They were already doing about $25,000 to 30,000 in sales a month.

> *I just sold whatever clients brought me. Being a PowerSeller was a nice benefit to my success with the business.*

Christopher lists about 100 items a day, as many as 1,100 in a week, but can do more if the merchandise is available for sale. The amount of items sold also depends on how much time it takes for research on the item and the type of merchandise it is. He normally starts his auctions at $.99.

> *Sometimes we list items with a minimum bid for clients. We are in the business of selling items for our clients where there is no emotional or financial attachment and so we prefer to start all items at the lowest possible price, hence the $.99. This starting price also saves eBay fees because eBay only charges $.20 to list an item below a dollar. Bids generate the "action" that raises this price to the item's market value.*

He finds keywords are the best way to draw people to his listings.

> *The keywords in the title of a listing are the magnets that attract buyers. Most buyers are searching specific words, such as a brand name or type of item. The keywords must be crafted in such a way as to attract buyers who are searching for that specific item. Titles are a bit of art and science. We use eBay Marketplace Research tools to determine what's hot and which keywords people are typing into eBay's search engine* **http://pages.ebay.com/marketplace_research**.

Christopher uses all methods of marketing since he sells for other people. He has an eBay store, auctions, "buy it nows," and sometimes he even sells vehicles. He finds most of the items they list nowadays through word-of-mouth.

We used business cards, networking, Chamber of Commerce mixers, printed advertising, and Internet ads to attract Trading Assistant clients.

He uses the listing software, Blackthorne Pro, and makes use of eBay's cross-promotion features.

We use an eBay Store which has features such as automatic cross-promotions to help up-sell items at the time a buyer completes his/her purchase. We also use the store's built-in search engine/price comparison engine optimization feature to allow other sites to pickup our eBay listings and present them to people during engine searches.

Time-ending with an auction isn't a big issue with Christopher anymore.

The ending time and day used to be pretty important before the advent of sniping software. These days most experienced bidders use sniping software to place a bid at the last moment before the auction ends so that they don't have to attend the auction.

When he has trouble with a buyer, he uses the eBay dispute console.

This allows you to file an Unpaid Item reminder to encourage payment. If that does not work, we file for a Final Value Fee request and the buyer receives an Unpaid Item Strike. If they get three strikes, they are "out" of eBay permanently and banned from further bidding. We then re-list the item. Re-listing usually gets a great price so it is not a problem.

All the items he lists are guaranteed as he has described them. If buyers are unhappy with items, he allows a return for a full refund and no expense.

Christopher said the best way he has found to save on shipping costs is by volume and size management.

Amazingly, all private carriers offer substantial discounts for high-volume sellers if you simply ask. We became an Authorized Shipping Outlet for UPS and they also give us a commission for accepting parcels from the public.

They do allow international buyers and will ship anywhere in the world. They use Express Mail as their primary shipping service.

With Express Mail there is no customer's brokerage fee charged to the buyer and many times they pay no duty if the parcel is small. We do not ship cheaper methods when we can help it because Express Mail gets there fast and reliably. More than 20 percent of our business is cross-border trading.

Christopher has found drop shipping to be a good method only if the margins are high.

It is better to list them as "buy it now" items aka SIF (Store Inventory Format) in your eBay Store to keep the listing fees lower. Keeping in mind the drop-ship services provider is very likely to be using more than one eBay seller; you will have more competition and you want to keep the fees low.

Not only do they use their eBay store site, they also have a site that is linked directly to it: **www.borntodeal.com**. They have found this helps drive people to their eBay store site.

*We put the vanity URL **borntodeal.com** on everything that we print and on e-mails. The URL forwards direct to our eBay Store. With the huge amount of marketing that eBay does to promote eBay Stores, we find most buyers discover the store from another location on eBay.*

A Final Piece of Advice

Trading Assistant work is a hot business right now. It allows a new member of eBay to become successful very quickly as a seller moving unwanted items for other people. No inventory and very little investment—a camera and a computer and perhaps an investment in business cards. I have sold more than $4,000,000 worth of items for other people and very few of my own items.

More Biographical Information

The most valuable item he has ever sold successfully on eBay was a rare Lenci porcelain figurine that fetched $17,100. The most notable item he ever sold on the site was a solid gold letter from William Randolph Hearst that was given to Louella Parsons in the 1940s. Spencer ultimately sold it to the Hearst Corporation in New York for $5,000.

When asked why a successful e-tailer would want to share his secrets for e-success, Spencer remarks simply:

There is enough business for everyone and the satisfaction of knowing you have made a profound, positive impact in a person's life is priceless.

Many of Spencer's pupils have followed him from city to city to see him over and over again, querying him about any new tips or tricks which may help their online endeavors. Quite a few of his pupils have gone on to become PowerSellers, the high-volume elite sellers on the largest e-commerce marketplace.

Spencer's view on the future of eBay is rather optimistic.

We have vaguely touched the tip of the iceberg in the arena of moving goods and services online. eBay has an astonishing number of users, over 180 million in all, but the world has billions of individuals who will eventually all become personal computer users. The potential for future growth is certain, as eBay's registered user base increases by over 90,000 new users each and every day. I know that moving items in this trading venue will become popular culture, just as everyone has enjoyed a can of Coke or Pepsi, so will their lives be affected by eBay. eBay is merely a computer system run by the caretakers who are the employees of eBay; however, in essence, eBay is the spirit of the loyal users who make it the greatest marketplace in history. Clearly, online trading is here to stay, and eBay is no longer an auction venue. Users can purchase items at a fixed price and sellers can create their own portals, called eBay Stores, to build their brand-loyal customer base alongside other large and small sellers. The costs and tools provided are the same for everyone, creating a leveling effect, making eBay easy for even a struggling student, housewife, or unemployed individual to compete with large corporations that use the eBay market to move their products and services. The basic listing costs only $.30, and there are no monthly fees, plus eBay is completely free to buyers. I think anyone can clearly see why it has become a profound cultural genesis of everyone's future trading habits.

Spencer's former affiliations have included vice president of the Wilshire Community Police Council and president of Dreams to Reality Foundation. He is currently a Petty Officer in the U.S. Naval Reserve force where he provides computer support for the Navy's operations.

Spencer has authored dozens of online training manuals for eBay and he has acted as a special consultant to eBay Motors, helping to construct course materials for sellers of autos, a multibillion dollar segment of eBay's business metrics. He is also the author of *The eBay Entrepreneur: The Definitive Guide for Starting Your Own eBay Trading Assistant Business*.

Spencer was born in Columbus, Ohio, and grew up in Falls Church, Virginia. He moved to California in 1985 and has been there ever since. He has lived in the Magnolia Park community of Burbank for the past 13 years, where he tinkers with computers and experiments with new recipes in his kitchen. He is an accomplished baker and gourmet and enjoys entertaining dinner guests from time to time when he is not busy at his offices or lecturing for eBay. Spencer owns an eBay Trading Assistant drop-off store as well as an antique shop in the community where he lives. He is a member in good standing of the Burbank Chamber of Commerce. Spencer also owns motels and rental properties throughout the country.

Contact Information for Christopher Spencer:
Christopher Spencer, President
The Spencer Company
3412 1/2 West Magnolia Boulevard
Burbank, California 91505
Direct: 818-630-5726
Phone: 818-567-4000
Fax: 818-475-1427

Frank Craven

Username:	with-a-twist
Name:	Frank Craven
E-mail:	admin@EASE-E-WAY.com
Classification:	Trading Assistant
Current Tier:	Gold PowerSeller
eBay Store:	The Endless Emporium
eBay Store Location:	www.stores.ebay.com/The-Endless-Emporium
Current Feedback Star:	Purple
Projected 2006 Sales:	$400,000

A Little Background

Frank Craven has been a member of eBay since October 1999.

Ease-e-Way is a three-employee business based in Nashville, Tennessee. We opened an eBay drop-off site in a retro-hip shopping district, comprised of 1930s houses turned into small businesses, and then we decided that working from home was less expensive, easier, and just as effective. It turned out to be a myth that we needed a storefront for customers to trust us with their belongings. We also sell our own items on eBay, and enjoy it thoroughly!

In the midst of political movement toward taxing all Internet sales and litigation promoting the requirement of eBay Trading Assistants to be fully licensed auctioneers in our state, we are very strong advocates of small business and of Internet commerce freedom.

Frank Craven—username with-a-twist—is a full-time Trading Assistant. He started selling on eBay after hearing about it and thinking it sounded like fun.

In 1999 I wanted to buy my first house, so I bought a PC, got an eBay account, and sold two MontBlanc pens for $4,200. I was hooked!

Although becoming a PowerSeller didn't start out as a goal, as the status became something obtainable, Frank began to see it as a goal. Once he started selling regularly, he earned PowerSeller status within three months.

Being a PowerSeller is nice (there really are benefits beyond the icon next to your username), but the money that you make from selling several thousand dollars per month is nicer!

Frank uses auctions, store-front, and eBay Motors to sell his items. He typically lists anywhere from 10 to 30 items a week, depending on what he is selling.

We just got a contract with a retail store to liquidate their overstock, so it will be more, now, and we help several auto dealers sell their cars on eBay Motors. Fewer items at higher sale prices is obviously better.

His average starting price is usually either $.99 cents or $9.99

with no reserve. Within his eBay store he does set the prices on his items. He said the best way to get people to notice his listings is through the gallery photo.

In addition to original artwork by several prominent artists, they are currently working on a line of metal lamps that will be made by Frank. Most of the items he sells now come from individual consignors, stores, yard sales, estate sales, and from his own suppliers. To list his items Frank uses Blackthorne, Selling Manager Pro, and Picture Manager. He cross-promotes his items through eBay automatically showing four of his items at the bottom of all of his auction pages. He said the timing of his auctions and time-ending is "VERY" important.

When he has not heard from a buyer, Frank will do the following:

> We send an invoice first, and then e-mail them twice. If we get no response, we file a non-paying bidder report. We also use eBay's blocking feature to prohibit bidders with low feedback from bidding on our items.

He does have a return policy that states:

> If we have made a significant mistake in the description of an item, which affects its use, such as listing a shirt as "Size Large," when it is, in fact, a "Size Medium," we will not only give you a refund, but we will pay for your cost in shipping it back to us!

> We're sorry, but we cannot accept returns due to "personal taste" (or size issues for clothing). Many of our items are sold through our eBay Trading Assistant service, and the money is given to the owner/seller when the item is paid for. Unlike browsing a retail store and being able to take something

home and then return it, unrecoverable shipping costs and eBay fees incurred upon the sale of an item prohibit us from being able to issue refunds without taking a loss. We will do everything within reason to assure that you are happy with your purchase!

To save on shipping costs Frank buys his shipping materials in bulk as well as recycling clean boxes and packaging materials.

We shred junk mail for packing materials!

He said that international shipping is absolutely good for business, although some areas are safer bets than others, regarding the safe and timely delivery of items. He does not find drop shipping to be a good method for selling items.

It's tough to find items that sell, especially items with enough profit margin. I've tried Wholesale Marketer/doba—no luck, but they have promised more items and new suppliers.

Frank places a link to his outside site, **www.Ease-e-Way.com**, on his "About Me" page. To draw people to his eBay store, he has found that having auctions and upgraded shipping is what gives him promotion on eBay.

A Final Piece of Advice

Charge enough for shipping to cover your time and expenses without violating eBay's new policy on shipping charges. Don't use a reserve, if at all possible.

Company Profile

Ease-e-Way sells a wide variety of items. We hold a

contract with a retail chain to liquidate their overstock, list cars for several auto dealers through Auction123, eBay Motors Dealer Assistant, and are authorized trainers and consultants through the Educational Specialist, Trained by eBay program. Our home on the Web is located at www. Ease-e-Way.com, and our eBay Store is called The Endless Emporium.

Contact Information for Frank Craven:

Frank Craven

eBay Educational Specialist and Trading Assistant

Phone: 615-297-eBay

Cell: 615-364-6282

www.Ease-e-Way.com

Suzanne Lampinen

Username:	EastgateDistributors
Name:	Suzanne Lampinen
E-mail:	Suzanne@hotspringseauctions.com
Classification:	Trading Assistant
Current Tier:	Gold PowerSeller
eBay Store:	Hot Springs e-Auctions
eBay Store Location:	www.stores.ebay.com/Hot-Springs-e-Auctions
Current Feedback Star:	Purple
Projected 2006 Sales:	$130,000

A Little Background

Suzanne Lampinen has been a member of eBay since July 1998.

Suzanne Lampinen is the owner of Hot Springs e-Auctions, an independent eBay consignment location in Hot Springs, Arkansas, operating under the eBay username: EastgateDistributors. Suzanne has been a member of eBay since 1997 and is currently a Gold PowerSeller. She is a registered eBay Education Specialist, one of only five in the state of Arkansas. She is also a registered eBay Certified Consultant and a registered eBay Trading Assistant. A 15-year veteran of big box retail management and e-commerce sales and marketing, Suzanne consults with existing brick-and-mortar stores to integrate eBay, e-commerce, and sales and marketing techniques into their regular business mix.

Suzanne Lampinen—username EastgateDistributors—is a full-time eBay Trading Assistant. She began selling on eBay because it intrigued her from the moment she became a member.

I learned early on that learning to buy on eBay was quite

easy; however, selling was a little more difficult. The challenge to conquer and my entrepreneurial spirit kicked in and I was hooked!

Becoming a PowerSeller was a goal for Suzanne and she said she wanted to do it smart. It took her only three months once she positioned herself as a real eBay seller and not just an occasional buyer/seller. She spent countless hours studying and reading other PowerSellers' ads just to find her own niche, and as she said, "It paid off!"

Knowledge is definitely power!

Suzanne uses all areas of eBay to market the items she sells: auctions, eBay store, eBay Motors, and real estate. Due to her consignment status, her number of items sold a week varies anywhere from 50 to 200. Her average starting price for her items is $9.99. She gave the following advice for the best way to get people to notice a listing.

The best way to get people to notice your listing is to be crisp, clean, and stick to keywords. Stay away from using symbols in your titles to try to make it stand out. It really turns people away rather than attracting attention. Always use a gallery photo and ensure that the photo is quality to make a potential buyer want to take a closer look at your listing.

Her Hot Springs eAuctions is an independent consignment location, so she receives the items she sells from all over the state of Arkansas. To list her items, she just upgraded her software to Resale World's Liberty 4 Trading Assistant.

It is fabulous! It features consignor management, photo hosting, internal accounting features as well an export for

QuickBooks, listing, and order management for eBay, and a point of sale system if you allow customers to shop locally, which we do. The software has replaced Turbo Lister all together.

She also cross-promotes her items using eBay's feature. It allows her to select up to 12 items for cross-promotion. She also uses her store banner and has navigation in each of her listings.

When it comes to the time and time-ending of an auction, Suzanne does not feel this is important. But she said there are exceptions to the rule depending on what you are selling.

I tell all of my students that they must consider who the target customer is for the item that they are selling. For instance, if the target customer is a stay-at-home mom then the ending time is definitely crucial. Her time is limited to midday while the children are either napping or at school. If you close the auction during after-school hours or early evening while they are doing homework and dinner, then you alienate her as a potential buyer.

When dealing with a non-responsive buyer, Suzanne said her company takes the "polite customer service" approach.

We realize that while we sit in front of our computers all day that all of our buyers may not. There are many new eBayers every day, and often they are slower to respond due to the sheer overwhelming amount of information on eBay as they learn to navigate around the site. Other factors include family issues, job issues, and working long hours. We have found that most of the late payments or slow communications were simply an oversight and the result of someone's not logging in to eBay daily to check the status of their auctions. Don't make the assumption that everyone is on top of their e-mail and eBay the way you are.

She does have a return policy, "as any good retail store does." She allows the customer three days to evaluate the item they purchased and will offer a full refund of the purchase price if the item was clearly misrepresented.

To save on shipping costs, Suzanne recommends setting up a FedEx or UPS account for regular pickup.

The discounts that you receive are a huge savings in the long run. We also recycle boxes by partnering with local stores. We go to the stores once a week to pick up the boxes from their shipments. Packing supplies and tape are purchased from other eBay vendors.

She does believe international bidders are very good for business and said that they ship approximately 10 to 15 items internationally per week.

While that doesn't sound like much, ask yourself the question "Would I have sold that item to only a U.S. buyer versus an international one?" Sell international! We call it revenue!

Suzanne does not believe drop shipping is a good method for selling items. She explored the idea and found it was not a good experience.

First, the companies that call themselves "drop shippers" are not real wholesalers to begin with. Anyone who sells a little below retail can actually call themselves wholesalers, but they are not. They are discount retailers and they offer these services at an additional charge. Real distributors do not charge this fee. My general rule of thumb for my students: If they do not ask you for a sales tax number they are not really a wholesaler. Find the real distributor or manufacturer of the product you want to sell for the best price.

When asked how she drives people to her eBay store, Suzanne had the following advice:

The first mistake that people make is they open an eBay account, then an eBay Store and wait for sales. It doesn't work that way exactly. Auctions drive people to your eBay Store and it is the promotion you do within those auctions that make the difference. We promote that we have a store using all of eBay features available to us like cross-promotion tools, additional links, and using the store header in our auctions. Keywords are used for the store items to help draw in customers through Internet searches like Google, MSN, and Yahoo!. These features literally scream "WE HAVE AN EBAY STORE. CHECK OUT OUR OTHER AUCTIONS."

Suzanne also has a Web site besides her eBay store that she uses located at **www.HotSpringsEAuctions.com**.

A Final Piece of Advice

The biggest piece of advice I have is to conduct yourself as a professional business person regardless of how small you actually are. Answer questions to potential buyers in a professional manner and in complete sentences, not short, choppy ones. Remember the rules of brick-and-mortar retail: say hello and thank you for looking, thank you for your purchase, or thank you for your bid. If you have an issue with a buyer, remember when you leave feedback that other people read it and it could affect your reputation. The way you respond to everyone tells others how you will handle issues if they arise with them and can make or break a bid. If it is not the way that you would like someone to address you in person, then don't address anyone in an e-mail that way.

Finally, "Think Outside of the Box." The greatest thing about eBay is that almost anything goes. Use your imagination and be creative.

Contact Information for Suzanne Lampinen:

Hot Springs e-Auctions
3970 Park Avenue, Suite C
Hot Springs, AR 71901
501-321-8199
www.HotSpringsEAuctions.com

Kelly Shew

Username:	salesbygetridofit!
Name:	Kelly Shew
E-mail:	kelly@getridofit.biz
Classification:	Trading Assistant
Current Tier:	Bronze/ Silver PowerSeller
eBay Store:	Get Rid Of It!
eBay Store Location:	www.stores.ebay.com/Sales-By-Get-Rid-Of-It
Current Feedback Star:	Red

Salesbygetridofit!
DON'T JUST THROW IT AWAY...GET RID OF IT!

A Little Background

Kelly Shew has been a member of eBay since April 2000.

Get Rid Of It! was started in June 2005 by owner Kelly Shew. Kelly, mother of three, attending college and working, was a frequent eBay user for the convenience of shopping with a budget and the lack of free time. She started selling on eBay to make a little money by getting rid of the extra stuff crowding her house. Drawn to her outgoing personality and knowledge of the Internet, friends and neighbors asked Kelly to act as a liaison between themselves and the Internet.

As word spread Kelly discontinued college and stopped working to focus on launching a business doing what she had previously thought of as just a hobby.

An avid seller, shopper, and Internet user, Kelly is a natural at helping people fully realize their unused assets.

Full-time eBay Trading Assistant Kelly Shew—username salesbygetridofit!—started selling on eBay just as her profile said: she wanted to get rid of household clutter.

> *I first started as just a way to clear out some oddball stuff that I didn't want to have to save up for garage sales. You know, get rid of things here and there—maybe one or two things a month. As my children were born, it became an easy way to make some money whenever I had a few minutes here and there. When it was too difficult to work outside the home with three kids, it just seemed natural to take what I knew about selling on eBay and offer that to other people.*

Kelly said it is much easier to attain PowerSeller status when you are a Trading Assistant because you are dependent on other people to bring you the items to sell. It only took her about six months to reach her Bronze PowerSeller status.

When I originally started selling, it seemed so far out of reach that I honestly never considered it. In June 2005, I opened a business from home that let me sell things for other people while being available for my kids. When that happened, I started trying to reach PowerSeller status.

She sells anywhere from 25 to 100 items a week and is a fan of starting her prices out low.

Get more people watching a low-priced item early, and you'll have lots of bids the last day. That seems to work best for me. If my client doesn't mind what the item sells for, I'll start it at $.99 with no reserve.

Kelly has found the best way to get people to notice her listings is by making sure not to go overboard with her title descriptions.

I keep my titles very searchable on keywords, but not crazy with funky, unused symbols; they just get overwhelming when looking through hundreds of listings for the same thing.

Although she has used eBay Motors, Kelly prefers to use the auction format with a "buy it now" price, as well as her store. She does not make items she sells, although she has sold a few items in the past that she made. These things are usually decorations from her children's rooms or quilts she made. She doesn't prefer to spend all day making the items. And, being a Trading Assistant, she doesn't have to.

Since I am a Trading Assistant, most of the items that I sell are brought to me. I do sometimes have a good find from garage sales or estate sales, but I wouldn't recommend it unless you're very familiar with what you're out to purchase and don't mind taking the time to find it.

When it comes to creating her auction and store listings, Kelly uses Turbo Lister.

It's free and easy to use—two very big points when trying to get a business started!

She finds the timing of the auction to be fairly important.

I think it's been shown that certain items tend to do better ending when the target buyer audience is home; that just makes sense.

Kelly sticks to the by-the-book approach when she has not heard from a buyer.

Have your selling policies clearly stated on your auction, and then the buyer can't argue about it. An e-mail when they win the item, a payment reminder e-mail if you haven't heard from them a couple of days later, and, if needed an Unpaid Item Reminder after that.

She does make use of a return policy for a specific kind of return only.

I have a return policy for items that arrive damaged or significantly not as described in the auction listing: I refund their full payment (original shipping included) as well as return shipping after I've received the item. I've found that most sellers only refund the auction price (not any shipping charges), and any buyers who have had to make use of my return policy have all been very pleased.

Kelly uses different methods of shipping depending on the weight of the item sold.

As a seller, be aware that it is not likely that any one carrier will be perfect for all of your shipping needs. I've found that for items under five pounds, it's cost productive to use USPS. For oddly shaped, large, or heavy items, UPS/FedEx/DHL are usually better.

She has never used drop shipping as a method. She does accept international bidders and believes they are absolutely good for business.

Easily 20 percent of my auctions are sold to people in other countries. There's a little more to learn for shipping to them initially, but especially now that international labels can be printed through PayPal, it doesn't take much to learn at all!

On her "About Me" page, Kelly does have a link to her non-eBay Web site, **www.getridofit.biz**. Her store site is **http://stores. ebay.com/Sales-By-Get-Rid-Of-It**. She finds she is able to draw people to her store by advertising it in all her listings.

Also, my business e-mail account points people there in the auto-signature portion.

A Final Piece of Advice

Always, always treat your buyers with respect! Even if they are just the worst buyer ever, be fair and professional in all of your e-mails, the same you would if they were your best buyer. Prompt responses to e-mails and any questions assure your buyer that you are serious about your eBay reputation.

Contact Information for Kelly Shew:
Get Rid Of It!
eBay ID: salesbygetridofit!
www.getridofit.biz
kelly@getridofit.biz

Angela Urbistondo

Username:	xena-angel
Name:	Angela Urbistondo
E-mail:	angelscloset@earthlink.net
Classification:	Trading Assistant
Current Tier:	Bronze PowerSeller
eBay Store:	Angel's Closet and Gifts
eBay Store Location:	www.stores.ebay.com/ Angels-Closet-and-Gifts
Current Feedback Star:	Red
Projected 2006 Sales:	$8,000

A Little Background

Angela Urbistondo has been a member of eBay since April 2000.

I am a wife, mother, manager at a Fortune 500 company (Rockwell Collins), and graduate student in addition to being an eBay PowerSeller. I am working toward my MBA at AIU Online (American Intercontinental University). I highly recommend both. AIU is a wonderful online university and Rockwell Collins is a great place to work. As a member of the eBay community, I am a Trading Assistant and Education Specialist. I don't teach large audiences, but I do teach individuals and small groups.

I try to keep majority of the eBay work confined to the weekends so I can spend weeknights with my family. Two or three nights a week I work on my homework toward the completion of my MBA, which I am attaining online. I frequently use eBay as a reference or example for my graduate level papers.

I sell what I have in the house, what I buy and then decide I don't want, and what family and friends ask me to sell for them. I am also a Trading Assistant, so if you like what you see and want some help selling your stuff, send me an e-mail and let's see what we can work out. My eBay store is called Angel's Closet and Gifts and I would love for you to stop in and browse: <http://stores.ebay.com/Angels-Closet-and-Gifts>.You can also reach me at angelscloset@ earthlink.net.

I only work in my eBay store part time. I was married for the first time in October 2005 and my son, Caleb, is my pride and joy. He even helps me with my eBay store and assists in spending the profits!

A part-time eBay Trading Assistant, Angela Urbistondo—username xena-angel—found out about eBay through a search on the Internet.

> *I did a general search on the Internet using a popular search engine. It pointed me to eBay for what I wanted. Once I got there I started browsing. I saw a doll of sorts selling for more than $50. I recognized it because I had the same one in my closet. I had no idea what I was going to do with it. I had gotten it for free when I made a purchase. It was a Bobblehead Buddy Lee and it sold for more than $50! I was hooked! You just never know what treasure you might have tucked away in a closet until you look it up on eBay! I also love to shop. I don't have much time for the luxury of shopping, but I know what I like, and eBay is the place to get it and frequently at the best price around.*

Becoming a PowerSeller catches up to Angela now and again. Her status does come and go as she is a Trading Assistant, and that is most of her business. She never is sure what kind of products she will have or how much.

> *I was a PowerSeller in 2004 before the hurricanes. I lost it when I did not have Internet access or very much to sell. I just got it back a month or so ago.*

Angela averages about one sale a day, with some days showing more sales, and other days less. Her sales come to about 30 a month. She considers herself a part-time seller as she only lists once a week, depending on her schedule. She does mail something almost everyday, and she checks her listings daily.

She said the best way to get her listings noticed is by posting them on the home page or featuring them in a category with a starting price, dependent on the type of product.

In general I would say the average starting price is $25. The starting price is much more for the expensive items like cars, motorcycles, and jewelry and much less for auctions of clothing, shoes, books, and children items.

Angela does not make her own items to sell. In the past she worked as a wedding planner part-time and lists a few of the wedding products she made during that time. Since she is a Trading Assistant, she sells mostly other people's items.

The rest of the stuff belongs to me or my family. I was recently married and we have two households, so we don't need as much as we had before getting together. If I see a good deal or sale on something that I think is unique or that I can sell, I will buy it in limited quantity and try it out. If it sells, I will go back and get more if that is an option.

When it comes to listing software, Angela uses Selling Manager Pro. She did try out Turbo Lister and Blackthorne, but she realized those were not for her.

Nearly everything I sell is unique, and when I am working on a listing I post it immediately. I find that Selling Manager Pro is the easiest tool for me to use and meets all my needs.

Angela uses the eBay automated cross-promotion tool on all of her listings and said that on a rare occasion she will also set up a custom cross-promotion on a specific item.

On the importance of time with an auction, and more particularly, the time-ending, Angela said:

> *This has been a topic of heated discussion over the years. My experience has been that ending day is important to higher dollars on the sales. Time of day is less important, but still there seems to be some linkage between the times of day. Mid-morning and afternoon does not appear to get as many sales as after work and late evening. Weekends are best for auction endings unless you have an established following. Since what I sell is different all the time, I try to stick to weekend evenings. I know other store owners who have a consistent product, such as estate sales or clothing, and they can have all their items end on a Wednesday or Thursday and they do great business because people specifically look at their store weekly for new finds.*

When she has trouble with the buyer of one of her items, Angela takes the approach of sending them a reminder.

> *I send them a polite reminder e-mail. I am usually patient and understanding. I know there are times when people don't read their e-mail because they are busy or their Internet connection is unavailable. I politely ask them to respond even if there is a problem. It's better to tell me than to let it go to a dispute.*

Angela does have a return policy, but she is unable to apply it consistently. This is due to her being a Trading Assistant.

> *Being a Trading Assistant makes it difficult to have a return policy that applies to everything. Once the owner of the item is paid, I would be out the money personally or stuck with a product that may or may not be something I can sell again. I try to limit returns to three days. This way I have time to*

work the issue with the owner of the item. In some cases where there is a high value item, the owner will refuse the return policy for fear of fraud.

Due to convenience and the variation in shipping, Angela finds it easiest and most reliable to use USPS to save on shipping costs.

They will pick up the items at my home for free from a designated location and they have a very consistent pricing scheme. Priority Mail and Flat Rate Priority Mail are the best value for me and the customer.

Angela does believe international bidders are good for business. She does not do many international sales herself due to high shipping costs, but she said every little bit helps and does at least one international sale a month.

When it comes to drop shipping, Angela finds that it does not work very well for her.

I find that being a Trading Assistant allows me the flexibility in pricing, shipping, and being responsible for the product from start to finish. I know it works well for others, but it just did not fit in with my way of feeling personally responsible for the products I sell.

Angela makes use of an "About Me" page and an eBay Store. She does not have a Web site outside of her eBay store site, but she has found this is all she needs for the types of products she sells. She finds using tools such as featuring items in categories or on the home page a good way to drive people to her eBay Store.

All I need is one good, interesting, or unique product listed in a featured area and that drives business to my store. eBay also does a great job of using popular search engines. When I go to Google or Yahoo and type in a key word from one of my listings, a link to my eBay listing frequently appears in the top three items of the search list. The better the key words in the title, the better the hits on the search engines.

She uses all areas of marketing: auctions, store-front, "buy it nows," and eBay Motors.

Being a Trading Assistant means taking what people want you to sell and doing your best to get the price they want. I've sold several motorcycles on eBay Motors. I try to list as much in the auction format as possible, since that is the most successful. In the case where an item is not selling or out of season, I will list it in my store. I want it to be out there, but I am not going to invest the money or that of my customer until the time and season are right. "Buy it now" is something I use when the seller will only accept one price and nothing less, or when there are similar items selling for "buy it now," and I can beat the price. Best Offer is a great addition to the eBay family of features. I would say 1 in 10 sales are based on a Best Offer as I accept all reasonable offers. It also goes a long way toward repeat business. If you haven't tried Want It Now, I recommend taking a look at it. I use it as both a buyer and a seller. The last time I used it, I hooked up with a seller who could get me a carbonated beverage product that my father missed from Italy, his birthplace. Now I have a way of getting it for him, and my husband is hooked on it as well.

A Final Piece of Advice

Many times I am asked to be a Trading Assistant because

the owner of the items just doesn't know how to be a seller on eBay. If they would like to be their own seller, I am more than happy to teach them how to do it. If someone is already a seller but would like more information on becoming a PowerSeller or Trading Assistant based on my experience, I am happy to share that information with them as well.

Oh! And if you get the chance definitely attend eBay Live!. It doesn't matter if you are a seller, buyer, or wannabe eBayer, it's an energetic event that will get you educated and excited about eBay.

Gina Scaletta-Nelson

Username:	geena
Name:	Gina Scaletta-Nelson
E-mail:	gina@ginabay.com
Classification:	Trading Assistant
Current Tier:	Bronze PowerSeller
Web Site:	www.ginabay.com
Current Feedback Star:	Turquoise

A Little Background

Gina Scaletta-Nelson has been a member of eBay since July 1998.

I am an eBay Trading Assistant as well as an eBay Education Specialist. I love to list and sell. I also enjoy teaching others how to do it themselves. I offer private lessons as well as group lessons. As a Trading Assistant, I am able to handle estate sales, warehouse liquidations, and general sales of items creating clutter! I started GINABAY in the fall of 2004 to make some extra money for family vacations, and business has been steadily increasing. I have had a high success rate in selling what I list. Selling on eBay helps me stay at home with my kids.

*If you would like more information on what I can do to help you sell, please contact me at gina@ginabay.com or visit **www.ginabay.com**.*

Part-time Trading Assistant and full-time mom to her two children, Gina Nelson—username geena—started selling on eBay after being a buyer for a while.

I decided to sell things around my house that I didn't need.

Gina's PowerSeller status was a surprise. It took her only about a year after she began actively selling on eBay. She also took three months off that year for the summer. She thought that her e-mail notice stating she was a PowerSeller was a hoax.

It was something I thought about but never thought that with the small amount that I sell, it would ever happen. It kind of caught me by surprise. At first, I thought the e-mail was a hoax, like a phishing e-mail, but found out in "my messages" that it was true. I was delightfully surprised.

Gina will list and sell up to 20 items a week. Her average starting price is between $.99 and $4.99.

The best way to get people to notice the listing is with a good gallery photo and a very low starting bid. I try to start at $.99 if I can.

Although she does not currently make the items she sells, Gina said she is in the process of purchasing a CNC Router and hopes to make items to sell. She finds most of the items she sells currently through friends and family.

You would not believe the things people have laying around their homes! I always tell people "Wait! Don't throw that out. I will sell it for you on eBay!" Now everyone brings me their stuff to sell!

Gina has found the listing software she prefers is Ink Frog and she also uses Auction Seller Solutions to keep track of everything. You can e-mail her for more information.

She does not really use any cross-promotions.

I use some of the eBay provided features like gallery photo and "buy it now," but not too many others.

Gina finds time and time-ending with auctions to be very important.

I usually begin and end my listings on Sunday nights at 9 p.m. Central Time. I do list on other weeknights, never on Friday or Saturday nights.

When she has not heard from a buyer, Gina takes the following approach:

If they have not paid for the item within seven days, I contact them per my TOS (Terms of Service). I am a very easy-going seller. If they need longer than seven days to pay, that is fine. However, they must let me know so I have an idea of when to expect payment. I once waited a month and then filed for my FVF. As soon as I filed, the payment arrived. I refunded his money to him and re-listed the item. It cost me my first negative for refusing his money.

She does not make use of a return policy. All of her items are sold "as is."

It is hard to offer a return policy when you are a Trading Assistant. If you give your client payment, it is hard to ask for the money back if the item is returned to me. Obviously if there was a gross error in the listing then I would consider it.

Gina uses several methods for keeping her shipping expenses to a minimum.

I use FedEx for anything over five pounds. They are the cheapest and fastest shippers in the business! I never buy boxes, I use only recycled boxes. I get boxes from all my friends and family. All my shipping supplies, from packing materials to scales, are purchased on eBay.

Although she personally does not allow international bidders, if someone e-mails her from another country and asks if they are allowed to bid, she always said yes.

Many other countries have some pretty strict rules about

what they will allow in. It is a lot more work filling out all the customs forms as well and most times, you do not have the safeguards protecting yourself when funds arrive from overseas.

She also believes drop shipping could be a good method for selling items.

You have to develop a good relationship with your drop shipper and really know their products. Drop shipping can break your business if you hook up with an unreliable company.

Gina does not have an eBay store at present. She has a non-eBay site that she is in the process of linking to her listings on eBay. It is **www.ginabay.com**. You can register to buy and sell on eBay through her Web site. She always uses auctions and sometimes she will also use "buy it now." She has also sold two vehicles using eBay Motors, as well as having purchased two vehicles through eBay.

Jodie McLaughlin

Username:	jodiemcl
Name:	Jodie McLaughlin
E-mail:	jodiemc@comcast.net
Classification:	Trading Assistant
Current Tier:	Bronze PowerSeller
eBay Store:	www.ragstorichesresale.com
eBay Store Location:	www.stores.ebay.com/Rags ToRichesUpscaleResale
Current Feedback Star:	Light Blue

A Little Background

Jodie McLaughlin has been a member of eBay since April 1999.

"That which doesn't kill us makes us stronger."

My determination and my conviction came from a relatively long string of bad life experiences, or looking back on it now, through a long string of tremendous blessings. I truly believe that our lives are a tapestry of our experiences and the choices we have made.

I am a cancer survivor, a single mother, and a victim of corporate downsizing early in my career.

I knew it was up to me to take control of my own life, my financial security, and my daughter's future. As a single mother, it was just too scary to leave my fate in the hands of anyone else; especially in middle management in corporate

America, which is a male dominated field. I began searching for businesses that I could do in my spare time, from my home that would eventually build to give me the options I needed and provide a backup to working for someone else. I tried a number of different businesses, which for various reasons, weren't a good fit. But I was determined to find something I would be successful at and that I could do part time from home.

The years of perseverance, my business background, and training paid off. As a registered personal Trading Assistant with eBay, I help people make some extra cash from things they want to sell. And as a PowerSeller and eBay store owner, my clients know I am an upstanding member of the eBay community. The best part is that I can do it all while being with my daughter and teaching her how to run a business. After seven years of learning eBay, I have now purchased a consignment and resale store-front and am an eBay drop off location. I am thrilled with the progress I have made in my business and personal growth and thank God for the lessons I have learned.

Currently an eBay Trading Assistant, and consignment store owner, Jodie McLaughlin—username jodiemcl—started selling on eBay because as a single mother, she is always trying to find ways to cut her expenses and build a home-business.

The best way I found was to sell the clothes and toys my daughter outgrew on eBay. Of course, once you have success with one particular item, you start selling anything.

After five months, PowerSeller status caught up to her.

I had been selling off and on for years. Then last year I decided to focus on building an eBay business as an alternative to working for someone else and to build financial security and to have an income after retirement. I took the Education Specialist training and focused on becoming a Trading Assistant. Once I had that focus, it didn't take long to become a PowerSeller.

The number of items usually sold in a week varies, but normally it is around 10 to 20 items per week. She prefers to list items into her eBay store. If she chooses to run an auction, she typically starts them at $9.99 and finds the best way to get people to notice her listings is by focusing on keywords, researching other successful eBay listings, and by eBay Pulse. eBay Pulse is a page on eBay designed to give an idea of that day's trends, hot picks, and cool things to find on eBay. The gallery photo option is the only extra feature Jodie uses.

Jodie does not make the items she sells. She finds most of her items as a result of being a Trading Assistant and gets her items from consignments. She also loves to shop at thrift stores, resale shops, tag sales, auctions, estate sales, and more. She has an eBay store and also does auctions.

I prefer my store. Stores are always "buy it now." I typically don't do "buy it now" when I auction.

She does not use any type of listing software or have a return policy. She does use the cross-promotions that eBay offers to her. When it comes to her timing of an auction and time-ending she finds they are somewhat important.

I usually schedule my auctions to end when the majority of people are not working, Sunday evening. However, from reviewing the times that people purchase things from my store, I think office hours might be something good to try!

Jodie has a Web site that is linked to her store, not individual listings, and finds she is able to draw people into her store through the following methods:

E-mail signatures, note cards enclosed with each purchase, business cards from my company Web site, and eBay listings.

When she hasn't heard from a buyer, Jodie waits a couple of days. If there is still no reply, she will send a follow-up e-mail.

If I still get no reply, I will e-mail one more time at the seven-day mark. On the eighth day from end of auction, I will file an unpaid item report. Eight days from then you can close the dispute and re-list the item.

To save on shipping costs, Jodie recommends purchasing a scale and weighing everything before listing.

She does allow international bidders and believes they are good for business. However, she does not like the idea of drop shipping.

You are at the mercy of the drop-shipping company. If they send a defective item to your buyer, the first you hear of it is from your buyer. I would rather have the item in hand; know that it is in good condition before my buyer ever sees it. I prefer to remain in control of the whole transaction.

A Final Piece of Advice

I really prefer having a store to the auctions. In a store, you can simply list your items and wait for the sale. If you feel you are getting a good return on your money with the price you set, then it is no problem. If you have an item that is in high demand, by all means do an auction. Then, the market will determine the value. But make sure you don't start it at a price you would be disappointed getting if the bidders are not there. You have to know the seasons, the trends, the brand names; RESEARCH, RESEARCH, RESEARCH.

Story: I had my largest amount of items running on auction in January of this year. Unfortunately, I didn't look at the calendar and I had them all scheduled to end on Sunday at 8 p.m. It was Super Bowl Sunday. I did not get ONE BID on anything!

eBay is a great business, but if you want it to be a business, it takes a lot of time. I have had a number of people consign items with me that they bought to sell on eBay but decided that it took too much time. Go into it knowing that to maximize your results from a listing takes research, great photos, a great description, the right price, and knowing the rules.

Company Profile

Rags to Riches Upscale Resale is located at 5716B Kennett Pike, in historic Centerville, DE 19807! Please come by! 302-654-5997

As your personal eBay Trading Assistant, I can help you with all your eBay needs.

Contact Information for Jodie McLaughlin:

Jodie McLaughlin
Rags to Riches Upscale Resale
5716B Kennett Pike, Centreville, DE 19807
Phone; 302-654-5997

jodiemc@comcast.net
www.ragstorichesresale.com

Stephanie Bass

Username:	cotton_tales
Name:	Stephanie Bass
E-mail:	sbassrdh@houston.rr.com
Classification:	Trading Assistant
Current Tier:	Bronze PowerSeller
Web Site:	www.cotton-tales.com
Current Feedback Star:	Red
Projected 2006 Sales:	$20,000

A Little Background

Stephanie Bass has been a member of eBay since December 2000.

Over five years ago our family gave birth to boy/girl twins. Ever since then I have been searching for an easier and less expensive way to clothe them. I found eBay to be the easiest since I didn't have to leave my home, and it was much less expensive than retail for same high quality items. Most items were starting at 75 percent off retail value or on excellent gently-used items.

Once the twins outgrew their clothing, I decided to resell them on eBay. That way my husband wouldn't worry where the money was coming from every month when I bought them new outfits or toys.

Once established with over a 500 feedback rating in June 2003, I started selling for others on eBay as well. Doing so has helped my very busy friends, neighbors, and hygiene organization make money and save time by not having to deal with garage sales or local consignment shops.

Now, I have a PowerSeller status and over 1450 100 percent positive feedback rating. I am also a Certified eBay Education Specialist who teaches the "Basics of Selling on eBay" to groups or individuals in my Fort Bend/Houston area.

*I can be reached on eBay at user ID: cotton_tales or my Web site at **www.cotton-tales.com**.*

Stephanie Bass—username cotton_tales—is a part-time eBay Trading Assistant. She does eBay more as a hobby-turned business. Her profession is as a Registered Dental Hygienist which she practices two days a week. When she had her twins, she realized going out and shopping with two little ones was hard so she began shopping on eBay. When they outgrew their clothes, she decided to sell them to buy more. That is how she got her start selling on eBay. Becoming a PowerSeller caught up to her. She wasn't really trying to become one, but after four years it happened.

I sold some items for my professional organization that were quite expensive and it pushed me over the limit for sales.

During a week, she averages around 27 auctions—her main market area for selling items. She has found the best way to get people to notice her listings is by her title keywords and the specials she offers like free shipping and handling. She generally starts her auctions at $1.99.

Lately I have been selling some higher priced items and starting them higher. My minimum is $1.99, and it just goes up from there. As a Trading Assistant, I try to set the prices according to what the market is selling or the consignee will ask for a specific price and I can accommodate the request.

She finds most of the items she sells from garage sales, as well as from others due to her Trading Assistant status. She does not make any of the items she sells. She uses only Turbo Lister to list her items. She also uses the automatically set up cross-promotions through eBay.

Stephanie finds the timing of an auction to be very important.

You have to know when the most people will be on eBay who will be interested in your product.

Her best advice when dealing with a non-responsive buyer: pick up the phone and call them. Stephanie does have a 100 percent satisfaction guaranteed return policy.

To save on shipping costs, Stephanie said to use Priority Mail materials and find the cheapest packaging materials that will "still do the job."

www.value-mailers.com is the cheapest I have found for poly bags for clothing.

Stephanie believes international bidders are absolutely good for business. Her auctions have been going higher recently thanks to international bidders. She cautions on only one thing: sometimes it is hard to track customers down when they do not pay because international calling is very expensive. As for drop shipping she said a big NO to it.

Most companies are a scam. You shouldn't have to buy into something to get a product. eBay's policy even states the items must be in hand to be able to sell it. A lot of people I hear that sell that way find that the products they are listings are no longer available (sold out) by the time the auction ends.

Stephanie does not have an eBay store; however, she does have a Web site: **www.cotton-tales.com**.

It gives information on my "The Basics of Selling on eBay" classes (I am a Certified eBay Education Specialist) and gives info on how to consign with Cotton Tales.

A Final Piece of Advice

Grammatical errors are a big turnoff; make sure you spell check and do the proper punctuation. And pictures are so important. Do not even list an item if you don't have a clear, cropped picture of your item. People do not buy sight-unseen items.

Maryann Lowden

Username:	onecrazyredhead
Name:	Maryann Lowden
E-mail:	maryannthefryinpan@yahoo.com
Classification:	Trading Assistant & Education Specialist Trained by eBay
Current Tier:	Bronze PowerSeller
Current Feedback Star:	Red
Projected 2006 Sales:	$2,000

A Little Background

Maryann Lowden has been a member of eBay since July 2000.

I am an Education Specialist trained by eBay and am qualified to conduct training classes on how to sell on eBay. Please be assured that you are dealing with an experienced eBay seller—I pride myself on selling quality items with prompt delivery. I have been an eBay member for more than six years and have successfully sold for several individuals as a Trading Assistant. My services include picking up your items; digital photo imaging; accurate, detailed listing description; I will handle all aspects of the auction from beginning to end. I will send out Winning Bidder Notifications and Handle all e-mail communications and will provide you with a spreadsheet that details dates, listing price, selling price, fees, and your net profit. I will prepare packages for shipment with tender loving care. Customer Service is my specialty. I have an outstanding feedback reputation. Please feel free to review the comments from both buyers and sellers.

A part-time Trading Assistant on eBay, Maryann Lowden—username onecrazyredhead—sells around 20 items per week. Her average starting price is $4.99 and she said her low price on her items is what she uses to draw people to her listings. She sells using auctions and "buy it now" option.

Maryann finds most of the items she sells through specialty/collectible stores and does not make any of her items. She does not use of any type of listing software. To cross-promote, she uses her eBay Education Specialist Logo.

Maryann believes that the time and time-ending of an auction are very important because most people "bid at the last minute." When she does not hear from buyers at the end of an auction, she will send them a reminder e-mail. She does have a return policy: "I will replace or refund."

To save on shipping costs, Maryann recycles her boxes and Styrofoam.

She does not believe international bidders are good for her business. Drop shipping is not something she believes is a good method for selling items as it is too costly.

Maryann attended eBay Live! 2006 in Las Vegas and plans to become more active in conducting classes and utilize her Education Specialist certification to assist people who are new to eBay on how to buy and sell.

A Final Piece of Advice

I have learned as a buyer to use the Watch Item function and to check the category several times to see if similar items have been newly listed in the same time frame that the item I am watching. Also always check the seller's feedback—it is vital!

As a seller, I list my items with as much detail as possible, including payment terms as a protection for myself if the bidder doesn't take the time to read through the listing.

chapter 13

PowerSellers with Multiple Classifications

Randall Pinson

Username:	rocket-auctions
Name:	Randall Pinson
E-mail:	sales@rocketauctions.com
Classification:	eBay/ Internet Business & Trading Assistant
Current Tier:	Platinum PowerSeller
eBay Store:	Rocket Auctions Incorporated
eBay Store Location:	www.stores.ebay.com/Rocket-Auctions-Incorporated
Current Feedback Star:	Shooting Yellow
Projected 2006 Sales:	$500,000

A Little Background

Randall Pinson has been a member of eBay since March 2000.

PowerSeller Randall Pinson started his eBay business almost by mistake. In the spring of 2000, he was managing a cell phone store. He came upon a large liquidation of cell phone equipment and snapped it up for a great price. He presumed it would be compatible with the service providers he was currently promoting. When he discovered the phones needed to be activated in New York and he operated the store in Utah, he had more than a little problem. A coworker suggested he try selling a phone on eBay. When the $25 phone sold on the site for $125, Randall was interested! It wasn't long before he was selling on eBay as his full-time job, and two years later he owned Rocket Auctions, Inc. Today he operates Rocket-auctions on the U.S. eBay site and Rockets-pockets on eBay in the United Kingdom.

Randall sells clothing, accessories, sporting goods, and toys. The company averages $45,000 in monthly sales between eBay and the other online sales channels Randall uses, which include Overstock.com. At the time of this writing, he employed one full-time and one part-time employee. Together they process an average of 50 packages a day.

I'm a minimalist when it comes to operating a business. I only hired a full-time employee when I realized that I was sacrificing money-making activities by spending hours pulling orders and processing shipments myself.

Randall keeps up-to-date when it comes to tools that will support his business. In the summer of 2005, he started using Shipworks from Interapptive. Interfaced with his auction management software, Marketworks, Shipworks has greatly reduced the time it takes Randall and his staff to process their shipments. He switched to Marketworks when he realized his business had outgrown eBay's Seller Assistant Pro (now Blackthorne).

This tool is significantly more expensive than the eBay branded auction management tools; however, the benefits that Marketworks has provided more than justify the expense.

He's a big supporter of using third-party providers for the tools that make a seller's life easier.

Not only are the costs justifiable but the quality of one's life improves as well

In November 2005, Randall wrote an article for eBay's own *Chatter Newsletter* about a trip he made with 24 other eBay PowerSellers to share their views with Congress about the Streamlined Sales Tax Project, a legislative measure that would require small sellers to collect taxes outside their own jurisdictions. According to Randall, that is the largest problem facing professional eBay sellers today. The group of 25 met with a number of representatives, both in a large group and for small group meetings. Randall had the opportunity to share his concerns in person and explain what this bill would do to the small business owner. It would mean that each seller would be required to collect taxes for 7,500 different taxing jurisdictions, keeping all the records straight and forwarding all the revenues to the correct agencies. The group was able to explain to the lawmakers why the current exemption they were considering for businesses generating $5 million or less per year was already inadequate for a large portion of sellers who depend on eBay for their livelihoods. They were also able to point out that not only are these small businesses good for the owners, but also for the communities they reside in. They provide jobs and generate business for USPS and for a variety of other businesses ranging from office supply stores to accountants. Randall wrote in his article about what a thrill it was to have a part in helping Congress research a bill and decide about legislation, opportunities that are not likely to happen to most ordinary citizens.

As for advice for other people wanting to become PowerSellers, I would say that if you're looking to get rich quick, you better go take a real-estate seminar. But if you're realistic about it you can start slowly, minimize your risks, and avoid the discouragement that many new sellers experience.

As for Randall, he's built a great life for himself and his family in Utah.

Art Sivertsen

Username:	auctionsteacher
Name:	Art Sivertsen
E-mail:	admin@auctionsteacher.com
Classification:	Internet/ eBay Only Business & Trading Assistant
Current Tier:	Gold PowerSeller
eBay Store:	PutterStore
eBay Store Location:	www.stores.eBay.com/putterstore
Current Feedback Star:	Red

A Little Background

Art Sivertsen has been a member of eBay since September 2002.

Almost three years later, I've had gross PayPal sales in 2006 reaching $86,000 and that is doing eBay as a part-time income while maintaining my eight to five job! My accomplishments in the past year include (keep in mind I've *achieved all of this while maintaining my full-time job!):*

- *Attaining eBay Gold PowerSeller Status*

- *Creating my own LLC company Southpaw Sales, LLC*

- *Creating and maintaining a golf Web site for retail golf putters*

- *Creating and maintaining my own Web site for Trading Assistance and Education Specialist Programs and **www. TheAuctionsTeacher. com** as well as my PowerU Portal with updates on future classes*

- *Creating and maintaining my eBay Store*

- *Maintaining a feedback score of 99.9 (currently 2100 positive feedbacks and 1 negative—that user is no longer registered on eBay)*

Accepted a professor position to teach "The Basics of Selling on eBay" at the University of Georgia in Fall 2006.

A part-time eBay seller and Trading Assistant, Art Sivertsen—username auctionsteacher—became a seller on eBay by accident. He found it to be a fun hobby and a potential second income.

Almost four years ago I was merely looking for a golf club for myself on eBay. I realized that the prices were much cheaper than in the golf shops. So I bought my first item. After I bought a few more things I thought that I would try my hand at selling some of my golf stuff. Then I started experimenting. I bought one World Series ticket on Ticketmaster, and I sold the one ticket to a buyer in New York. At that point it was getting to be a hobby. Since childhood I have been into golf, so I decided that my niche would be mostly golf equipment. I approached some local golf shops in my town and asked them if they wanted me to sell any of their overstock or trade-ins for them on eBay! I had no idea what they would say, but they said, "Yes, we don't currently have anybody doing that, and we really need somebody to do that for us," especially since they said that they had no idea how to sell on eBay.

Art didn't really set becoming a PowerSeller as a goal. It just kind of happened for him. It took him about a year and a half to reach PowerSeller status.

I never thought I would generate $1,000 in gross sales in a month to become eligible. Now I'm doing $10,000 per month.

He sells high-end golf equipment, with around a $100-$150 value. He sells about 30 items a week and said the best way to draw people to his listings is by using good titles, correct keywords, gallery photos, and using the correct categories. The average starting price for his listings is $.99 cents. He does not use any kind of listing software.

Art finds the items he sells at golf shops, golf wholesalers, and from individuals who need a Trading Assistant. He does not make his own items.

When it comes to cross-promotions, Art is in.

I use my cross-promotion tools to promote similar items; I also use hyperlinks from the eBay description page to create links to certain things in my item description.

Art does not have a specific time that he prefers to end his auctions.

I don't really have an ideal time, but most sellers say Sunday is the best day to finish an auction. I don't necessarily agree with that. For example: I was selling Xbox 360s last Christmas, and I was buying them late at night, Sundays included, and I was paying about $510 for the core systems and reselling those exact systems in the daytime for about $650 so there was a $140 difference by selling them during work hours as opposed to late night hours.

When he hasn't heard from a buyer, Art takes this approach:

Get their contact information (through the contact form on eBay) and call them. If it's a fake number, file an unpaid item dispute.

Art sometimes allows returns on his new merchandise with seven days exchange time. He doesn't drop ship as he hasn't found the time to search for a good drop shipper as he keeps busy enough with his golf items. He does allow international shipping on his items.

I sell most of my golf equipment to Australia, New Zealand, UK, Canada; it really helps your bottom line.

Art does not really use anything major to drive people into his eBay store. He does make use of a Web site outside of his eBay store **www.Putterstore.com**.

I really don't drive them hard except through my regular

auction listings, trying to get them into my store. I would rather spend marketing dollars on my regular Web site because the fees are much less. I don't want to spend money to promote eBay, because that's what the eBay fees are for!

He markets his products using auctions, fixed pricing, and his eBay store. He said he doesn't usually use "buy it nows," just a fixed price.

The Education Specialist Program

Art is currently the only featured eBay instructor in Georgia. There are only 17 Featured Education Specialists trained by eBay currently in the United States.

I became a Trading Assistant a few years ago, but I didn't enjoy helping individuals as much as I thought I would because they would have to pay me commissions and they didn't know how to describe their items very well. Sometimes they didn't actually know what they were selling. I had a guy who was trying to sell a computer and he didn't know how much memory it had or what type of processor he had. I also noticed that a large company called iSold It opened in the city that I live in. So when I looked up eBay University, I saw the Education Specialist program and I thought, "I know I can teach people how to eBay!" so I turned my focus away from Trading Assistant and directly on my eBay business and the Education Specialist program. I was so excited I took and passed the test as fast as was humanly possible!

The reason I decided to teach this curriculum was because I didn't want people to give 30 percent to 40 percent of their profits to a company such as iSold It when it's so easy for them to do it themselves. So I began teaching the Holiday Buying Class at the Library, and I also taught the Selling Class free at the Library so I could get some practice in. Since then I have received a feedback of 20, and I have maintained a 93 percent feedback rating through power U. So my goal coming in to this program was three fold:

- To become a featured instructor

- To teach (when I become eligible in a few weeks) the Beyond the Basics and (in a few months) the new Business Consultant Program

- To become an eBay University Instructor.

A Final Piece of Advice

If you are just starting out, make sure you take a class on how to sell on eBay by a Certified Education Specialist Trained by eBay at **www.ebayuniversity.com**.

Contact Information for Art Sivertsen:
Art Sivertsen
Gold PowerSeller
www.TheAuctionsTeacher.com
www.PutterStore.com
www.Stores.eBay.com/putterstore
Phone: 877-968-GOLF
PO Box 222, Fayetteville, GA 30214

Thomas Adinolfi

Username:	auctionseast
Name:	Thomas Adinolfi
E-mail:	auctionseast@msn.com
Classification:	Internet/ eBay Only Business, Brick-and-Mortar Store Using eBay, & Trading Assistant
Current Tier:	Gold PowerSeller
eBay Store:	AuctionsEast
eBay Store Location:	www.stores.ebay.com/AuctionsEast
Current Feedback Star:	Red
Projected 2006 Sales:	$400,000

A Little Background

Thomas Adinolfi has been a member of eBay since July 2000.

AuctionsEast was founded in the attic of my parents' home and has grown faster and bigger than I could have ever imagined. A few years back I left my job on a leap of faith. Not knowing what to do, I sold a few items on eBay for some quick cash on the advice of a friend. I started to sell a few personal belongings, and to my surprise by my second week, I made as much as I would if I were still at my old job.

A little time goes by and I recognize the unlimited potential behind this company. eBay stimulated the creative mind, and it shows the power of people and the mind.

In the middle of running this new little enterprise that I have created in my attic, my mom was diagnosed with breast and bladder cancer. I dropped everything in my life to care for and aid my mom. We stood strong! I used eBay as a catalyst for happiness. I had her boxing items and writing DVD lists to keep her mind off of her illness. And being a thinker and not a sleeper, in the middle of the night I would research and work toward the concept of what I thought I was inventing. It turns out drop off points out west were already a huge industry, but had yet to boom. And had yet to come east. Hence AuctionsEast. Fast forward. My mom fought through the cancer, is totally well, and checks out healthy now. Thank the Lord! By the way that is all that really matters in this world, not only in times like this but as a life mission!

So through all of that this brainchild was born, and I swore to myself once all of that smoke cleared with my mom, I was to move forward with this idea. And better days were ahead. Now we are Staten Island's/New York's foremost eBay connection. September marks my first full year open to the public. We have hosted the first eBay Roadshow, been featured on NY1 local news, acknowledged by the local paper, The Staten Island Advance, Time Warner Cable, Our Lady of Good Counsel, Staten Island Academy, Wagner College, St. Johns University, Industry Magazine, and everyone else who has taken notice of our vision.

I would just like to thank eBay and the local community and my virtual neighbors and customers. Thank you for changing my life and believing in me, my idea, company, vision, and hard work. Thank you for allowing me to accomplish more at this young age of 26 than I could have ever thought possible. I am so grateful for what you have given me. But more importantly, God. It is funny how things happen on God's time. During one of the worst times of my life—no job, my mom had cancer—it was the love for each other and the presence of eBay that got us through that horrible course of events. I work so hard now that I have this brick-and-mortar store location: 13- to 14-hour work days with no days off! I have faith in God, eBay, and you. I would say that is good enough company. See you on eBay! Thomas Adinolfi, AuctionsEast Founder.

Thomas Adinolfi—username auctionseast—is a full-time eBay seller. He left his job as a mortgage broker feeling unfulfilled. When a friend mentioned selling on eBay to earn a little extra cash, he did. Once he realized what a PowerSeller was, he set earning the status as a goal. It became one of the first eBay-related goals he set for himself.

And now I set new and fresh goals on a monthly basis with a higher bar than the last. Goals are important in life's evolution.

It took him about four or five months to earn PowerSeller status. He said it takes about a month just to learn the eBay system and getting the hang of it.

The second month you will begin to build your brand/name, and learn a few tips and pointers. By the third month you will have a good feel for everything and by the fourth month you will be on your way. Judging on your sales total average you will be awarded any day after.

Thomas sells about 30 items a day or 180 items a week with an average starting price for most of his items of $49.99. He believes variation is the best way to get people to notice his listings.

> *Use Online auctions, "buy it now" auctions, store inventory branding. It is important to use the featured and gallery option, as well as the eBay home page option. Yes, it may cost a little bit more to list the item, but if it is a reasonably high priced item, it will well be worth your while. Like anything else, you sometimes have to spend money to make money. Also, when listing be efficient and professional. It isn't a race so take your time and present the item accurately.*

Thomas markets his items, his company, and his brand in every way through eBay. He has live auctions running from one to ten days, with "buy it now" as an option. He also recommends opening an eBay store.

> *Begin to build your own brand with widely diverse item selection that will also get an occasional impulse buy. We sell about one car every seven to ten days and a boat every five months. We sell a motorcycle every six months.*

The items he sells are drop-offs at his brick-and-mortar store or from appointments made for home visits. Sometimes he will also buy overstock items from Staten Island businesses. He does not make his own items that he sells, but said eBay is a great venue for those wanting to do so and create a buzz about their brand and items and to also test the market to see how the public will take to the item. To list his items, Thomas uses an Andale. They offer free counters that show up at the bottom of the auction ad. He does cross-promote.

> *When cross-promoting, you can show other similar related*

items that are available in your store. Showing a variety will ultimately increase the sales rate of the items.

Although he does feel the time and time-ending of an auction are important, he does not believe they affect the price dramatically.

You always want to list at night, preferably after dinner. And weekend auctions are always best. Remember to think like a buyer when marketing an item from start to finish including auction time to list. When will people be home? Nights and weekends.

When he hasn't heard from a buyer, he will send an additional invoice accompanied by a follow-up e-mail. If he still has not heard anything, he will send the buyer a non-paying bidder alert via eBay's Auction add and dispute console.

And then you can also perform an advanced search through eBay with a User ID Request. You will get the address and phone number of the buyer. If all else fails, get the Final Value Fee Request Form and fill that out. You will leave the buyer a non-paying bidder strike, and will recuperate the Final Value Fee.

Thomas does offer a return policy that states that satisfaction of his clients is of the utmost importance. He will work to resolve any problems that may arise.

Full money-back returns will be determined when the item returned shows proof of complaint. Shipping and handling costs for returns will be the responsibility of the buyer. There is a $3 restocking fee on all returns. International bidders will incur a shipping surcharge.

To save on shipping costs, Thomas recommends developing a relationship with a local store or grocer to use boxes they are discarding for shipping your items. If you don't want to purchase bubble wrap or peanuts, he also recommends using newspaper to secure the item in the box. He does suggest using the bubble wrap or peanuts for pricey items.

Our company also sells bubble wrap and peanuts as some of the cheapest prices on the Web are with us, AuctionsEast. You can also contact USPS via eBay Shipping Center for free priority boxes.

Thomas believes international buyers are good for business. He suggests not selling internationally until you have a feel for eBay and the system.

If you are not prepared, it can cost you, literally. I have paid dearly and lost money because of shipping miscalculations and errors such as package surcharges and customs charges, which should always be paid by the buyer, and insurance forms not being filled out. Insure anything and everything fragile, please.

He said drop shipping is a good method for selling items if you want to venture into that territory.

The sky is the limit with eBay, and really any and everything only becomes what you make it. I have made a vision a tangible store/entity.

To drive people to his eBay store, Thomas has built a wide variety of brands and items, quality service, and thorough strategic cross-promotions.

Be creative; offer deals and promos. Make sure the items

are related by category, keywords, and genres.

Company Profile

AuctionsEast is a recognized eBay Professional PowerSeller Trading Assistant and Certified eBay Teacher. We'll even teach you how to become a CEO out of your own living room, if you so desire. All you have to do is call us or drop your item off. Sure, we all have stuff that we no longer use or that has been tucked away, waiting for this very day to come. We turn your clutter-collectibles into cash! We are all now more liquid-worth than ever before. Look around the very room in you are in, I bet you can find something in less than five minutes, unless you thought of an item already that you could cash in on. We all have them. Your new or used goods will be all professionally handled by AuctionsEast—We do all the work, from start-to-finish:

- *Research and competitive pricing*

- *Photography*

- *Marketing the eBay way*

- *Professional Listing Ad with all the bells and whistles to help sell your item*

- *Handle all correspondence and offers.*

- *Boxing and shipping upon the items' sale*

You can sit back and reap the profits. The easiest and laziest way to eBay. If you are interested in finding out more about our services please call or e-mail us. We specialize in:

- *Diamonds, gold, and other fine quality jewelry*
- *Comic books and collectibles*

- Musical instruments
- Tools
- Retro, collectible toy and hobby items
- Disney and vintage dolls
- Vintage and new train sets
- Cars
- Boats
- Motorcycles
- Homes
- Property
- Asset and business liquidation
- Estate sales
- Antiques and vintage goods
- Packaging supplies
- Furniture
- Baseball, fan/sport memorabilia
- Autographed items
- Sports and exercise equipment
- Collectible figurines
- Art
- Clocks
- War memorabilia
- Designer and luxury goods
- Consumer electronics
- Knick knacks/ Bric-a-brac

And it goes on and on to the bizarre and wacky. It is not just a job. It is a hobby and an education. Use our expertise and cash in today!

Dave Cook

Username:	highbidexpress
Name:	Dave Cook
E-mail:	Highbidexpress.sales@gmail.com
Classification:	Internet/ eBay Only Business & Trading Assistant
Current Tier:	Silver PowerSeller
eBay Store:	High Bid Express
eBay Store Location:	www.stores.ebay.com/High-Bid-Express
Current Feedback Star:	Red
Projected 2006 Sales:	$150,000

A Little Background

Dave Cook has been a member of eBay since March 2005.

I am the founder and CEO of High Bid Express, Inc., a Sandy, Utah-based company.

High Bid Express was founded in May 2005. In just four months it became one of eBay's fastest growing Trading Assistants. The company has been awarded eBay's prestigious Silver PowerSeller status and has become an official Education Specialist trained by eBay.

Before founding High Bid Express, I worked for Sprint (a Fortune 100) company for 14 years. At Sprint, I was responsible for leading the development of multi-million dollar high-tech projects from concept to market launch.

As an eBay Education Specialist we teach others how to sell on eBay. You can learn more and about and register for classes at http://highbidexpress.poweru.net.

Dave Cook—username highbidexpress—is a full-time eBay seller and Trading Assistant. He worked for a Fortune 100 company for 14 years and then was laid off.

After looking at a large number of different kinds of self-employment opportunities, we decided the selling on eBay could provide us with the income and the flexibility we needed.

Dave became a PowerSeller almost immediately because his company took off pretty quickly from day one. Making use of every area on eBay to sell—auctions, "buy it nows," eBay Motors, and store-front—he sells about five or six items a day with an average price that varies depending upon the item.

Do your research on eBay's completed listings and see what others are doing for the same or similar items.

Dave recommends three ways to get people to notice your listings: putting the item in the correct category, using keywords in the title that the buyers will enter in a search, and always using a gallery photo.

Because he is a Trading Assistant, Dave gets 99 percent of the items he sells from his clients. He does not make any of the items he sells. To list his items he uses Blackthorne and Selling Manager Pro. He cross-promotes all of his items.

Dave said he hasn't found the time of day to be too significant when dealing with auctions.

We run almost all our auctions for seven days so each listing always runs through a weekend.

When he hasn't heard from a buyer within three days after sending an invoice, he will send them a reminder e-mail directly from his account.

If they haven't paid within seven days we'll send another reminder. If we do not receive a response to our e-mail, we have eBay send them an e-mail with a reminder of their obligation to pay for the item. If this still doesn't produce payment or an appropriate response, we will file an unpaid item dispute with eBay. Please note we have had very few problems in this area.

Dave does offer a return policy. It states that items must be returned in the same condition as received. Items that were sent with insurance must be returned in the same manner. He does not refund shipping, handling, or insurance. Refunds are issued promptly upon receipt of the merchandise at his offices.

He does believe international bidders are good for business. He has not tried drop shipping. To save on shipping costs, he has the following advice:

■ *Use the calculated shipping option when listing your item*

- *Use packaged weight*

- *Have at least one other carrier beside the USPS.*

To draw people into his eBay store he will make sure to list his items with titles that buyers will enter when searching for items. He also has a Web site: **www.highbidexpress.com**.

We link from our Web site to eBay, not vice versa. We have an eBay store and all eBay auction formats appear in our eBay store.

A Final Piece of Advice

We have a brick-and-mortar location for our business. We feel that having a physical business location adds credibility and makes people more comfortable in doing business with us.

Be sure you understand all the various selling fees that relate to your listing and sale of your items.

Understand USPS Mailing Guidelines and Rates, especially for international sales.

Be sure that you buy your items for the right price. You make money on eBay just like anything else—you make money when you buy, not when you sell.

Contact Information for Dave Cook:
High Bid Express, Inc.
9460 S. Union Square #220
Sandy, Utah 84070
Phone: 801-495-1400
Highbidexpress.sales@gmail.com
www.highbidexpress.com

Donna Bond

Username:	online-auction-princess
Name:	Donna Bond
E-mail:	donnabond@comcast.net
Classification:	Internet/ eBay Only Business & Trading Assistant
Current Tier:	Silver PowerSeller
eBay Store:	Donna's Fashion Diva Boutique
eBay Store Location:	www.stores.ebay.com/Donnas-Fashion-Diva-Boutique
Current Feedback Star:	Red

A Little Background

Donna Bond has been a member of eBay since August 2001.

Once I saw this was going to be a sure success, I made the decision to give up my career as a nurse to eBay full-time, teach eBay classes, and spend more time with my family.

I sell ladies fashions of all kinds full-time on eBay. I also am an Educational Specialist Trained by eBay and teach 'Basic' and 'Advanced' classes. Recently, I was chosen as one of the top 'Featured' instructors by PowerU.

Last year I had an eBay store consultation with one of eBay's best to contact me to analyze my store as I was not selling much. By the time he got done with my store and I made all the changes he suggested, my store has been a total success ever since! The 'offer' option has been awesome! I have sold more out of my store in one year with his help than ever before. Now I don't have to work as hard since my eBay store is working hard for me and is set up correctly. Now that I'm an educational specialist trained by eBay and have been teaching for almost a year, I now share this vital information to hundreds who attend my eBay classes. The response I get from my students after I help them set up their store the right way is unbelievable! Their exact words include sayings such as: 'It would have taken me months/years' and 'I would have never figured this out.' This alone makes me feel great knowing that I have probably caused another future 'eBay success story!'

Future challenges of mine include staying on top of my competitors. I have already accomplished two of my goals by becoming successful on eBay and launching my eBay classes. My next goal is to move up to the next level of the PowerSeller tier on eBay and travel the United States teaching my eBay classes. I'm in the process now of upgrading my store to the next level as I know it will pay off. I just opened up a 'Pro-Store' to get more business coming into my eBay store.

Like many other Education Specialists and eBayers, my passion for eBay and teaching has developed into the fun and freedoms that eBay has allowed many of us. My classes sell out every time, but I want to share my passion around the United States. My five years of eBaying has sure paid off!

It has made a significant impact in my life and I enjoy nothing more than spreading the word. My experience and *success as a trainer and seller and my enthusiasm for eBay work well together and it shows through in my classes and sales."*

A full-time eBay seller, Trading Assistant, and Education Specialist trained by eBay, Donna Bond—username online-auction-princess—decided to become an eBay seller after she realized the success she could have with it. She quit her job as a nurse to become a full-time seller on eBay in 2001.

Becoming a PowerSeller was a goal she had set for herself. She realized that goal within only three months.

Donna sells around 100-plus items a week. Her average starting price for her items is $9.99. She finds that the best way to get bidders to notice her listing is by attractive designing and professionalism. She finds most of the items she sells through private suppliers and eBay.

She does not use any type of listing software, rather she customizes her listings herself and she always uses cross-promotions. She finds the timing for an auction to be very important.

When she has not heard from a buyer, Donna tries to rectify the situation by sending several invoices and making phone calls to the buyer. She says this is the best approach for her.

She does have a return policy. It states the following:

Exchanges & or In-Store credit will be given on returns. Full refund if the item is in any way misrepresented. Please read Measurements of any item. Mis-measured items can not be exchanged or credited. All items are measured more than once for accuracy. Items must be received back to me within seven days. No refunds on shipping. If you send an item back for an exchange or store credit, you are responsible for additional shipping and handling unless the item was misrepresented in any way."

Donna finds the best way for her to save on shipping costs is to buy her supplies wholesale. She does allow international bidders. In fact, 30 percent of her customers are international. She absolutely does not feel drop-shipping is a good method for selling items.

When it comes to driving potential bidders to her store, Donna has found using the right keywords and marketing to be the approaches that work best for her. Her Web sites include: **www.fashiondivaboutique.net, http://home.comcast.net/ ~donnabond/wsb/html/view.cgi-home.html-.html,** and **http://stores.ebay.com/Donnas-Fashion-Diva-Boutique.**

Donna uses all the marketing areas when selling: auctions, store fronts, and "buy it nows".

A Final Piece of Advice

I always hated sales and I was the type of person who would not go to school the next day if I had to give a speech as I had that fear. Look at me now! Selling and teaching…all for eBay! eBay has totally changed my life, plus my income is double what it was being a nurse!"

Web Addresses for Donna Bond

eBay Store:

http://stores.ebay.com/Donnas-Fashion-Diva-Boutique

Donna's About Me Page through eBay:

http://members.ebay.com/ws/eBayISAPI.
dll?ViewUserPage&userid=1968titans

PowerU/ eBay University Featured Instructor site:

http://www.poweru.net/ebay/instructor/
insFeaturedArchive.asp

Student comments from those she has taught:

http://www.poweru.net/ebay/student/
searchComments.asp?id=71595249

eBay class schedule:

http://www.poweru.net/ebay/student/
searchResultsInsDetail.asp?id=71595249

Trading Assistant Program:

http://tradingassistant.ebay.com/ws/eBayISAPI.dll?Trading
Assistant&zipCode=37128&streetAddress=&Country=US&st
ate=&page=profile&profileId=157082825&city=murfreesboro

Donna's Non-eBay Sites:

www.online-auction-princess.com

Jeff Edmunds

Username:	silvercreekconsignment
Name:	Jeff Edmunds
E-mail:	jeff@onlinepowerbrokers.com
Classification:	Brick-and-Mortar Store & Trading Assistant
Current Tier:	Silver PowerSeller
eBay Store:	SilverCreekConsignment
eBay Store Location:	www.stores.ebay.com/SilverCreek-Consignment
Current Feedback Star:	Purple
Projected 2006 Sales:	$84,000

A Little Background

Jeff Edmunds has been a member of eBay since April 1999.

I have a small business called MAILPLUS of West Jordan—we

are a mail and parcel-shipping center. We offer UPS, FedEx, DHL, and postal services as well as printing, faxing, and copying. We have been in business and in the same location for 14 years. About three years ago our shipping business started to decline dramatically. The Internet has changed our industry by making online shipping easier for everyone. The USPS has their click-and-ship right online and will even schedule the postal carrier to come pick up your items. A lot of our old business customers now have their own accounts, and we have just become a fancy air-conditioned drop box for them.

So to make up a new profit center I started to offer to sell our customers' items on eBay for them. I had personally been selling and had been an eBay member at that time for four or five years. I rearranged the store, put in a new counter and some storage racks, and started to advertise and tell all our existing customers. Things took off real fast; we had a lot of stuff coming in—some good, some not so good. We found ourselves wasting a lot of time on the not so good items and finding that the customers had an unrealistic value for their items. They had heard all the stories about how well old games and vintage clothing sold on eBay. Well, some old board games like Mystery Date, Battlemasters, and Bladerunner, but the games we were getting in were none of these. Don't get me wrong though. We did and do get in some real good stuff on occasion.

In the process we have had some manufacturers come to us and have started to work out some agreements to sell their locally manufactured items online. This I feel is the better way to do business. We have also contacted other manufacturers and begun to manufacture some of our own items. If I could go back in time I would have started this way years ago and not done the drop off business. The overhead, employees, store-front, and customer issues, and for the percent that the eBay drop-off stores charge (15 to 38 percent), I really don't see how we can make it. In fact, I have seen three competing eBay drop-off stores open and go out of business just within the last year. They had great locations, nice stores, media coverage, TV, and radio, but without charging at least 50 percent—and customer balks when you tell them 28 percent!—I don't see how it will play out.

*We are converting our drop-off store to a consignment store—thus our new name "SilverCreekConsignment." We have joined a national organization—**NARTS.org** (National Association of Resale & Thrift Shops). In the near future you will see kiosks in all sorts of stores wanting to sell your stuff on eBay—but how cool is the local consignment shop with all their neat antiques, retro style kitchenware, old furniture, name brand clothing at a quarter of retail? Will your customers want to leave their stuff at some drop-off kiosk or with you in your awesome little shop?*

*If you want to avoid the retail scene I am working on a book/manual that will have a detailed list of items to look for at yard sales, thrift stores, estates sales, and local auctions. My new Web site is **www.silvercreekconsignment.com**.*

We have become Education Specialists trained by eBay and are teaching classes on how to sell on eBay.

Jeff Edmunds—username silvercreekconsignment—began selling on eBay to increase his revenue. He is seeking to sell full-time on eBay. He set becoming a PowerSeller as a goal and after eight months, he realized that goal.

Jeff sells about 60 to 90 items a week with an average starting price of about $3.90. He finds that interesting pictures are the best way to draw people into his listings. He uses auctions as his avenue for selling on eBay.

He finds most of his items through consignments and manufacturers as mentioned in his bio above. He does make some of the items he sells as well. Jeff currently is manufacturing hunting benches and fly rod cases.

Jeff uses Store Manager Pro G2 by: Auction Wagon in his drop-off business. He also has a 100 percent customer satisfaction return policy and so far he has refunded the shipping costs as well.

He has found cross-promoting to be helpful and uses it in his listings. He also thinks that the timing of an auction and ending time of an auction are very important. When he hasn't heard from buyers, Jeff tries to e-mail them, hoping for a response.

He does allow international bidders.

To save on shipping costs, Jeff does the following:

We use flat rate envelopes when we can and we buy large rolls of brown kraft paper for packing material—it's cheaper than bubble wrap and protects the items a lot better. We also buy used boxes.

He does have a Web site that is linked to his listings:**www. silvercreekconsignment.com**. To get people into his eBay store, Jeff purchases key words (from eBay and Google). He hands out flyers locally and uses a vehicle wrap.

A Final Piece of Advice

My suggestion is to find a product or products that you like yourself—a niche. This way you can become a real expert on the items, know the value, find the manufacturers, go to yard sales, local auctions, estate sales, put ads in the local paper, and let your friends know that you are looking for these particular items. Once you have products you can start to target market your items. Find out who your customers are, where they hang out, and what their hobbies are so that you can focus your marketing and sell related items—all on a budget.

Here's an example of an item you can find at yard sales for under $20 and sell for up to $150 on eBay: Vita-Mix Blenders (almost any model will do), they sell great online. Old rotary telephones can be purchased for a couple of bucks and can sell for way over $50 each. The list goes on.

If you have interests in starting an eBay drop off store—I would check out some of the local consignment shops. They were in business way before eBay and they have a 50/50 split and can choose to put your item in their store or list online—their choice. They set the sale price and have the option of reducing the price if it doesn't sell within the first 30 days.

Contact Information for Jeff Edmunds:
Jeff Edmunds
SilverCreekConsignment
E-mail: jeff@onlinepowerbrokers.com
Web site: www.silvercreekconsignment.com

Lorne Counter

Username:	list4uonline
Name:	Lorne Counter
E-mail:	Lorne@list4uonline.com
Classification:	eBay Only Business, Trading Assistant, & eBay Education Specialist
Current Tier:	Silver PowerSeller
eBay Store:	List 4 U online
eBay Store Location:	www.stores.ebay.com/List-4-U-online
Current Feedback Star:	Red
Projected 2006 Sales:	$115,000

A Little Background

Lorne Counter has been a member of eBay since September 2000.

I got started selling for others about three years ago when I started selling for my friends and family. I've gone from being a Sunday part-time seller to a super silver seller. The nice thing about selling for others is there is no need to go out looking for things to sell; they come to you. And if you do a good job those people will tell their friends and the business grows by leaps and bounds. I'm not only selling for people but companies with liquidation items as well as new products.

Now as far as keeping yourself happy, try reading everything on eBay you can, including this great book. Knowledge is power and power equals money and money equals happiness. For me, if all goes well I should break $100,000 this year. Not too bad for a guy who stumbled into this selling for his friends.

A full-time eBay seller and Trading Assistant, Lorne Counter—username list4uonline—started selling on eBay after getting talked into selling some items for a friend. After that, he was hooked and spending every spare minute on eBay.

After about a year and a half Lorne became a PowerSeller by accident as he just began selling more when more people wanted him to sell for them on eBay. He is a silver tiered PowerSeller but is climbing towards the gold tier.

He averages about 80 to 100 items sold every week. He said to get people to notice the listings the best methods are keywords in the title and a gallery photo. He suggests the seller think like a buyer and use as many words in the title line that will attract the biggest bidding audience. When it comes to his average starting price, he tends to stick to $.99 if it is not a "buy it now" item.

Why give eBay extra money in fees if you have done your research on the item you are selling and know it always sells for $250? Why start your bid at $249.99 and only get one bidder when you can start it at $.99 and get a lot of *people into your item when the price is low? And if all works right they will get in a bidding war and maybe make you more that that $250 mark, plus saving you a lot on listing fees which add up over a year's time.*

Lorne does not make any of the items he sells and as a Trading Assistant, he gets most of his items from people bringing them to his consignment store. He does spend at least one day every week when he goes "combing the hills" for items he can sell for himself.

To list his items, Lorne has used Turbo Lister and Auction Wizard. He also tried MarketBlast, but because it was still in Beta testing, he didn't like all the bugs still in the program. Currently, he makes use of Blackthorne software.

It manages everything from feedback to all my consignment customers, which was key to me.

Cross-promoting is very important to Lorne.

I sell a lot of secondary items that are only in my store and all the little add-on sales really add up fast.

He finds the timing of an auction to be important depending on the type of item he is selling.

If I am selling ladies' items I would want them to close in the late morning to mid-afternoon as this is the time when the kids are in school and a lot of house moms are at home possibly surfing eBay for one of my items. Other than that I like my auctions to close on weeknights around 6 p.m. PST, which means it is not too late on the East Coast. Time zones play a very crucial part in planning. But my all-time favorite time is Sunday around 3 p.m. Everyone is back from church or family gatherings and at home.

When he hasn't heard from one of his buyers, Lorne tries to be patient and sends out a reminder e-mail after two weeks.

After three weeks I file a non-payer with eBay and if that runs its course I will leave feedback and collect my fees back. If the person has contacted me and needs more time, I will bend to accommodate the customer as I hope they will come back and buy from me again.

He does have a return policy because he feels it is important to give the buyer a sense of trust.

In five years, I have only had one person return an item.

Lorne allows international bidders, and 15 to 20 percent of his business comes from overseas. He believes that not only should you ship worldwide, but also accept every type of payment possible to allow more bidders on your items. He doesn't drop ship and doesn't feel it would be a good option.

I like to have the item on-hand because if my drop shipper messes up, it is my feedback on the line and my PayPal account that gets the fees charged back—not the other company. They risk nothing and you risk all. All my wholesale items I buy myself in bulk so I never sell anything I don't have in stock.

To save on shipping costs Lorne, recommends using Priority Mail as it is the best you can get for the price. It allows the item to arrive quickly to the buyer—this means good feedback. It is only a few cents more than Standard Rate Mail but a lot cheaper than the UPS two- to three-day delivery service.

The only other way to ship and save money is if it is Media

Mail. Using the media rate a ten-pound bag of books will ship for around $5. If you ship any amount of books over four pounds overseas be sure to use the little known M-bag; it is $11 for the first four to 11 pounds and then only $1.05 per pound after that.

Lorne does have a Web site that is linked to his auctions: **www.list4uonline.com** and finds the best way to draw them into his store is by cross-promoting.

A Final Piece of Advice

In conclusion, just keep all your customers happy. No one likes surprises. Do your research to ensure the highest possible bids and that will mean more money for you and any consignment customers you may work with. Now as far as keeping your bidders happy, never misrepresent an item that someone gave you to sell just to get a higher bid (negative feedback will haunt your bidding down the road), take lots of pictures, and DON'T OVERCHARGE ON THE SHIPPING! Be fair; it's ok to make a few dollars extra but there is a limit.

Contact Information for Lorne Counter:

Lorne Counter

Owner of List4Uonline

www.list4uonline.com

20025 Heathers Place SE

Monroe, WA 98272

Phone: 425-442-2679

Maggie Potenza

Username:	frednmag
Name:	Maggie Potenza
E-mail:	truelife@ptd.net
Classification:	Brick-and-Mortar Store Using eBay & Trading Assistant
Current Tier:	Silver PowerSeller
eBay Store:	Truelife Finds
eBay Store Location:	www.stores.ebay.com/Truelife-Finds
Current Feedback Star:	Purple

A Little Background

Maggie Potenza has been a member of eBay since November 2004.

> *I recently opened an eBay drop-off and consignment store in my town. Items that have little or no eBay value go on consignment. Of course consignment items are added daily to my eBay store to help increase the chances of selling consignment items. I tell anyone who comes into my store, I am the only local consignment store open for business 24 hours a day seven days a week internationally.*

A part-time eBay seller and Trading Assistant, Maggie Potenza—username frednmag—got started selling on eBay because of her husband. After about a year of selling, she reached her goal of becoming a PowerSeller.

Maggie sells about 20 to 25 items a week with her average starting price at $29.99. She uses eBay auctions and her store-front to market her items.

She does not make the items she sells, but being a Trading Assistant gets her items from her customers. She doesn't use any listing software. She does make use of the cross-promotion tools eBay offers as well as a return policy.

When she hasn't heard from a buyer, she tries sending an e-mail to get their attention.

> *I send a friendly e-mail saying "I do hope your item has arrived to you safely. Please let me know you are happy with it by leaving positive feedback. If for some reason you haven't left feedback please let me know why so we can make this a positive transaction."*

The timing of auctions and the ending-time of auctions are something Maggie finds very critical.

> *Different items cater to different people, and it's important to know when these people are home.*

To save on shipping costs, Maggie has customers who will bring in peanuts and boxes and other packaging material for her use. When it comes to international bidders, she said that they can be a good thing for business. She does not use drop shipping as a method for selling items.

To drive people to her eBay store (**http://stores.ebay.com/ Truelife-Find**s), Maggie does the following:

> *I pass out my business cards everywhere. On the back I show people how to find me by searching on Google for my*

eBay store name Truelife Finds.

Contact Information for Maggie Potenza:

My store is located at
103 Roberts Lane
Milford, PA 18337
Phone: 570-296-2545

Available at my store Tuesday thru
Saturday from 10 a.m. – 4 p.m.

Marylou Garcia, ISA, ASA

Username:	southend-estate-sales
Name:	Marylou Garcia, ISA, ASA
E-mail:	SouthendEstates@aol.com
Classification:	Brick-and-Mortar Store, eBay Business, & Trading Assista
Current Tier:	Silver PowerSeller
Current Feedback Star:	Red
Projected 2006 Sales:	$75,000

A Little Background

Marylou Garcia has been a member of eBay since August 1999. She is an accredited senior appraiser with International Society of Appraisers & American Society of Appraisers.

I am a Trading Assistant and eBay Educational Specialist with over 1900 feedbacks and still 100 percent positive!

A part-time eBay seller and Trading Assistant, Marylou Garcia—username southend-estate-sales—started selling on eBay because she saw it as an outlet for the types of items she was selling a little slower at her store Estate Liquidation shop.

I sell only old, antique, vintage, collectible, or interesting items.

Marylou didn't make becoming a PowerSeller a goal, but was happy when after about a year she earned the status.

She does things a little different when it comes to how she sells her 50 to 100 items a month.

I list throughout the month to have all items sell on the same day. The day I pick fits into my business and personal schedule, so I know for that week I will be answering questions just prior sale, then after sale packing and shipping.

Most of the time her auctions start at $.99 without any reserve set. She does this even when she knows the item will sell for thousands of dollars. She calls herself a "true liquidator" because she is not above taking a loss. But she said most of the time her items reach the correct level. To draw people into her listings, she does a few different things.

I like listing many of the same type of item together; whether it is antique silver, fly fishing gear, vintage cameras, or Christmas plates. If a bidder sees one of my items, with discounted shipping of multiple items they will look at other listings. Over time, I have developed a following of people who have me on their favorite seller list.

Marylou uses eBay's cross-promotional tools. She also mentions her listings in her other listings. She sells books also on Half.com. She finds the time and time-ending of her auctions, she finds this to be very important. Her advice is to think about who the buyer is and when he or she would be online. When she doesn't hear from a buyer after the closing of the auction, Marylou does the following:

Now I have what I do in my listing and on the invoice; at three days they will get second invoice, at seven days the non-paying bidder process starts, at 14 days the sale is canceled, I get the final eBay fees back and item is re-listed or offered to under bidder—depending on price. I will block bidder from buying again and most important, I don't worry about it. It's just part of doing business.

Once a man did not pay nor contact me until several months after the sale. He had had a serious heart attack and felt so bad that he had not got back to me. That made me think that non payer may be having problems I would not know about, so I just hope they are well and carry on without getting upset over it.

Marylou does have a return policy. She said it is very important to have one and hers is a no question return within seven days. The item has to be in the same condition in which she shipped it out for the purchase money to be returned. She does not return the shipping costs.

She has looked into drop shipping as the theory sounds good to her, but she has yet to try it out. She does allow international bidders and said it is worth all the extra work to pack, do customs forms, and stand in line at the post office. Marylou said it is hard to save on shipping costs but has a few ideas she does herself.

Having good, clean lightweight packing material and good boxes is a good start. I love the free USPS Priority boxes; have a couple of shop owner friends save the popcorn packing their shipments come in. I buy large amounts of bubble wrap at a time. I use stamps.com, with extra costs of monthly fee and labels, but the service gives a well-packed appearance and saves so much standing in line time at the post office, it is so worth it.

Marylou also said that running an eBay business is ideal for a military spouse; her husband is US Marine Corps Gunnery Sergeant Dennis Garcia.

The spouse can work long hours during deployments and do an easy business-restart after moves.

A Final Piece of Advice

- *Research "completed listings," to have an idea range of selling prices your item or similar items generally sell for. You will also see what information sellers of similar items have found important to include.*

- *When you get an e-mail about your item from a*

knowledgeable person or expert, appreciate their time in writing you about it

■ Pack well.

■ Ship ASAP.

■ Take good pictures without clutter in background and use as many pictures as necessary.

■ Have all needed information in listing: age, condition, material, and size.

■ Answer questions promptly and politely.

■ Cool off before answering rude e-mails.

■ Always be nice.

■ Use "Block Bidder" for any non-payer or anyone who is just plain nasty or rude. Great tool to save sellers' sanity!

■ Have fun e-meeting faraway people.

Company Profile

We are a very active Estate Appraisal and Liquidation business in the heart of Palm Beach County, Florida. Each week the contents of several homes come in to our South Dixie Highway facility. We get anything that can be found in a home: china, porcelain, books, pictures, silver, plates, jewelry, upholstered furniture, old furniture, modern furniture, fun furniture, junk furniture, fine antique furniture, great paintings, good art, and even cars, boats, or motorbikes.

On eBay we have sold a bronze sculpture for $9,000,

Autographs of all four Beatles together for $10,000, and an important Tiffany silver piece for $4,500.

Osvaldo Garcia

Username:	yardleyplace
Name:	Osvaldo Garcia
E-mail:	yardleystudios@earthlink.net
Classification:	Internet/ eBay Only Business & Trading Assistant
Current Tier:	Silver PowerSeller
Current Feedback Star:	Purple

A Little Background

Osvaldo Garcia has been a member of eBay since September 1999. He has a Bachelor of Marketing from East Stroudsburg University in Stroudsburg, Pennsylvania. He is currently the President of Auction Works of Puerto Rico. The company does marketing and sales of liquidation surplus for retailers and wholesalers via Internet Marketing and Sales. The sales are obtained through Internet Auctions on eBay.

Osvaldo also is an Education Specialist certified and trained by eBay. He offers workshops and seminars on "The Basics of eBay Selling." Find out more about this at **www.auctionworkspr. com**. He teaches how to buy and sell on eBay in a professional manner.

A part-time seller on eBay, Osvaldo Garcia—username yardleyplace—got "high on the first sale" on eBay. After that he was totally addicted. After two years he reached PowerSeller status.

> *I have to admit it was on the back of my mind but making the money was first; PowerSeller just came along!*

Osvaldo uses auctions and "buy it now." He averages two or three items sold a day, with average sales of about $150. His starting prices vary per item. He believes that to get people to notice his listings he needs to have a good product at a good price and a professional listing.

> *Just be professional.*

Although he would love to make some of the items he sells, he doesn't at this time. He finds most of his items from wholesalers and just about everywhere because he is also a Trading Assistant. To list his items he uses the Seller Sourcebook and Turbo Lister. He makes cross-promotions standard in his listings.

Osvaldo finds the timing of an auction to be very important.

Very. Only end auctions Monday thru Thursday and Sunday at 8 p.m. PST.

When he hasn't heard from a buyer, Osvaldo will wait the amount of time listed, then try a friendly e-mail and then telephoning them. Although he does not advertise it, he does have a return policy.

I back all my products with an unconditional money-back guarantee.

When it comes to shipping, he has found that using Priority Mail within the United States and USPS Global Express for international shipments are the best ways to save on costs. He does believe international bidders are good for business. He believes drop shipping is a good method for selling items but with an "established a trustworthy relationship." Otherwise, he said it is risky and will only ship what he inspects.

A Final Piece of Advice

Be honest, offer a money-back guarantee, research your products, and most of all have good customer service—use the phone!

Stephanie Inge

Username:	stephintexas
Name:	Stephanie Inge
E-mail:	stephintexas@gmail.com
Classification:	Internet/ eBay Only Business, Trading Assistant, Certified eBay Education Specialist, eBay Consultant, & eBay Mentor
Current Tier:	Silver PowerSeller
eBay Store:	TEXAS STATE OF MIND
eBay Store Location:	www.stores.ebay.com/TEXAS-STATE-OF-MIND
Current Feedback Star:	Red
Projected 2006 Sales:	$75,000

A Little Background

Stephanie Inge has been a member of eBay since March 1999.

> *I am most proud of the fact that my eBay classes were the first of their kind to be offered at the college level and way before eBay developed their Education Specialist program. I became certified by eBay shortly after the inception of the program and I am very proud that I have taught more than 2,000 students since 1999. I am also a member of the eBay*

Mentor program and moderator of two eBay groups.

My store, Texas State of Mind, specializes in vintage cowboy boots and Texas memorabilia of all kinds. As a registered Trading Assistant, I get a wide variety of items, so I usually have a very eclectic assortment on auction and in my store. My eBay "About Me" page recently underwent a complete overhaul and its sole purpose is to provide eBay sellers with hundreds of free tips, tricks, and tools to enhance their eBay experience.

Highlights of my eBay career:

- *First college level eBay instructor in the nation (March 2003)*

- *Seven-plus years tenure as eBay PowerSeller*

- *eBay instructor for Dallas and Tarrant County Community College Systems as well as other colleges throughout north Texas*

- *Regular speaker for eBay Days (seminar) sponsored by eBay, Small Business Administration, and the United States Postal Service*

- *Founder of the most active eBay Sellers' group, Dallas eBaybes & eMales, in the nation, recognized by Business Week Magazine, March 9, 2006*

- *Meetup.com Organizer of the week, May 2005*

- *eBay's PowerSeller of the month, February 2006*

- *Member of eBay Voices 34*

- *eBay University teacher*

- *Registered eBay Trading Assistant*

■ *Own and operate full-time eBay consulting business*

Stephanie Inge—username stephintexas—is a full-time eBay seller, instructor, consultant, and Trading Assistant. After being in the antique business and tiring of the slow sales, Stephanie decided to give selling on eBay a try. After her first sale, she was hooked. She earned PowerSeller status in January 2004, just a few months after switching from selling part-time to full-time. She had set becoming a PowerSeller as a goal but it was difficult for her to reach that as only a part-time seller.

After being laid off from my job in 2003, I decided it was time to kick up my career several notches as a PowerSeller, eBay Instructor, and Trading Assistant! I was so tired of dead-end jobs and ruthless employers, that I made the decision to create my own job. The first step was to create a syllabus for my eBay classes and start contacting the local colleges. To my surprise, they jumped at the chance to add my eBay classes to their schedules and by 2003 year end, I was teaching at 12 local colleges, as well as other venues.

I also began marketing myself as a Trading Assistant and eBay consultant by using all the tools that eBay provides to their Trading Assistants. The results have been amazing and occasionally I have to turn business away.

Stephanie sells most of her items through online auctions. If they do not sell, she will move them to her eBay store which she uses as a clearance center. She sells about 300 to 500 items a month with an average starting price of $9.95 or below.

Low starting prices encourage early bidding and bidding

activity increases visibility, which usually results in bidding wars and drives selling prices through the roof.

She said the best way to get people to notice her listings is by using effective keywords in the auction title and always including a gallery photo.

Stephanie enjoys the "thrill of the hunt" when searching for items she will sell and is an avid fan of estate sales, yard sales, and thrift stores.

I usually don't buy at flea markets or antique malls because the dealers have the items priced too high for resale. Occasionally, I will find bargains on eBay, but you have to know how to find them and when to look.

She has tried many different types of listing software: Andale, AuctionWatch/Vendio, and AuctionWorks just in the past seven years. Because most of them continued to increase their pricing and it became too much, Stephanie shifted away from them.

I started using eBay's Selling Manager Pro in 2005 and have been very pleased, but now I have learned that I must make the switch to Blackthorne, and there are so many bugs that still need to be worked out that I am thinking about finding an alternate management service.

Stephanie uses many different types of cross-promotion tools available to her.

I use eBay's cross-promotion. I also advertise on Craig's list, I always up-sell and cross-sell when corresponding with customers, or potential customers, I advertise my other listings in all of my auctions, and I encourage visitors to shop in my store by providing several links in all of my auctions.

Stephanie said the timing of an auction is key!

You want to make sure that your target audience is sitting in front of a computer, since most bids are placed in the last few hours, or even minutes, of an auction.

When she hasn't heard from a buyer, Stephanie will start out sending the buyer a gentle reminder. She will wait a day and if she still does not receive a response, she will file an unpaid item dispute through eBay.

If you do not receive payment after ten days, you can file for a refund of your Final Value Fee and the deadbeat bidder will receive a black mark on their account.

Stephanie does allow returns on items that have been misrepresented but said that she stands behind everything she sells and would never misrepresent.

So basically I never have an unhappy customer, and I am happy about that.

To save on shipping costs, Stephanie uses USPS as she said that is where she receives the least expensive domestic and international shipping rates and where she can get her shipping materials free.

In addition, you can print all of your mailing labels and receive the delivery confirmation for free!

When asked about international bidders' being good for business, Stephanie replied that global marketplace said it all.

Why would you limit yourself to one country when you can have the whole world shopping in your store? I love doing business with international customers, and most of them are extremely appreciative!

She is not a fan of drop shipping.

I pride myself on customer service, which includes a handwritten thank you note, immediate shipping, and careful packaging. Drop-shippers don't offer any of that, and many times the item you sold is on backorder for weeks. This is a quick way to ruin your eBay reputation and it sounds like a no-risk way to make a lot of money, but there are many risks, so I've never tried it.

To draw people into her eBay store, Stephanie has placed links within her auction listings. She advertises on Craig's List, uses keyword campaigns, and joins new groups. She uses her non-eBay Web site to promote as well.

eBay does not allow linking to third-party Web sites that sell the same item, but I do have links to several different Web sites: my "About Me" page, my eBay class schedule, my eBay sellers' group, Dallas eBaybes & eMales.

A Final Piece of Advice

Provide clear, close-up photos and honest descriptions with lots of details. Remember to take the photos as if there were no description and write the description as if there were no photographs.

Great customer service will set you apart from the competition and create a life-long customer. I can't tell you how many times I've received a poorly packaged item with nothing inside but old, crumbled newspaper and not so much as a thank you note, or receipt. It is very easy to print out a receipt/invoice/packing slip through PayPal, or eBay and requires no typing.

Never overcharge on shipping! Whenever I see an exorbitant shipping charge, I immediately think that seller is a scammer and I would never want to be put in that classification.

Always answer e-mails promptly, and that doesn't mean 24 hours! That person may be waiting to bid on your item and if you wait too long, you may lose that customer.

Give your customer more than they expect! I like to include a Hershey's Kiss, or a miniature Snickers Bar, or whatever kind of candy I may have available! Everyone loves chocolate and I want them to remember my auction with a smile and hopefully, add me to their favorites.

Contact Information for Stephanie Inge:

stephintexas@gmail.com
Phone: 214-232-8046
Fax: 972-463-1148
Store: http://tinyurl.com/k4jva
Auctions: http://tinyurl.com/mrymc
Free Auction Tools: http://tinyurl.com/eb42h
Dallas eBaybes & eMales: http://ebaysell.meetup.com/119/about/
Class Schedule: http://stephintexas.poweru.net/

Sharron Harris

Username:	dprintersink
Name:	Sharron Harris
E-mail:	sharron.harris@verizon.net
Classification:	eBay/Internet Business & Brick-and-Mortar Store
Current Tier:	Silver PowerSeller
eBay Store:	D Printers Ink
eBay Store Location:	www.stores.ebay.com/D-Printers-Ink
Current Feedback Star:	Green
Projected 2006 Sales:	$85,000 eBay only

A Little Background

Sharron Harris has been a member of eBay since July 2001.

I began this business locally, and it found me, rather than my finding it. I was working for a national retail office supply company when a woman came in one evening in desperation over an inkjet refill product that wasn't working. Since I was on company time and was very familiar with the product and its disadvantages, I suggested the customer contact me later when I could assist her. She did and that evening

I walked her through re-filling. I already had personal experience with the high cost of replacing cartridges, having used some of the refill kits that were on the market at that time, in the early part of 1995, when I was doing research for our family tree. The printing cost of the information we were obtaining was getting a bit out of control, and when you start going through several cartridges a week, it can get pretty expensive.

From there my husband and I spoke about it and decided to look further into the ability to buy the products and revise instructions, which I found poorly written. Having family in the printing business, I started there. Once I was able to determine who I could buy supplies from and who wouldn't sell to me because I was nobody, I did some manipulating, and started producing my own refill kits. Then I began thinking of a name and again went to relatives. Actually, I stole my name from one of their businesses, with a slight modification, and came up with the name, D' Printer's Ink. My main concern during the beginning was that I be able to show people "how to" and not just sell the kits. I started out weekends in a local flea market and during the first few years, the business blossomed. September 11th, 2001, began a downtrend in sales, and I was looking for other options when the thought of selling on eBay came to us.

With the encouragement of a relative who had sent me several hundred ribbons, we began our eBay ads. From there I dabbled in posting the kits, and it took off faster than I could have imagined. My husband now assists me with running the local store, and my son and daughter-in-law also help with much of the re-bottling of the inks. I have since added a line of remanufactured cartridges, and am beginning to bring in toner and laser cartridges as well.

*We still run a storefront and have a Web site at **www. dprintersink.com**. We are still in a local shopping mall, but eBay is about 70 percent of the business. I firmly believe that quality products are important, but being able to assist and show a customer is what gives us the edge over other companies producing similar products. I believe that you have to know what you are talking about when you sell a product; I have used every product we sell. I know what can go wrong and know how to correct the problem personally, and I am able to assist my customers because of the direct knowledge. People who have questions or concerns regarding refilling can reach us at 727-861-5058 or e-mail us at sales@ dprintersink.com.*

Our eBay ads and sales have also produced a secondary business for us and that is in assisting others to sell on eBay. I started teaching family, friends, and business associates, and at their encouragement, went on to become a Certified eBay Training Representative in spring 2005.

Sharron Harris—username dprintersink—became a PowerSeller pretty quickly after starting to sell on eBay. Becoming a PowerSeller wasn't her main goal because in the early stages of selling on eBay she was focusing on her feedback score—and still does somewhat; she just broke 5000 in feedback scores with a recent sale. She now is a full-time seller.

We started part time, and then a family member became ill and needed constant attention, so I left my full-time job to care for her and continued eBay part-time during that period. When we eventually were unable to care for her ourselves, we made the decision to revise many of our listings and within a couple of months we were doing it on a full-time basis.

She uses mostly "buy it nows" and store-front to sell her items, with a few auctions thrown in as well. All of her items are consumable and she has a rate of 15 percent returning or repeat customers. Anywhere from 125 to 150 pieces are being shipped a week. She has found that to get people to notice her listings, it most important to have proper keywords in the description.

To make the items she sells to her customers, Sharron will buy in-bulk from manufacturers and then break them down to sell to her customers. She also will purchase some of the "needs items" through the Internet or locally. When selling her items she will use cross-promotion. To list her items, she uses Turbo Lister.

We have used Blackthorne, but for the most part we found Turbo Lister to be just as efficient to suit our needs. We also use eBay's Accounting Assistant program and then export our sales into QuickBooks. We further use Stamps.com and are able to import our customers' addresses into it, making shipping a bit quicker and more streamlined.

Over time, Sharron found that customers are shopping in peak periods. Because of this, she finds Monday to be her best day and evenings produce sales better than mornings or during midday.

But knowing others who also sell on eBay, I am told they have different days when they do their best selling. I would guess product would have a lot to do with it as well. This is something that I think most sellers will have to do as trial and error.

When she hasn't heard from a buyer, she will send a reminder notice. Even after the reminder, she said it usually takes a non-paying bidder notice for the item to be paid for, and still one in five will end up not paying for the item. She does have a return policy that states:

All Ink Refill Kits listed under "D' Printer's Ink," contain Cartridge Specific Ink. At D' Printer's Ink we take pride in the products we sell. We use only ink designed specifically for use in the cartridges the kit is designed for. Please do not use the ink in any other cartridge than that which it was specifically designed for, as it will void our guarantee. Using refill kits, remanufactured or compatible cartridges will not void your printer warranty. We guarantee our products to be free of material- and workmanship-defects. If you have a problem with any Kit or Cartridge Purchase, let us know immediately. You must notify us within 14 days of the receipt of your purchase for any type of refund and/ or exchange. Refunds on kits will be issued based on the amount of ink still in the kit, upon receipt of returned kit. All items included in the kit must be returned with the kit for refund. We are not responsible for any damage to personal property due to the use of refill kits or remanufactured or compatible cartridges. Cartridges are subject to testing prior to any refunds. Cartridges must be returned in the original box and with any clips that came on the cartridge at time of purchase. If a cartridge is returned to us empty we will not issue a refund. We do not refund shipping charges.

She does believe international buyers are good for business as she does a large amount of international shipping herself. She does not do drop shipping—"at least not with eBay buyers"—but said that she supposes with the right kind of company, it may be profitable. She isn't sure if there is a best way to save on shipping costs but does say the following:

Most of our items are less than five pounds so we use USPS as it is less expensive than UPS for those weight constraints. USPS also supplies you with boxes if you ship Priority, and luckily we are in close proximity to another eBay member who sells shipping and packing supplies. Since we can pick them up locally, we save the cost of shipping them. Since most of the items are the same size and weight we have been able to manipulate to some degree the USPS weight restrictions, and will use Flat Rate packaging when possible. Stamps.com also has reduced rates for tracking and this also helps reduce the cost, but we do pay a monthly fee so unless you are doing some type of volume, then this won't necessarily help reduce the cost. I believe this is something that individually one will have to do a trial-and-error method to determine what works for them.

Sharron does have an external site besides her eBay store site, as stated in her bio, which is located at **www.dprintnersink. com**.

As much as possible we cross-promote our items, and we have a search box within our ads to encourage our customers into our store.

A Final Piece of Advice

I would like to tell people who are considering selling on eBay to find a product that they have an interest in, something they find enjoyable to deal with, and something they believe in. I always suggest someone who is just starting out or who may ask me what they might be able to sell to begin with things they have around the home that they might sell in a yard sale. This way they can build up some feedback and get a feel for the whole process. I also tell them not to be too disappointed if something doesn't sell and not to give up. Just because it doesn't sell this week doesn't mean that two weeks from now it won't sell.

I also suggest that they determine whether the item they are selling is seasonal. I believe everything we sell fits into some particular season whether we think it does or not. For example: selling a collectible baseball during football season probably won't get many people looking at them. But sell them at the start of baseball season and you will get bombarded. So seasonal isn't necessarily determined by winter, summer, spring, or fall. Know when your product sells and push it heavily during its peak period. Also, when creating a description for your products, ask someone who isn't all that versed in it to describe it for you. Ask several family members to tell you how they would look for the item. These will be your title and description keywords. Take close-up pictures for your ads. Pictures do wonders. Be honest in your descriptions and be thorough. I don't believe anyone can ever be overly descriptive in an ad.

Marilyn Paguirigan

Username:	islandmele
Name:	Marilyn Paguirigan
E-mail:	hi.mele@hawaiiantel.net
Classification:	Internet/ eBay Only Business & Trading Assistant
Current Tier:	Bronze/Silver PowerSeller
eBay Store:	MELE'S MENAGERIE of Cool Things
eBay Store Location:	www.stores.ebay.com/MELES-MENAGERIE-of-Cool-Thing
Current Feedback Star:	Red

A Little Background

Marilyn Paguirigan has been a member of eBay since January 2003.

I am an Education Specialist trained by eBay with a distinction of being a featured instructor on the Education Web site sponsored by PowerU.

Aloha Everyone! I would describe "eBaying" as neither my job nor career...but rather, my full-time PASSION!

I have been an eBayer since January 2003. My experience with eBay began as a browser. Then I graduated to eBay buyer—and as with most eBayers, I became unabashedly ADDICTED! I was convinced I could sell ANYTHING on eBay when one day I sold my old cell phone and some used plastic hangers that a local department store was getting ready to bring to the garbage dump.

Prior to eBay, my only experience with the Internet was my limited flirtations with e-mail. From those beginnings, I have built a business that allows me to do work that I find fun and fulfilling.

Fast Forward: I am now a PowerSeller; an authorized eBay Trading Assistant; owner of a featured store on the U.S. site; an international featured store owner on the eBay Australia site; and a top ranking writer of reviews and guides on eBay. I am also the founder and leader of the No Ka Oi Sellers Group, an active network of Hawaii-based sellers on eBay, the majority of whom are my prior students. To date, I have successfully completed more than 10,000 transactions on eBay!

It's an honor to add yet another dimension to my eBay repertoire as an Education Specialist trained by eBay. It is my pleasure to be able to parlay my experience and knowledge in assisting others to be successful buyers and sellers on the world's largest on-line marketplace.

A full-time eBay seller and Trading Assistant, Marilyn Paguirigan—username islandmele—starting selling and became addicted to eBay. Here is her story of how she got her start:

I really could find everything possible on eBay and at competitive prices—much better than regular retail. Then one day, I just started selling things around my home (items that would have otherwise gone to the trash bin) and I quickly found there was a buyer for things that I no longer needed nor wanted.

I learned quickly that the power behind eBay was that a seller could sell something for more than he or she expected and a buyer could get that very item at a price he or she thought was a bargain. It's a "win-win" situation for both parties, who in the end both end up happy!

When I realized that I literally could sell "anything" on eBay (I quickly was convinced I could sell spit on eBay), I started to consider selling on eBay to supplement my income—more than just a hobby.

I got wind that department stores threw away a lot of their old hangers. When a customer is offered the hanger with the apparel or garment that they purchase, and they decline, those hangers are thrown away. Most garments already come on a hanger when they come from the manufacturer or distributor so when they are removed after a purchase, they are disposed of because they are no longer needed. Being resourceful (recognizing an opportunity for obtaining product at "zero" cost), I approached department stores and offered to pick up their old hangers. On the flip side, it saved the stores precious storage space and the cost and time of sorting and throwing these bulky items away. As an added benefit, if I could resell these hangers, we could save some space in the landfills and another thrifty business could benefit from the low cost of these "used" hangers. These hangers were such a hot commodity on eBay that I soon found myself sending boxes of hangers all over the world! And that's how my eBay selling tenure began."

It didn't take Marilyn long to become a PowerSeller. She had not really set it as a goal, but as soon as she really starting selling heavily, she got the invitation to become a PowerSeller.

Marilyn averages about 100 to 150 items sold per week. She uses all formats that are available to sell in: auctions, "buy it nows," Best Offer, Worldwide shipping, Store-front with her U.S. site, and international store-front, as well as Want It Now. Her starting price for her auctions is always set at only $.99, but she finds this works well for her.

There are risks involved with this strategy as you as a seller are obligated to sell an item if $.99 is in fact the highest bid—so you leave yourself vulnerable to selling an item for less than your cost. Retailers apply this strategy on a regular basis—using the loss leader strategy during their sales.

But low starting bids tend to encourage bidding. On the upside, at $.99, you really allow the market to determine the value of your item—as an item is only worth what a willing buyer will pay. While there have been occasions when I've sold items at $.99, I've also sold items that ended at over a $1,000 with a $.99 cent starting bid.

This has also worked as an excellent marketing tool for her as people are more willing to begin bidding on the $.99 auction.

That brings me a lot of hits that I wouldn't otherwise get. This strategy drives potential buyers and a stream of traffic to my eBay store which leads to instant (BIN) sales where I command premium prices for the same or like items as those at auction. I capitalize on the fact that some people are willing to purchase the item at a fixed price rather than wait for an auction to end or risk losing the bids.

Marilyn used to sell items she made herself, but due to time issues, she now purchases most of her items from other crafters and resells them. She gets her items from many different sources including wholesalers and drop shippers. She also sells items she gets from her customers as she is a Trading Assistant as well. To list all of these items, she makes use of the Selling Manager Pro listing software.

She uses cross-promotions on her listings as much as possible and in every way she can find to cross-promote her store.

I cross-promote items within my own auctions/store using eBay's cross-promotional tools. I have cross-promotion connections with other sellers. I have a cross-promotion connection between both of my eBay stores as well.

Furthermore, each of my listings has a clickable link embedded in the description to my other items, my eBay store, my eBay guides, or a link to sign my store up on the buyer's "favorite's list."

Recently eBay launched a Reviews and Guides program. I currently have 11 guides on eBay and plan to write more. The majority of my guides cross-promote my store or specific item listings. I am currently ranked as a top 100 writer of

Reviews and Guides on the eBay U.S. site.

Marilyn said that finding and identifying the most ideal times to end an auction are very important because they are a big determinant in the final price.

> *I check my traffic reports and hits on a regular basis to help me determine the best end times for my market. I've determined that my customers are those eBaying from work so most of my listings end during the week during normal work hours.*

She will make every effort possible to try to communicate with a non-responsive buyer. She sends out e-mails to remind them at the end of the auction as well as payment reminders on the third and seventh days after the end of an auction.

> *I only file NPB reports as a last resort. Often I have to give a little more time and consideration to new eBayers as they aren't accustomed to the etiquette of eBay buying and selling as are the more experienced eBayers. Patience usually pays off because the customer is very excited about their purchase from a non-traditional venue, and they soon recognize the advantages and convenience of buying on eBay! More often than not, these customers become return customers.*

Because customer service is Marilyn's top priority, she does have a return policy in effect. It allows for a full refund if the buyer is not 100 percent satisfied, and there are no exceptions to this.

> *I boast an amazing 50 percent rate of return customers and repeat business. Between 20 and 30 percent of the traffic to my eBay store is from customers who have bookmarked me. My own business mantra is to instill loyalty in my*

customers—it is a lot easier to RETAIN customers than to get new ones!

Marilyn has saved thousands of dollars every year by taking advantage of PayPal to print off labels and get her delivery confirmation free. She does believe that international bidders are good for business because since they are adding to the number of buyers able to bid on an item. They drive the price of the item higher and higher. She also thinks that drop shipping can be a good method for selling items for some people.

To be effective, it is imperative that a seller research their potential drop-ship partners. Because your reputation is on the line (not the drop-ship company), you have to develop a rapport and relationship with RELIABLE and efficient businesses. If there is a problem with the fulfillment end of the transaction, it will reflect poorly on the eBay seller.

When it comes to having a Web site linked to her listings, Marilyn follows eBay's policy of not linking them directly to her listings. She does make use of eBay allowing the "About Me" page to include any of these types of links.

I have a clickable link to my other Web site which happens to be my Education Web site. I am also an Education Specialist trained by eBay and I offer full-day seminars on how to sell on eBay. Information about my seminars and the link to this Web site is on my "About Me" page.

Soon I will include another link to a "Shop Hawaii Virtual Mall" site that I established. This site features a group of Hawaii-based eBay sellers and their stores. It also features stores that sell Hawaiian and Island-themed products. Every storeowner featured on this site is a member of the No Ka Oi Sellers Group, an eBay community group that I founded and am currently the leader of. This is a powerful marketing tool for our group as many islanders and islanders-at-heart actively support other islanders in their businesses. We as sellers can also share customers and refer customers to one another. This is especially significant to residents of Hawaii who make purchases on-line as they tend to display a very strong "Buy Hawaii" sentiment. This is an extension of a campaign in the islands that encourages residents to support local businesses. Members of the group will also be permitted to feature this link on their "About Me" page. This will undoubtedly bring more exposure to all of our individual eBay store sites and well as promote our group.

To drive people into her eBay store, Marilyn first off promotes her store in all of her auction listings. She also uses the cross-promoting as mentioned earlier between her two stores. She also has a mailing list of all her customers to whom she sends out newsletters at least once a month and tells of her new items or of any special promotions she may be holding at that time. On top of that, Marilyn also has a domain name jump that goes directly to her store. She prints this site on her business cards which she makes sure are dropped into each package as it is shipped. She also puts links to her store on the eight blogs she has and another independent site she uses as well. Finally, Marilyn said she tells EVERYONE about her eBay store!

A Final Piece of Advice

I am convinced that the most successful and effective sellers are those eBayers that began their eBay experience as eBay buyers and became successful and effective BUYERS first, before trying their hand at selling.

If you are an experienced buyer on eBay, you are empowered with some valuable knowledge—that knowledge transfers into powerful tools that you can implement in your own selling to become an effective seller.

Here are some other tips and tricks that I can offer other aspiring PowerSellers or to those that may want to grow their business aggressively.

On Paypal: *Instead of just letting your funds sit in your PayPal account, sign up for an interest-earning money market account on PayPal. The upgrade is free and easy. Apply for the PayPal debit (not CREDIT card) and use it to pay for your cost of goods sold, postage, and everything related to running your eBay business. This will streamline your bookkeeping. But there is also another advantage. Every time you use your card you will get an instant cash back rebate. No waiting whatsoever. You will see the cash credited to your account immediately! Apply for a volume discount on your PayPal transaction fees. There are certain thresholds whereby if you reach a certain volume (determined by the amount coming through your PayPal account over a span of a month), you are eligible for a discount on transaction fees.*

Second Chance Offers: *I use this option at every opportunity I can. Since I carry multiples of the items I list, I offer second chance offers to all non-winning bidders after the auction ends. I offer the second chance immediately after the auction ends to take advantage of the non-winning bidders that still have a high interest in the item. The longer you wait to make your offer, the more the interest in the item wanes so do it right after an auction ends. This strategy is very successful especially after there is a "last-minute bidding frenzy" or last-second sniping going on. Those who lose the auction* *have another opportunity at obtaining the item at their highest bid and you can move your inventory faster! With this strategy, you can take advantage of securing additional sales without the added cost of additional listing fees or additional waiting time as you would in a regular auction listing! This alone can generate enough revenue to raise you into PowerSeller status!*

Company Profiles

Site: eBay USA

User ID: Islandmele
Store Name: Mele's Menagerie of Cool Things
E-mail: hi.mele@hawaiiantel.net

Our specialty includes local island crafts, Hawaiian money & ribbon leis; wedding & party favors; Hawaiian jewelry; flower fimo hair accessories; aloha-inspired treasures & gifts; Luau needs & Hawaiian island snacks. We also offer money saving coupons for Hawaii visitors. While Hawaiian and Island-themed products are our specialty, we also offer a melange of cool things. Our product line is always expanding to offer you a dynamic shopping experience!

I am also a Trading Assistant and if you are a resident of Oahu, Hawaii, I can sell your items for you!

Site: eBay Australia

User ID: Frangimad
Store Name: Hawaiian Island Bungalow
E-mail: frangimad@yahoo.com

Aloha to all you Hawaiians and Hawaiians at heart and

mahalo for stopping by Hawaiian Island Bungalow. It is my pleasure to offer Hawaiian and Island-themed accessories, novelties, and gifts to the online shopping aficionado in YOU! Having been born and raised in the islands, it is my goal to bring a little island flair to you wherever you are! We ship globally and send all shipments with lots of aloha!

We specialize in Hawaiian treasures including unique Handmade in Hawaii products, Hawaiian jewelry, Hawaiian leis, local crafts, floral hair accessories, beach and surf themed items, Hawaiian style wedding and party favors, kitchenware, home decor, and supplies for your next luau or hula event!

Especially to my Aussie friends, I offer many beach and surf-themed products. For those who are mad about FRANGIPANIS (Plumerias, to us Islanders), end your search here, my bungalow is your Frangipani Heaven!

*Shop Hawaii Virtual Mall Site: Site featuring Hawaii-Based Sellers from the No Ka Oi Sellers Ohana, an eBay community group—**http://shophawaii.blogspot.com**.*

*Education Web site for those interested in taking my seminars on how to sell on eBay as well as getting tips and tricks from an eBay pro! Learn how to sell on eBay utilizing the same up-to-date materials as eBay University and register for a seminar today: **http://HawaiiEd.poweru.net**.*

Carla Edwards

Username:	cedeed
Name:	Carla Edwards
E-mail:	ebaycarla@yahoo.com
Classification:	Internet/ eBay Only Business, Trading Assistant, Education Specialist Trained by eBay
Current Tier:	Bronze PowerSeller
Web Site:	www.e-auctionhelp.net
Current Feedback Star:	Red
Projected 2006 Sales:	www.e-auctionhelp.net

A Little Background

Carla Edwards has been a member of eBay since October 1997.

My name is Carla Edwards and I retired from business and

*took up eBay as a hobby to earn some part-time income and keep me busy. Well since 1998 I have maintained PowerSeller status and enjoy hunting bargains in collectibles and antiques to offer to the eBay buyers. I sell under the ID cedeed. In addition to being a Powerseller, I am a Registered Trading Assistant, Leader of the eBay group Wyoming eBayers and an Education Specialist Trained by eBay. I can teach you how to be a PowerSeller, too! Visit my Web site at **www. e-auctionhelp.net** for the exciting details or e-mail me at ebaycarla@yahoo.com. Yours in Trading, Carla Edwards*

An eBay seller, Education Specialist Trained by eBay, Trading Assistant, and a teacher for those wanting to learn how to sell effectively, Carla Edwards—username cedeed—looked into eBay as more than a hobby when she was getting ready for retirement.

When I moved to Wyoming I had a big need for new décor. I happened to like antiques and the thrifty side of me dictated my buying. I went to a live auction and was hooked! I just knew these items they were letting go had more value than the auctioneer was bringing, and I could certainly see the earning potential right away. I had done some buying on eBay but here was a venue I could really get my teeth into. I was close to retiring, and this was a great way to occupy some time and make a few dollars every month.

Carla became a PowerSeller within only four or five months.

I earned PowerSeller status almost immediately. I loved every aspect of buying and selling. It didn't take long.

When it comes to selling, Carla said she usually manages to

have around 12 to 20 listings up most of the time. She also uses a few ideas to get people to notice her listings.

A good title with descriptive hit words and a Gallery photo— these are the "must-haves" of any successful auction.

Most of her auctions start at only $9.99, and she does not put a reserve on them.

I usually have a good idea of the value of an item before I buy it, and I trust that the eBay buying public will tell me what it's worth. A low starting bid will have bidders circling like sharks in anticipation of a good deal, and thus begins the bidding frenzy!

Carla finds most of her items as live auctions, garage sales, and flea markets. She does not make her own items for her auctions. When asked if she does create her own items, she had this to say:

"Who, me? I am so creatively challenged!"

After eight years of trying all different kinds of listing software packages available for helping with her auctions, Carla chose a system she finds works best for her.

My preference is simply to list on eBay's sell your item form and track my auction sales with Auctiva's eBud, a small subscription program for one-click year-end bookkeeping. It's very simple and easy to use.

She does promote her own listings but does not promote other seller's listings.

Why would I want my buyers to shop some place else?

When it comes to the timing of an auction, especially time-ending, she said that it is very important.

> *Who would be silly enough to end an auction at 3 a.m. or on a holiday? I like to create my listings at my own leisure and have them end at a specified time by using the auction listing options. The best day to have an auction run is Sunday to Sunday but other days come a close second. When I list a consignment item for someone else (I am a Trading Assistant) I list to open on a Thursday and close on the Sunday after 10 days' exposure for maximum results.*

When she hasn't heard from a buyer, Carla has found an approach that works well for her.

> *When I send an original invoice at the close of the auction, I remind my customers they have 10 days to pay. At the 11th day I like to send a polite e-mail inquiring as to the status of their payment. The next step would be to contact them via telephone using eBay's contact member forum. A polite phone call usually does the trick. Often it's a case of the buyer simply having forgot, or having some legitimate reason.*

Carla saves on her shipping costs by using the free Priority Mail boxes and other supplies from USPS. She does have a return policy as she said it helps the buyers make decisions when all the rules are "spelled out."

When it comes to international bidders, she finds them absolutely good for business. To help her items appeal to overseas buyers, she uses AltaVista's Babel Fish translator which can be found at (**www.babelfish.altavista.com**). This site will allow you to type in a phrase (International Buyers Welcome!) and then it will translate it into whatever language you are gearing your auction toward (Bienvenue Internationale D'Acheteurs!).

I then paste that right onto the auction page. They love it!

Carla does not find drop shipping to be a good method for selling items.

It's difficult to find a reliable shipper who understands the eBay feedback policies, and it does not allow for the gross profit margin I like to have.

She does not have an eBay store at this time, but she does have a Trading Assistant site through eBay and an "About Me" page, both of which you can locate by searching for her username on eBay.

A Final Piece of Advice

■ *eBay is a fabulous venue for people to earn a second income. My best advice is to learn, learn, learn! Know your product and sell what you know. Remember, as a seller you make your money on the buy. For example, if you purchase a collectible glass tumbler for $10 and it sells for $12, well, that's just not good business. However, if you pay $.50 for that same tumbler, your profit margin is much higher.*

■ *Think like a buyer. If you are a seller, read and re-read your item description and details and make sure you've covered all the questions a buyer might have.*

■ *Take GREAT pictures. Learn to work with your camera and photo software; don't short-change this important step. There are many articles to be found on eBay on great photo techniques.*

Gloria McClain

Username:	glorsstore
Name:	Gloria McClain
E-mail:	glorsstore@optonline.net
Classification:	Internet/ eBay Only Business & Trading Assistant
Current Tier:	Bronze PowerSeller
eBay Store:	Glor's Store
Web Site:	www.glorsstore.com
Current Feedback Star:	Red

Glor's Store

A Little Background

Gloria McClain has been a member of eBay since September 2000.

My belief is that every job and skill that you have in life comes in handy again somewhere down the line. Every day as a PowerSeller, I appreciate the fact that over the years, I have held the following jobs: part-time bookstore clerk (how I paid my way through college), elementary school art teacher (graduated with a BA in Art and Education from City University of New Jersey), advertising agency employee (everything from administrative assistant to account executive, including media buyer, traffic coordinator, and bull pen artist), public relations and marketing, graphic designer, and freelance writer.

A full-time eBay seller and Trading Assistant, Gloria McClain— username glorsstore—decided to become an eBay seller for a few different reasons.

My husband and I ran a graphic design business together, and... well... oil and water don't mix, so to speak. I had heard from a friend about a woman who had sold her children's used clothing on eBay, and, being fond of holding garage sales to sell off unwanted household items, I decided to give it a try. I still have the printout from my first eBay auction page from a "lot" of my daughter's clothing. And, the rest is history.

Gloria had becoming a PowerSeller as a goal for herself and although it didn't happen overnight, she became one in October 2004. She is currently a Bronze, but is working towards the Silver tier.

I had been selling on eBay on and off on a part-time basis since September 2000, on a "steady" basis since early 2004.

She uses a variety of the areas in which eBay has for selling.

I use a combination of auctions and store items, and sometimes use "buy it nows," especially when listing new gift items. I've never used eBay Motors, but hope to do so soon with my own car.

Gloria sells about 18 items a week with an average starting

price for her auctions of $9.96. She has found a way to get people to notice her listings.

I've noticed some success with "cross-promoting" my listings using simple HTML between my auctions and my store.

She finds her items in a variety of ways, including:

Estate sales, garage sales, things that I "find" (don't ask), items purchased from store sales, and items purchased from wholesalers.

Gloria also has a line of items she makes herself.

Currently, I make and sell custom-made "poodle skirts" for women and girls. This is an area that I've been building upon since last fall, and hope to "branch out" with.

Gloria does make use of listing software for her auctions.

Just Turbo Lister and Selling Manager (free for eBay Store owners). I've done free trials with multiple other programs, but haven't used anything yet that warranted a purchase.

She finds timing to be very important with auctions.

Timing is everything. Occasionally, I'll go against my Thursday and Sunday evening rule, and have an auction end another day or time. I almost always say to myself: "Had this ended Sunday evening, it would have bid up higher."

When she hasn't heard from one of her buyers, Gloria tries her own approach.

Personally, I find the Non Paying Buyer program to be a little harsh in its wording. I prefer a "kinder, gentler" e-mail first, if I haven't heard anything within four or five days.

She does have a return policy, but with limitations.

> *I used to have an "open" return policy and had people return items for all sorts of reasons. Now I limit the time and amount of money that is returned.*

To save on packaging and shipping costs, Gloria has a system in place that works well for her.

> *I try to package as securely as possible, for the lightest weight possible, in the smallest box possible. It's almost a science at this point. I am a "Top 5,000 Reviewer" for a Guide that I wrote about packing (within eBay's "Reviews and Guides" section. It can be found at **http://reviews.ebay. com/Packaging-101-Thinking-Inside-and-Outside-the-Box_W0QQugidZ10000000000067929**).*

Almost all international bidders are welcome in Glor's Store. She finds they are good for business.

> *By allowing international bidders, my auctions will bid up higher. Awaiting payment and shipping is a bit more work and time-intensive, though. I started out by adding Canada until I got my feet wet, and now ship almost anywhere internationally.*

When it comes to drop shipping, Gloria does not really find it to be a good method of selling items for her.

> *I'm too picky with when, and how my packages leave.*

Making use of a "jump" (in other words, if someone types in **www.glorsstore.com**, it opens my eBay Store home page), Gloria finds that driving people into her store is becoming easier.

> *Actually, eBay has been making that easier lately with*

various changes made in favor of store sellers. One of the best is that my unique store categories now appear on every auction page. This change is too new to realize the impact but I'm certain it makes it easier for potential buyers to see what else I'm selling. Also, as previously mentioned, I use simple HTML within my store and auctions to cross-promote.

A Final Piece of Advice

The Importance of Finding a Niche: *Initially, I listed everything and anything I could get my hands on. I tended to look for items to list based upon collectibles that I was familiar with, or had some success selling previously. It wasn't until I stumbled upon a Halloween costume that I found my specialty. I didn't realize it at first. Seeing a girl's 1950s "poodle skirt" style dress for sale for $1 at a yard sale, I purchased it. It was a typical costume, not especially well-made, but it had character and style, none-the-less. Although a one-piece garment, the top was solid black, the bottom a black and white checkered plaid, with the standard "poodle and leash" motif. When there was a little bidding war toward auction end, and it sold for $50, I decided to find a simple pattern and try my hand at making poodle skirts. A little research on eBay showed that there was, indeed, a market for this item. Using my basic sewing skills, I put together a poodle skirt, and I've been slowly building up an inventory within my eBay store, carrying a variety of 1950s sock hop items in my "poodle skirt" department. My goal is to open a dedicated Web site based on this theme. Finding my "niche" has helped me set goals and it has given me a "direction" as far as future sales and inventory.*

Contact Information for Gloria McClain:

Glor's Store

57 E Willow Street
Beacon, NY 12508
Phone: 845-489-2613
E-mail: glorsstore@optonline.net

Stephen A. Banks

Username:	a-deal-4-u-2
Name:	Stephen A. Banks
E-mail:	Info@IeBayForYou.com
Classification:	Internet/ eBay Only Business & Trading Assistant
Current Tier:	Bronze PowerSeller
eBay Store:	A Deal For You Too
eBay Store Location:	www.stores.ebay.com/A-Deal-For-You-Too
Current Feedback Star:	Red

A Little Background

Stephen A. Banks has been a member of eBay since December 1998.

I'm Stephen A. Banks, Sr. All my friends just call me "Banksy,"
a former corporate middle management clone who escaped

the nine to five Slave Grave thanks to downsizing! I'm now an eBay PowerSeller, stay-at-home husband, and father of a handsome son and beautiful daughter.

A registered eBay Trading Assistant, we offer consignment services that can develop into dependable and predictable income generating stream very easily and very simply.

We've recently been trained by eBay as one of their Education Specialists and can now offer our one-on-one and group specialized eBay workshops and private consultations.

We've been selling on eBay full time for the last five years, and while I'm not going to make Bill Gates shake his head at my "Incredible Overnight Wealth," my family is comfortable. More important, I'm willing to share all the truly "money saving, time saving shortcuts, don't make the same mistakes insider secrets" that other PowerSellers refuse to share.

Stephen A. Banks—username a-deal-4-u-2—began selling on eBay after corporate downsizing and the need to be able to feed his family. He has been selling full time since 2000. He didn't set becoming a PowerSeller as a goal, but said that once the status came he has tried to maintain at least bronze level. Once he became serious about selling on eBay full time, it only was about a year before PowerSeller status came.

Stephen sells through all different areas of eBay: auctions, store-front, "buy it nows," and eBay Motors. He sells anywhere from 35 to 50 items a week with an average starting price of either $.99 cents or $9.99. He said the best way to get people to notice his listings is by his keyword-rich auctions titles and good gallery photos.

He finds the items he sells in various places including: garage and yard sales, antique and thrift stores, consignments, local auctions, and he is even given items for free. He does not make any of the items he sells. To list his items he uses Vendio.com and SpareDollar/ InkFrog software. He always cross-promotes.

Stephen doesn't believe that the timing and time-ending of an auction are very important anymore.

I don't think so much anymore with all the good auction "sniping" software tools available, but back in the early days of eBay it was VERY important! With that said, I still list for auctions to close on Sunday, Monday, Wednesday, or Thursday nights.

When he hasn't heard from a buyer after three days, Stephen will send a Payment Reminder Notice and then a second Winning Bidder Notice.

If I've still not received a response, I'll keep sending the above two e-mail combination every 48 hours.

He does offer a money-back guarantee (less the shipping and handling), but also "must be contacted within seven days of the item being received. I only refund if the auction description is not accurate."

To save on shipping costs, Stephen said to have the buyer pay them. As for drop shipping, he used to do this almost exclusively when he first began selling on eBay, but when his source dried up he no longer used this method. As for whether international bidders are good for business:

35 percent of my merchandise goes out of the USA."

Stephen just opened his eBay store **www.stores.ebay.com/A-Deal-For-You-Too**. He also has two other Web sites: **www.IeBayForYou.com** and **www.StephenABanks.com**.

A Final Piece of Advice

While making money on eBay is simple, it is NOT EASY! Anyone thinking of making millions on eBay overnight after buying an e-book or "Info-Product" is in for BIG disappointment.

Selling on eBay is like selling anywhere else, know your product, know your market, and plan on hard work, and then you can build a successful business.

Company Information

We handle 100 percent of the work involved with the promotion, customer service issues, not to mention the entire fulfillment and all the shipping headaches; we do all the work, and all the consignor does is cash checks! Lots of checks!

I'll show you how to make money within 24 to 72 hours of setting up your account on eBay; yes I said you can make money on eBay within a few hours and I'll show you exactly how to do it step-by-step! Get the facts now.

Contact Information for Stephen A. Banks:

Stephen A. Banks

456 Main St.

PO Box 113

Franklin, NY 13775

Phone: 607-829-6921

Toll-Free: 866-822-6921

E-mail: Info@IeBayForYou.com

www.IeBayForYou.com

www.StephenABanks.com

chapter 14

Follow-up Interview with Dan Glasure

Sitting down with dans.train.depot

Dan Glasure took the time to sit down with me for a little while. Here we delve further into his interview.

Angela: What are your Web sites?

Dan: **Danstraindepot.com** and **Brasstrains.com**. **Brasstrains. com** is our selling site and **Danstraindepot.com** is our corporate site that offers information about our business and directions to our store. We are working on a revamp for both sites right now.

Angela: Do you only sell trains?

Dan: For the most part, yes. We branched out a couple of times and fell on our face. In the past we sold some radio controlled cars and accessories. We also sell all different scales of trains, but we have been most successful when we stay within our niche, which is HO scale model trains.

Angela: What all kinds of trains do you sell?

Dan: As noted, mainly HO scale model trains, which is the most common scale around the world. Brass trains, our biggest sellers, are made in Korea and Japan by hand. A tremendous number of man hours go into producing them. They are very limited runs—only 50 to 300 were made of some types. One time we sold a single brass locomotive for almost $4,000, but the average selling price is $200 to $1,000.

We also offer plastic train cars that sell anywhere from $10 to $50. Anything that costs less than $10 is not worth selling on eBay for us, since the profit margin doesn't mesh. We also sell all kinds of accessories, books, and other model-railroad related items. Model railroading is like any hobby. It's a lot bigger than you realize until you get into it. Trains have been around since the beginning of the last century, and they've captured people's imagination.

Angela: Do you do cross-promotions?

Dan: Yes, but my eBay manager, Doug, handles most of them. I do know eBay is constantly striving to make it easier, and it is a valuable selling tool.

Angela: What would you say is the best way to save on shipping costs for you as a seller?

Dan: First, it is important to have to have the right size box. We fill our boxes with Styrofoam peanuts around the item, and they cost money. So the right size box can save us some money in packing supplies. Whenever possible we use a Priority Mail box because they are free. If you're using other boxes, buy in bulk. You can save at least 25 percent of the cost if you buy in large enough quantities. We buy several pallets of each box size we use, and we also have our company logo on all of the boxes we purchase.

We use UPS and USPS for our shipping. We have had bad experiences with FedEx's home delivery. FedEx express works well, but when we were using Home Delivery we found it slow. It has been a few years since we used them, so this situation may have improved. We got some fantastic rates with them at the time, but our customers just weren't happy so we dropped it.

Angela: : You mentioned that you don't do drop shipping.

Dan: It certainly can create all kinds of problems. We sell only what we have in stock. I've seen companies that do it and are successful for a while but I don't think I've personally ever seen a company with long-term success doing drop ship. To me it seems to be a poor man's way out; it's nice not to have to pay for your merchandise until you sell it, but in our experience you have to spend money to make money.

The other problem is that if you're drop shipping, the person next door can do the same thing and beat your prices and you lose your competitive edge. Also if the company's out of something and you already sold it and the customer is then told it is not in stock it can create problems. Imagine how you would feel if you ordered it and then they say "Oh, sorry, we don't have that." You may get a refund but you've already paid for it, stopped shopping for it, and you're waiting for it. Then a week (or more) later you get a call saying it is not available, and it would make you upset. So I'm quite adamant against it. We have had a chance to try this method. We were going to be set up with a Web site that has everything a certain distributor carries, and we would have been drop shipping all kinds of packages every day. We looked into the infrastructure, but the company would not guarantee that everything would be in stock. So it was just too many chances for problems and we dropped the idea.

I will say that if somebody drop ships and they're successful, they probably have a niche. They have a certain small company that they deal with for their particular product. If the company guarantees them that they have it in stock, and they have an efficient system worked out, then I could see how it COULD work. But as far as just dealing with a large company, I personally would advise against it.

Angela: How much harder do you think it is now to have a brick and mortar store?

Dan: In my opinion the mom and pop store does not lend itself to the current economy. There are people selling out of their trunks at trade shows or selling on eBay with no overhead. Many are happy to make $5 profit so they're selling stuff dirt cheap, and it is hard for a store with overhead to compete. You've got to have a competitive edge in a niche market. It's the only way to survive on eBay or in a brick-and-mortar. It's the same business principles. The only thing with eBay is it's easier to control your inventory and overhead. You can have a small inventory and be successful on eBay and nobody knows; whereas you walk into our brick-and-mortar store, people expect to see half a million dollars worth of stuff. Otherwise, they consider it a little store.

Angela: Do you sell everything you have in your store on eBay?

Dan: Often what goes to our brick-and-mortar store goes on eBay eventually if it does not sell in the store, but we do not have anything listed on eBay that is in our brick-and-mortar store. Again, what if something is listed on eBay, and then somebody walks into the store and buys it at the same time that somebody buys it on eBay. That would lead to an unhappy customer!

Angela: So you keep that separate. That's a good idea. You first started on eBay seven years ago because you wanted extra income. What advice do you wish somebody had given you that first time you put something on auction?

Dan: The best advice given to me was to use auction management software. Seven years ago that was not real prominent. We started then using Seller Assistant. Recently eBay bought out this software, and now it's called eBay Blackthorne. A lot of people don't think it's the best program. For people doing new inventory or for people wanting the best inventory management program (listing the same type of item over and over again), I don't think it is the best program. It's very buggy, and for that we hate it, but we just haven't found anything better for us. It could be wonderful. We keep hearing promises of how eBay is going to get it right, so we hope to have a bug-free program to use one day!

There are many types of software available. eBay Blackthorne is very inexpensive: I believe it is only $15 a month. However, many auction management solutions can become quite expensive. Some of them require a monthly percentage of your eBay auctions and other fees that can really add up.

Angela: What do you think was the worst mistake you ever made or when you first started?

Dan: There were many mistakes, such as trying new stuff. But then trying new stuff is how you make a lot of money, too. The worst thing you can do is buy merchandise that you're not acquainted with, venturing out into categories that you're not thoroughly educated about. Educate yourself before you buy. Things may appear to be a great deal but end up being the opposite. One time we bought a huge amount of photography equipment, because we were convinced it was worth a fortune, but we ended up losing a huge amount of money. I have definitely learned to research to learn the market before making a purchase.

Angela: What was your most successful sale or the one you're most proud of?

Dan: We're up to 60,000 to 70,000 feedbacks now (counting repeat buyers). Not everyone leaves feedback so that's probably 100,000 auctions. So I would say I am more proud of that and our customer satisfaction of 100 percent, than any one particular auction.

Angela: You put your links everywhere to your Web site. Is that your most successful marketing strategy?

Dan: That is certainly one part of our marketing strategy. We have put out advertising in national trade magazines for a long time. One costs $6,000 a month for a one-page ad. There was a time that eBay would kick back 25 percent when you advertise with their specifications, so we did that a lot. We have spent a lot of money in advertising, more than we probably should have, but it did help get our name out there. We have a custom eBay store page and our "About Me" page as well.

Angela: On the "About Me" page, have you found that to be a good benefit to your business?

Dan: I think you should definitely have it. It's probably good to put a picture of yourself up there. I've never really liked doing that, but I think people like seeing the face of the business owner. Often they will feel more comfortable dealing with you if they can see your photo and read a little about your business. There's a lot of fraud on eBay so that anything you can do to help put the customer at ease is important.

Angela: Where do you see yourself going from here?

Dan: Our company was fairly large for a while. I had 13 employees. We were right on the fringe of being a titanium PowerSeller. But for us that was just too big, our overhead was really high, and that put a lot of pressure on the business. My goals now are not oriented on our gross income, but on our profit.

Angela: Is there something on eBay that not many people may know about that you would like to mention?

Dan: There's this thing called eBay guides now. I can go to my specific category and say people are looking for a brass train. I can educate them and let them know what to look for when buying a brass train. I plan to do that because I do think it's important to educate people about eBay.

Angela: What advice do you have for eBay beginners?

Dan: Selling on eBay is a lot of hard work. It's not a get-rich-quick scheme. That's the good thing about it because those never work anyway. You get out of it what you put into it. Plan to work some pretty long hours. But the hours are flexible. I think most people who are successful have figured out a way to put in long hours or use employees to their advantage. We've done a little bit of both.

Angela: Does your family help with the business?

Dan: My wife does little stuff, my dad used to help, and my mom does much of my packing.

Angela: You have seven employees. Do most of them have a specific job?

Dan: Yes, we have a full-time packer, full-time photographer, full-time customer service, a guy who runs the brick-and-mortar store, and we have two subs who fill in where needed.

Angela: For someone just starting out, what would you tell them when they're listing an item?

Dan: Have lots of high quality photos. Be honest. If something has a problem, don't try to hide it, be very upfront. We try to downplay our items, if anything. You want the customer to get it and be happy. You don't want to deal with a refund. Remember the goal is to have happy repeat customers.

Angela: How much of a percentage are your repeat customers?

Dan: We currently have 17,000 unique feedbacks and more than 70,000 total feedbacks so everybody is returning on the average three plus times. However, many customers have returned many more times, and feedback is just a guide to that. Not everyone leaves feedback for each item they won.

Angela: Do you send them a newsletter?

Dan: No, but that can be a very good idea. Week in and week out we just have stuff they're interested in. If we had dry spells where we don't have anything to keep them, we're going to lose their attention. We list DTD in all our titles so they can tell that it's us, without even clicking on the title link. We get more for an item than most people just because the customer knows we are going to give them good shipping costs, good packing, and it's going to be at least as good as described. We strive to give great customer service. We do our best to ship out the same day. I personally would pay 20 percent more for that kind of service, and I think that's how a lot of our customers feel too.

Angela: What would you say to encourage the readers of this book?

Dan: You have to know your goals. Instead of having a garage sale, you better have a business plan, make a budget, and when the money rolls in don't treat it as your money. It's your business's money. Pay yourself a salary and reinvest the rest in your business. I educated myself like crazy before I started. Every time we make a deal I learn something. Know your product and know your competition. I don't know who all of my competitors are, but I do know the average prices that things are going for. And like anything in life, if you work hard enough at it, everyone has a great shot at running a profitable eBay business!

chapter 15

The Future of PowerSelling

What's Next

Where does eBay, and PowerSellers, go from here?

First, common wisdom agrees eBay will keep expanding worldwide. Today, in about 15 percent of transactions, the buyer and seller are in different countries. eBay managers have floated the opinion that their international trade might become 50 to 60 percent by 2015. That means a growing range of opportunities for PowerSellers able to find niches to market to both the Third World and the industrialized world.

Second, eBay will find other means of selling beyond auctions and eBay Stores. A typical example has been the recent launch of a classified ad-type service overseas, called Kijiji. (It means "village" in Swahili.) Learning new ways to reach new markets outside of the current auction base is another source of broad opportunities for the thoughtful PowerSeller.

Third, eBay will continue to expand PayPal, the part of eBay that lets individual sellers take credit cards for purchases. Many think PayPal someday will become a finance company, making loans to buyers. There is already some movement that way, with PayPal offering limited financing on the eBay Motors portion of the site. It lends amounts on qualified car purchases. Within a few months or years buyers could soon start using PayPal financing to purchase wedding gowns or X-ray machines.

The growth of broadband Internet connections will also have a big impact on eBay's plans. eBay listings are now static Web pages. New technologies may soon have sound and video options to broaden the texture of product listings.

One aspect Omidyar has talked about is looking at using eBay for small-time finance. His idea is to develop a way of making small loans to impoverished individuals so they can start a business or plant a crop. Perhaps a Web site could link people who want to make loans to those who need to borrow.

Perhaps the greatest challenge facing eBay is brought by governments. Many governments look longingly at the vast amounts of money changing hands within the eBay community. They long to reach out and tax it. Many governments already place sales tax or value added taxes on eBay transactions. Many more do not but want to.

Expect more government regulations and taxation in the not too distant future.

So what is the future of eBay in general and PowerSellers in particular? It's really the same it always has been since eBay was created. eBay has always been expanding in size and into new areas and new markets.

PowerSellers have always been the most adaptable of eBay's sellers. They find opportunity and respond to it. The coming years of eBay promise greater and broader opportunities as eBay continues to reach towards its full potential.

About the Author

Angela Adams was born in Indiana. She went to college in Cleveland, Tennessee, where she received her Bachelor of Arts Degree in Communications from Lee University. She also received minors in Religion and Christian Education.

Angela is currently the Assistant Editor for Atlantic Publishing Company and resides in Ocala, Florida. She enjoys reading, writing, and playing around on her computer. Most of her writing has been poetry, but beginning with this book, she hopes to move that up a notch to larger projects.

A non-stop reader during her growing up years, Angela always made it known she loved to write and one day wanted to write books in her spare time. This book is her first step in realizing that goal. Although still relatively new to eBay—she has a feedback of only 12 on eBay—she would love to take some of the tips and techniques she has learned during the writing and compiling of this book in the future on eBay.

You can reach Angela by e-mail at angela.c.adams@hotmail.com and through her Web site: **www.acafreelance.com**.

Charts and References

Star Ranking Percentages

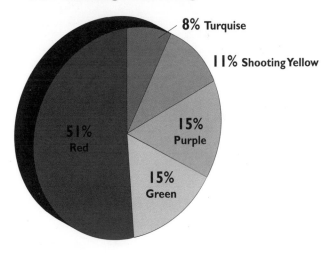

8% Turquise

11% Shooting Yellow

51%
Red

15%
Purple

15%
Green

About Me Pages

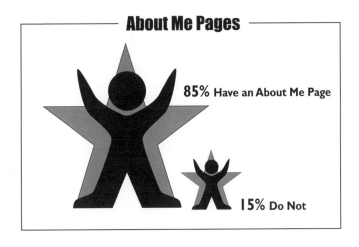

85% Have an About Me Page

15% Do Not

Participants Per PowerSeller Tier

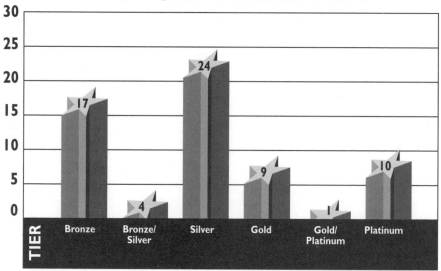

Percentages of Participants Per PowerSeller Tier

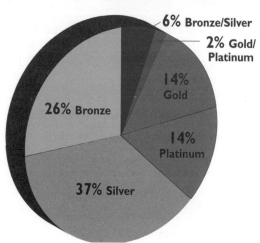

Is Drop Shipping a Good Method for Selling Items?

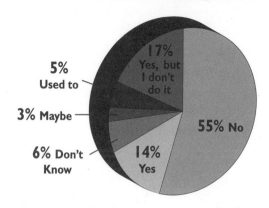

Are International Bidders Good For Business?

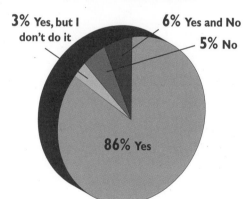

Participants That Cross Promote

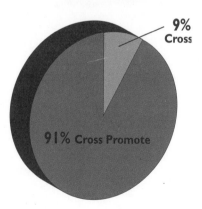

Web Resources

Shipping Resources

DHL	www.dhl.com
eBay	http://pages.ebay.com/services/buyandsell/shippingcenter9.html
	http://pages.ebay.com/services/buyandsell/shippinginternational.html
Express Mail	www.usps.com/shipping/expressmail.htm
FedEx	FedEx.com
Greyhound Express	www.shipgreyhound.com
Media Mail	www.usps.com/businessmail101/classes/packageServices.htm
Priority Mail	www.usps.com/businessmail101/classes/priority.htm
Stamps.com	www.stamps.com
Selling Manager Pro	http://pages.ebay.com/help/sell/printing-invoice.html#bulk_printing
Uline	www.uline.com
UPS	UPS.com
U.S. Postal Service	U.S. Postal Service.com

Listing Software

AAA Seller	www.aaaseller.com
All My Auctions for Sellers	www.rajeware.com/auction/index.html
Alysta AuctionMaker Standard	www.alysta.com/software/auctionmaker.htm Andale
	www.andale.com/corp/products/products.jsp
Auction Hawk	www.auctionhawk.com
Auction Wizard 2000	www.auctionwizard2000.com
AuctionGenie	www.luxcentral.com/auctiongenie
AuctionHelper	www.auctionhelper.com/ah/main/main.asp
AuctionSage	www.auctionsagesoftware.com
AuctionSound	www.auctionsound.com
AuctionTamer	www.auctiontamer.com/atindex.htm
AuctionTeller	www.auctionteller.com
AuctionWagon Store Manager G2	www.auctionwagon.com
Auctiva Power Tools	http://classic.auctiva.com/products/Download.aspx

AuktionMaster.NET	www.pages.auctionWeb.info
bidmachine	www.bidmachine.com
Blackthorne	www.pages.ebay.com/blackthorne
CARad	www.carad.com
ChannelAdvisor Merchant	www.channeladvisor.com/solutions/merch_overview.asp
ChannelAdvisor Pro	www.pro.channeladvisor.com/pro/default.asp
Consignment Companion	www.auctionadvantage.biz/Products/ Consignment%20Companion.htm
CORESense for eBay	www.coresense.com/products/sbebay/index.html
DEK AuctionManager	www.dekauctionmanager.com
Easy AuctionTools	www.auctiontools.net
eSellerPro	www.esellerpro.com
Estates-On-Line.com	www.estates-on-line.com
ezebase	www.ezebase.com/products/index.htm
Hungry Gopher	www.hungrygopher.com
Infopia Marketplace Manager	www.infopia.com/products/mm.shtml
inkFrog	www.inkfrog.com
kAuction	www.kinem.com
Kyozou	www.kyozou.com
Liberty TA Resaleworld	www.resaleworld.com/L4TA.php
MarketBlast	www.marketblast.com
MarketPlacePro	www.marketplacepro.com
Marketworks	www.marketworks.com
Meridian	www.noblespirit.com
Mpire Launcher & Builder	www.mpire.com/products/launcher.html
My Auction	www.database-central.com/myauction/index.html
Picture Manager	www.pages.ebay.com/picture_manager
Seller Sourcebook	www.sellersourcebook.com
Seller's Assistant	www.pages.ebay.com/sellers_assistant
Selling Manager	www.pages.ebay.com/selling_manager pro
SendPal	www.sendpal.com/public/service.aspx
ShipWorks	www.interapptive.com
Shooting Star	www.foodogsoftware.com
SpareDollar	www.sparedollar.com/corp
SpoonFeeder	www.spoonfeeder.com
Trak Auctions	www.jwcinc.net/Info/AuctionManagement.aspx
Turbo Lister	www.pages.ebay.com/turbo_lister/download.html
Turbo Lister 2	www.pages.ebay.com/turbo_lister/
Vendi	www.vendisoftware.com

Vendio Sales Manager	wsacp.vendio.com/my/acp/promo_choose.html
You Can Bill Me	www.youcanbillme.com
zdrop	www.ztradingindustries.com/products/zdrop.aspx
Zoovy	www.zoovy.com

Search Engines

AllTheWeb	www.alltheWeb.com
AltaVista	www.altavista.com
AOL Search	http://search.aol.com/aolcom/Webhome
Ask Jeeves	www.askjeeves.com
Google	www.google.com
HotBot	www.hotbot.com
LookSmart	www.looksmart.com
Lycos	www.lycos.com
MSN Search	www.msnsearch.com
Netscape Search	http://channels.netscape.com/search
Open Directory	http://dmoz.org
Yahoo	www.yahoo.com

eBay Resources

"About Me" Guidelines	http://pages.ebay.comhelp/policies/ listing-aboutme.html
"About Me" Page	http://pages.ebay.com/help/account/about-me.html
Become an Education Specialist	http://www.poweru.net/ebay/index.asp
Best Offers	http://pages.ebay.com/help/sell/best-offer.html
"buy it now"	http://pages.ebay.com/help/sell/bin.html
Cross-promotions	http://pages.ebay.com/help/sell/cp-overview.html
eBay Keywords	http://pages.ebay.com/keywords/
eBay Live!	http://pages.ebay.com/ebaylive/
eBay Motors	www.motors.ebay.com
eBay Pulse	http://pulse.ebay.com/
eBay Store Promotions	http://pages.ebay.com/help/specialtysites/ promoting-your-store.html
eBay University	http://pages.ebay.com/university/index.html
Final Value Fees (FVF)	www.pages.ebay.com/help/sell/fvf.html
Fixed Price	http://pages.ebay.com/help/sell/fixed_price.html
Half.com	www.half.com
Marketplace Research	http://pages.ebay.com/marketplace%5Fresearch/
PowerSeller	http://pages.ebay.com/services/ buyandsell/welcome.html

PowerU Education Specialist Directory	http://www.poweru.net/ebay/student/searchIndex.asp
PS Criteria	http://pages.ebay.com/services/ buyandsell/powerseller/criteria.html
TA Directory	http://tradingassistant.ebay.com/ws/ eBayISAPI.dll?TradingAssistant&page=main
Trading Assistants	http://pages.ebay.com/tradingassistants/ hire-trading-assistant.html
Unpaid Item Process	http://pages.ebay.com help/tp/unpaid-item-process.html

Other Online Resources

PayPal	www.paypal.com
iOffer	www.ioffer.com
Babel Fish Translator	www.babelfish.altavista.com
Google Adwords	http://services.google.com/marketing/ links/ US-HA-CMBNINE2/

Participants' Usernames with Store/Web Address

1968titans	www.stores.ebay.com/Donnas-Fashion-Diva-Boutique
3buttons*n*2bows	www.stores.ebay.com/3-Buttons-N-2-Bows
accessoriessusan	www.stores.ebay.com/AccessoriesSusan
a-deal-4-u-2	www.stores.ebay.com/A-Deal-For-You-Too
appealingsigns	www.stores.ebay.com/Appealing-Signs
auctionseast	www.stores.ebay.com/AuctionsEast
auctionsteacher	www.stores.eBay.com/putterstore
bidmentor	www.BidMentor.com
borntodeal	www.stores.ebay.com/The-Spencer-Company
catsmagick	www.stores.ebay.com/catsmagicalshoppe
cedeed	www.e-auctionhelp.net
celebglasses	www.stores.ebay.com/Celebrity-Glasses
ClassicCarWiring	www.stores.ebay.com/Classic-Car-Wiring
collectibledecorandmore	www.stores.ebay.com/ Collectible-Decor-and-More
cotton_tales	www.cotton-tales.com
direct210	www.stores.ebay.com/direct210
divinefinds	www.divinefinds.com
dprintersink	www.stores.ebay.com/D-Printers-Ink
eagleauctionsusa	www.eagleauctionsusa.com
EastgateDistributors	www.stores.ebay.com/Hot-Springs-e-Auctions
eauctiongurus	www.stores.ebay.com/eAuction-Gurus

eBargainNow	www.ebargainnow.com
enkorestuff	www.stores.ebay.com/Enkore-Stuff
expressdropchicago	www.stores.ebay.com/ExpressDrop-Chicago
ezauctioning	www.stores.ebay.com/ezAuctioning
frednmag	www.stores.ebay.com/Truelife-Finds
geena	www.ginabay.com
gerardsbike	www.stores.ebay.com/Gerards-Bike-Shop
glorsstore	www.glorsstore.com
golfingaddict	www.stores.ebay.com/Golfingaddict-Sales
hamstore	www.hamiltonstore.com
hatterassurfer	www.stores.ebay.com/Hatteras-Surfer-Shop
highbidexpress	www.stores.ebay.com/High-Bid-Express
houstoncharlie2	www.stores.ebay.com/Texas-LeatherCraft
islandmele	www.stores.ebay.com/MELES-MENAGERIE-of-Cool-Things
jodiemcl	www.stores.ebay.com/ Antiques-Collectibles-Designers-etc
justcuriosities	www.stores.ebay.com/Just-Curiosities
list4uonline	www.stores.ebay.com/List-4-U-online
matrixmedical	www.matrixmedical.com
mhswope	QuickSellOnline.com
michauctionsales	www.stores.ebay.com/Michigan-Auction-Sales
mistymae	www.becausescraphappens.com
onecrazyredhead	www.sellitb4youmoveit.com
pacificquest	www.stores.ebay.com/Sell-Online-ART-ANTIQUE-Consignment
poodles*	www.stores.ebay.com/POODLES-Fashions-and-Passions
rocket-auctions	www.stores.ebay.com/Rocket-Auctions-Incorporated
salesbygetridofit!	www.stores.ebay.com/Sales-By-Get-Rid-Of-It
scorebid	www.stores.ebay.com/Siegels-Diamond-and-Gold-Outlet
serendipity_gift_boutique	www.serendipitycollection.com
sharptradingcompany	www.stores.ebay.com/Sharp-Trading-Company
silvercreekconsignment	www.stores.ebay.com/SilverCreekConsignment
stephintexas	www.stores.ebay.com/TEXAS-STATE-OF-MIND
sunnking	www.stores.ebay.com/Sunnking
thebetterbaglady	www.stores.ebay.com/Tongue-In-Chic
thebiglittlestore	www.stores.ebay.com/the-big-little-store
themesnthings1	www.stores.ebay.com/THEMES-N-THINGS
Webauctionexpert	www.Webauctionexperts.com
with-a-twist	www.stores.ebay.com/The-Endless-Emporium
xena-angel	www.stores.ebay.com/Angels-Closet-and-Gifts
yardleyplace	www.auctionworkspr.com

Index

U

W

Learn to take advantage of the INTERNET